Improving Teaching and
Learning in Physical Education

Improving Teaching and Learning in Physical Education

Harvey Grout and Gareth Long

Open University Press

Open University Press
McGraw-Hill Education
McGraw-Hill House
Shoppenhangers Road
Maidenhead
Berkshire
England
SL6 2QL

email: enquiries@openup.co.uk
world wide web: www.openup.co.uk

and Two Penn Plaza, New York, NY 10121—2289, USA

First published 2009

A catalogue record of this book is available from the British Library

ISBN-13: 978-0-33-5234066 (pb) 978-0-33-5234059 (hb)
ISBN-10: 0-33-523406-2 (pb) 0-33-523405-4 (hb)

Typeset by Kerrypress, Luton, Bedfordshire
Printed and bound in the UK by Bell and Bain Ltd, Glasgow

Mixed Sources
Product group from well-managed
forests and other controlled sources
www.fsc.org   Cert no. TT-COC-002769
© 1996 Forest Stewardship Council

FSC

The *McGraw·Hill* Companies

Contents

Acknowledgements

Thanks must go to the following for their time and expertise in contributing to the content of the book.

For their help in providing the sample interview questions:
> Steve Dinnie: Assistant Principal and Director of Sport/Health/Extended School at South Dartmoor Community College
> Jason Trevarthen: Assistant Principal and Director of Sport at Paignton Community and Sports College
> Dave Walters: Assistant Principal at Clyst Vale Community College

For their help with specific lesson plans:
> Darren Laver: International Street Soccer Association
> Donna Ramus: Advanced Skills Teacher in Dance

For her help in arranging for sports performers to answer our questions:
> Louise Calton: Sporting Champions

For Mum and Dad

HG

For Kathy

GL

Introduction

This book is for trainee teachers of physical education (PE) and is about the PE lessons they teach. Although a school's curriculum extends and expands beyond 'lessons' (e.g. out-of-hours learning and the organization of school routines), it is arguably the lesson itself that demands the majority of the trainee teacher's time, effort, focus and concerns.

Improving Teaching and Learning in Physical Education is about helping you as a trainee PE teacher to plan, teach and evaluate effective PE lessons. It is also about you beginning to develop an understanding of your own personal teaching philosophy and pedagogy. For your pupils, it is about you helping them to become successful learners, confident individuals and responsible citizens. Ultimately, this book is about helping you to become the teacher you want to be. Soon you will be joining the teaching profession and your journey to achieve qualified teacher status (QTS) has probably already begun. What is guaranteed is that you will be joining an incredibly rewarding, yet hard-working profession.

This is a great time to be a PE teacher; the subject is seen as having an important role in helping young people succeed in achieving the aims of the national curriculum as well as securing for them the outcomes of the Every Child Matters policy. Furthermore, as the Physical Education, Sport Strategy and Young People Policy (PESSYP) seeks to have an impact on high-quality PE and school sport, debate continues over the important place of PE in the curriculum. Increasingly, PE is recognized as having the potential to contribute positively to pupils' personal, social, emotional, cognitive as well as physical development.

The changes to the National Curriculum have at the very least provided an opportunity for PE teachers to reflect and question what they do, how they do it and why they do it; this is perhaps most evident in the lessons we teach. In turn, research (Armour and Yelling, 2003) suggested teachers found continued professional development in PE to be effective when it was:

- practically based;
- relevant to the National Curriculum;
- relevant to teachers' lives and contexts in which they worked;
- designed to be workable;
- to encourage critical reflection of current teaching practice;
- designed to facilitate the sharing of experiences and ideas.

(adapted from Armour and Yelling, 2003)

Therefore, this book and its features have adopted these wishes and should assist you in your own continued professional development.

Features of the book

Lesson plans

The lesson plans that follow each chapter have been included to highlight principles discussed within the chapter. They are not intended to be seen as 'exemplar' lesson plans, and if you find some ideas you like in them and wish to put them into practice then great, but remember that they were not written with you or your pupils in mind. So our advice is to read them to recognize the key messages of the chapter and use these to inform your own lesson plans.

Teachers' stories

Even the many excellent teachers that you get to observe on your school-based placements will have made or will make the same mistakes as you. In turn you will also begin to experience the successes that they enjoy. The teacher's story feature introduces the topic to be discussed within the chapter with a 'real voice'.

Reflect boxes

These provide time to 'pause for thought' and relate the content of the chapters to your own thoughts and experiences. They are tasks that require you to question, assess and evaluate your practice in order for you to progress. For many of the reflect boxes there is not a 'correct answer', but rather opportunities for you to justify what you do and plan to do in the future.

QTS standards

Each chapter outlines the relevant new QTS standards. However, it is unlikely that the chapter is limited to just these standards as principles transcend across chapters, but the standards highlight the focus of specific chapters.

Lesson observation notes

In this feature written comments from subject mentors and higher education tutors highlight some of the common problems and successes associated with trainee PE teachers' lessons. You are not alone in the experiences you are facing and it is useful to recognize the experiences of other trainee PE teachers.

Sample interview questions and developing a personal teaching philosophy

Soon you will have an interview for your first job where you will be asked a simple question, for example, "Why will you make a good PE teacher?" and suddenly you may fluster and waffle! This feature is not only a chance for you to practise sample interview questions but, more importantly, to spend time considering your own philosophy of teaching PE. By answering the questions you will be much better prepared in an interview because you have spent time to formulate, question and verbalize what you believe in.

What makes a good PE teacher?

To understand what your pupils perceive to be a good PE teacher is powerful. Here we asked elite sports performers what they felt made a good PE teacher. Do not be afraid to ask your own pupils!

How to use this book

This book is designed to support and supplement the guidance you will be receiving from your HE institution and placement schools. It is intended that you can use this book to inform your teaching and/or to find answers to specific questions that may arise when you are planning or evaluating your PE lesson.

The best way to read this book is the old-fashioned way of starting from the front cover and finishing at the end! It was very difficult to decide on how to separate this book into chapters as undoubtedly the principles and messages need to be seen as connected. The eight chapters in the book are unfortunately not the only eight aspects you need to understand in order to become an excellent PE teacher; in fact, they are not even the most important. Your professional and personal attributes will shape much of the teacher you become and there are many excellent books that discuss this. Nevertheless, you will all want to improve the actual PE lessons you teach and the following chapters and features are designed to help you do this.

This book should be seen, therefore, as an aid to help you in your journey to gain QTS. We hope that you will find at least one thing (but hopefully more!) in this book that will cause you to question what you currently see and do, to try something new and then reflect upon its success (or weakness) and then improve it further.

1 Planning teaching activities to increase pupils' learning

Harvey Grout and Gareth Long

A teacher's story

I always thought teaching football would be easy. I had played myself at a high standard and also coached adult football teams so teaching it to Year 7s should have been simple! It was a few years into my career when I began to evaluate what I was doing and wondering why my 'football lessons' were not going as well as most of my other ones. It soon became apparent that I was replicating the football lessons that I had been taught as a pupil and, to a certain extent, the football sessions I now coached. I was giving little thought to why I was teaching football and what I wanted the pupils to get out of my lessons, and as a result I was predominantly focusing upon skill development and then playing unrelated games at the end. This hadn't been much of a problem to the pupils as they seemed comfortable with this approach and were happy as long as they got a 'big game' at the end. However, was I teaching them anything?

Once I had recognized this, I was able to adapt my teaching. I had much clearer and more focused lesson objectives that went wider than the development of a football-specific skill, and I also began experimenting with a 'games for understanding' approach. I believe that these changes contributed significantly to the pupils learning within the lesson; they were becoming a lot more involved in their own and other's learning and appreciated a different approach than the one they had been used to.

The PE programme of study helped me to refocus my philosophy further and recognize that there was a lot more potential to develop pupils' learning other than solely developing skill.

David, Head of PE, age 29

The learning outcomes of the chapter are:

- ☑ To understand how the national curriculum informs planning of PE lessons
- ☑ To understand that lesson objectives can develop pupils' 'personal development and well being' as well as their 'achievement and standards'

☑ To understand that a range of teaching methods and styles can be employed to help pupils achieve lesson objectives
☑ To understand that creative and challenging lessons will be more successful in motivating pupils to learn

The professional standards for qualified teacher status (QTS) addressed in this chapter

Q14:	Have a secure knowledge and understanding of their subjects/curriculum areas and related pedagogy to enable them to teach effectively across the age and ability range for which they are trained.
Q22:	Plan for progression across the age and ability range for which they are trained, designing effective learning sequences within lessons ... demonstrating secure subject/curriculum knowledge.

The aims of the curriculum

PE should contribute to the aims of the National Curriculum by helping young people become:

- successful learners who enjoy learning, make progress and achieve;
- confident individuals who are able to live safe, healthy and fulfilling lives;
- responsible citizens who make a positive contribution to society.

(QCA, 2007b: 189)

Therefore, the PE lessons you plan need to progress pupils towards these aims. This chapter looks at some of the ways in which this can be done. Methods include setting appropriate lesson objectives, including the activities chosen to teach these objectives, through to the format and structure of the lesson plan. In essence, this chapter introduces factors to consider when planning *what* to teach (content) and *how* to teach it (methods).

Although this book is specifically focused on the lesson, it is important to understand how the individual lesson fits in with longer-term planning. The PE department you are working within will have schemes and units of work that identify the medium- and long-term planning of what they want the pupils to learn over a set period. By using the department's schemes of work you will be able to identify important aspects to help you with your lesson planning. For example, what are the aims and objectives of the schemes? What prior learning has taken place in previous schemes and what is planned in subsequent schemes? What facilities, time and resources do you have available? How will the pupils be assessed? It is when you know the answers to questions like these that you can begin to ensure that your lesson plans relate to the 'big picture' of what the pupils should be learning within PE and begin to contribute to the aims of the curriculum. By doing this, you as the teacher will be better placed to build on pupils' previous experiences and have a more focused view of what pupils are expected to learn. Clearly, then, it is important for you to become familiar with your department's schemes of work in order to inform and enhance the process of your lesson planning.

The schemes of work your department use will very much depend on their philosophy and how they have interpreted the National Curriculum and planned their PE curriculum. So while one particular department may base their PE curriculum around the subject's importance statement and curriculum opportunities, others may start from the key concepts or the key processes. Notice that all these methods move away from using the range and content as the starting point.

Reflect:

- Ask your department how they went through the process of beginning to plan their PE curriculum. What decisions did they need to make and what factors influenced these decisions?
- How do they embed other aspects of the curriculum into their PE schemes and units of work, such as the personal, learning and thinking skills and functional skills?

Although this book does not make any judgement on which approach is 'better', it does use the key processes to highlight decisions and principles relating to lesson planning. This decision links directly to the assessment chapter as the key processes are more overtly linked to the National Curriculum attainment levels. As traditionally the PE curriculum has been dominated by an emphasis on games (OFSTED, 2005), this particular chapter takes 'outwitting opponents through invasion games' as its range and content focus, and provides examples of how they can be planned to reflect the aims and objectives of the curriculum. The idea of this is to show how the most 'traditional' of activities can still embrace the 'new' ideas and aims of the curriculum, not that the range and content should be the main focus of planning.

Reflect:

Read the example provided of a basketball lesson.

- What evidence of good practice do you see?
- What aspects would have needed to have been considered in the planning of this lesson?

An example of teaching and learning basketball skills

The changing rooms were networked and contained screens so that the teacher was able to show edited clips to illustrate teaching points. A basketball lesson started in the changing room with video clips of lay ups, slam dunks, set shots and drives to the basket on a loop. Questions drew key technical aspects of skill acquisition from pupils which led into an introduction to the lesson's aims and objectives.

The pupils moved into a well-equipped sports hall and immediately into warm-up activities involving everyone with a ball free shooting into designated baskets. Revision of dribbling skills from one side of the court to the other at speed, changing hands and direction as they moved, was refined into a series of relay drills with differing challenges as they crossed the court. Mobilisation exercise consisted of working the ball around the body, through the legs, pivoting and leaping, extending and landing.

Good knowledge of the pupils' ability was used to set them a series of tasks, which allowed the most able to extend themselves, whilst also encouraging the less able to experience some success. For example, a shooting drill for lower ability pupils involved static shooting with a smaller ball and lower net from a short distance whilst the most able had to dribble, stop and perform a jump shot with a player defending the basket.

The teacher's deep subject knowledge and experience enabled him to communicate confidently and expertly: complex skills were broken down into accessible segments, with a strong emphasis on correct technique and the quality of movements. The teacher's empathy put the pupils at ease. They responded well to praise and authoritative feedback which helped create positive relationships and productive learning.

(OFSTED, 2006: 9)

Reflect:

What do you think were the basketball lesson's aims and objectives? Write it down as you think it would appear on your lesson plan.

Before moving on to look at what to teach in PE, a relevant question may be to ask, what do you want the pupils to achieve? The curriculum aims outlined at the start illustrate what we hope the pupils will become at the end of the journey but it is also helpful to look at what this might look like on the way.

Table 1.1. Characteristics of pupils who are becoming successful learners, confident individuals and responsible citizens.

Outcomes of high-quality PE and sport (DfES, 2004). 'Young people who ...'	Every Child Matters outcomes (DCSF, 2008). 'Every child ... to have the support they need to ...'	Ofsted criteria (AfPE, 2008) 'Learners ...'
Are committed to PE and sport, both in and out of school	Be healthy	Like PE and take part in all it offers
Know and understand what they are trying to achieve and how to go about it	Stay safe	Are normally interested in or excited by their work in PE
Understand that PE and sport are an important part of a healthy, active lifestyle	Enjoy and achieve	Are keen to achieve as well as they can
Have the confidence to get involved in PE and sport	Make a positive contribution	Behave well in PE lessons and are willing to undertake work of their own accord
Have the skills and control that they need to take part in PE and sport	Achieve economic well-being	Have a good understanding of how to lead a healthy lifestyle and take up opportunities to do so with enthusiasm
Willingly take part in a range of competitive, creative and challenge-type activities, both as individuals and as part of a team		Develop good work-related skills in line with their personal qualities in PE
Think about what they are doing and make appropriate decisions for themselves		Respect and value each other, which is demonstrated by their positive attitudes
Show a desire to improve and achieve in relation to their own abilities		Make good progress in skills, knowledge and understanding in all areas of the PE curriculum
Have the stamina, suppleness and strength to keep going		Achieve well compared with their prior attainment and compared with pupils in similar schools

Table 1.1 (Cont.)

Enjoy PE, school and community sport	Demonstrate good skills, knowledge and understanding ... in the PE attainment target and across most areas of activity, with little or nothing that is unsatisfactory in terms of standards Do not underperform in PE Are involved in school, regional and national teams and/or activities

---

Reflect

The AfPE (2008) place these outcomes into two categories of 'Personal development and well being' and 'Achievement and standards'. Which of the two categories do you mainly focus on in your lessons? Can the table also stimulate relevant lesson objectives for your lessons in addition to the content of the PE national curriculum?

Lesson objectives and teaching methods

As a trainee teacher it is important that you focus on what needs to be learned in relation to your department's schemes of work and the ability of the pupils, but a good premise to begin with is to start with what you (and your pupils) feel the pupils need to learn and work backwards from this (e.g. what are the pupils' existing strengths and weaknesses?). However, it is useful to be aware of 'trends' in what PE teachers have often 'wanted pupils to learn'. The 2004/5 QCA report on curriculum and assessment in PE (QCA, 2005b) revealed that in Key Stage 3 the acquisition and development of skills remained the focus of the PE curriculum. Furthermore, teaching and learning activities often lacked progression and challenge that impacted upon pupils' attainment (QCA, 2005b). Thus, this chapter uses the key processes (QCA, 2007a) to explore lesson objectives and content in addition to the development of skill, and provides examples of how these can be achieved through creative teaching activities. Although already stated, it is important to reiterate that your lesson objectives will be decided through a raft of different factors and that it is not simply a case of selecting one of the key processes and deciding to teach that! It is also important to recognize that key processes do not have to be taught in isolation and that links and connections between them should be made apparent. Moreover, it is not being claimed that all the key processes (e.g. the four subsections of 'making and applying decisions') can be taught in one lesson or indeed throughout one unit of work.

Reflect

Go back over some of your previous lesson plans and look at the lesson objectives:

- What percentage have focused predominantly on skill development?
- Consider how would your planning and teaching of a key process (or part of one) differ from a Year 7 to a Year 9 group?

Key processes in PE

Developing skills in physical activity

Pupils should be able to:

a) refine and adapt skills into techniques;
b) develop the range of skills they use;
c) develop the precision, control and fluency of their skills.

(QCA, 2007a: 192)

As already mentioned, skill development has been the traditional focus of PE lessons and although this chapter argues that in the past the teaching of skill has dominated lesson objectives, it also recognizes the importance of its contribution to developing the physically educated pupil. Furthermore, it argues that skill development should not be a static activity where pupils simply repetitively practise the skill.

This section of the chapter takes 1 v 1 skills inherent in invasion games to highlight its argument.

Turning in football is often a skill taught to develop a pupil's competency in 1 v 1 situations. As such, a lesson objective may read 'to improve the pupils' ability to turn with a ball'. Commonly seen teaching activities include the teacher demonstrating a turn, for example, a Cruyff turn and then the pupils having a go at practising it by dribbling to a line, turning and dribbling back to a classmate. This process is often then repeated with other common football turns (e.g. drag back, inside hook).

Reflect

Would you include the teaching activity described above in your lesson plan? Justify your reasons.

The above teaching activity can probably be improved to enhance pupils' understanding, learning and development of skill. So, let us look at another way of introducing/developing turning in football. Starting with the lesson objective a more focused one may be 'to develop the precision, control and fluency of the pupil's ability to perform a turn when they are face to face with a defender (180 degree turn)'.

Reflect

How does a more focused lesson objective help you in planning the rest of the lesson?

The purpose of the following example of a teaching episode is certainly not to claim that it is exemplar practice, but instead to move away from skill development simply being repetition of a skill. Conversely, it should provide opportunities to develop the key concepts of competency, performance and creativity.

Sample teaching episode for 'developing skill in physical activity'

Teacher: *'Dribble to the line with a ball and perform any turn of your choice, I want you to imagine that the line is (insert name of the current England centre back) coming towards you'.* Here the pupils are allowed to either perform a turn that they are comfortable with or one that may not be a 'traditional' turn. This enables the teacher to step back and have a look at the turns being performed (successfully as well as unsuccessfully). This way the pupil now has a choice but also an opportunity to be creative.

'Let's have a look at Jo's turn and then Alison's turn – watch what part of the foot they use to turn with (Jo – inside of the foot and Alison – sole of the foot). I would now like you to continue, but experiment using different parts of the foot to turn'.

If the teacher wants to they can 'name' turns that they see or get pupils to demonstrate ones that are less familiar. All pupils will now have practised at least four turns (inside and outside of the foot, the sole of the foot and the heel). The teacher can extend pupils by asking them to perform the turn with their weaker foot and at a quicker pace, and they can assist other pupils by asking them to perform the turn stationary or walking.

'Now let's look at Andy and Lee's turns which use different parts of the feet. I would like you to look at the similarities of the two turns and why they are good turns'.

Here the 'teaching points' can be explored, for example, the disguise used before turning, quick turn with the ball close to the feet and acceleration away from the defender. And the pupils can now focus on developing these teaching points in their own performance.

'Let's put your own turns under a bit of pressure now. I would like you to dribble as fast as you can while keeping the ball under control, and turn between the two cones set out. You can make the gap smaller or wider whenever you like. Your partner will observe and tell you what you did well and what you need to improve on'.

Now the pupils are challenging themselves and personalizing the level of that challenge. The skill is now more realistic to how it would look in a game situation (i.e. turning away from a defender). Pupils are also required to evaluate the performance of others.

'Now we are going to put your turns into a realistic game situation and work on the moves we looked at last week for beating a defender. Tracey is going to dribble towards Julie and when they enter the middle zone Tracey has a decision to make. Tracey will decide to either turn and dribble the ball back to line A, or try and go past Julie and dribble to line B. Whatever Tracey decides Julie will try and get control of the ball before Tracey can get the ball under control past either line'.

Now a defender has been added the pupils should be able to recognize the context of decision making regarding 'when to turn', as well as 'how to turn'. In addition, they are able to link the lesson content with last week's.

Reflect

- What aspects of the key concepts of PE are covered here?
- What would you improve further if this was your lesson plan (is dribbling/turning in a straight line realistic to the game)?
- After a warm-up had taken place could the teaching activity involving Tracey and Julie have been the first one?
- Could some of the teaching points have been incorporated into a warm-up?
- Take another 'skill' from any activity and think how you would teach the key process of 'developing the precision, control and fluency' of the skill.

Making and applying decisions

Pupils should be able to:

a) select and use tactics, strategies and compositional ideas effectively in different creative, competitive and challenge-type contexts;
b) refine and adapt ideas and plans in response to changing circumstances;
c) plan and implement what needs practising to be more effective in performance;
d) recognize hazards and make decisions about how to control any risks to themselves and others.

(QCA, 2007a: 192)

Pupils' ability to make and apply decisions can relate to their own individual performance and/or with their application of tactics, strategies (in this example) and compositional ideas in group situations. With regard to invasion games an example of an activity often used to promote decision making alongside the skill of passing is a 4 v 1 practice.

Reflect

How do you as a teacher design a 4 v 1 practice?

A traditional way of teaching a 4 v 1 is outlined below:

- 4 v 1 in a 15 x 15m square;
- the four players in possession of the ball keep the ball away from the defender; if the defender touches the ball they become an attacker and the player who made the mistake becomes the defender;
- play continues until the teacher stops the activity.

Within this set-up common decisions players need to make include:

- the attacker in possession of the ball – whether to keep possession of the ball or pass the ball? Who to pass to and what type of pass to execute?
- the attackers not in possession of the ball – how to support the player in possession and whether to get in position to receive a pass?
- the defender – whether to tackle the player in possession, whether to intercept or whether to mark another player?

A more creative approach to such a teaching and learning activity could enhance the pupils' decision-making abilities. For the purpose of this example, we will use a lesson objective of 'improving the pupils' ability to recognize when and how to support a player in possession of the ball'.

Sample teaching episodes for 'making and applying decisions'

Activity one: Five players in a set area (shape and size decided by the pupils) all wear a different coloured bib. When the teacher shouts out a colour that player becomes the defender. If the defender gains possession of the ball (e.g. ball in two hands, two touches on the ball, dribble the ball out of the area) they gain 10 points and give the ball back to an attacker. They stay as the defender until the teacher calls out another colour (the pupils can change the size and shape of the area whenever they like). If coloured bibs are a problem, the pupils can be numbered 1 to 5 and when their number is called they pick up and hold a bib or cone to signify that they are the defender.

Rationale: By doing the above set-up and frequently changing defenders, it overcomes the motivational problems that can occur if a defender cannot gain possession of the ball, or the attackers cannot keep possession of the ball. See Chapter 5 on differentiation to read ideas on how to make the activities easier, harder and more inclusive.

See this activity 'in action' at www.sport-IQ.com

Activity two: Using the same set-up as the first activity, the pupils are set the challenge of passing the ball between them until each colour (or number) has been in possession of the ball for a set number of times (e.g. twice). When they achieve this (or have had five attempts) they change the defender.

Rationale: This activity will 'force' pupils to attempt to move into space as they know they must receive the ball at least twice for the challenge to be achieved. Pupils will need to decide when and how best to provide support for the pupil in possession. In addition, when in possession of the ball players must look up and quickly select the colour that they are trying to pass to.

See this activity 'in action' at www.sport-IQ.com

Activity three: Again, one defender is 'on' and this time five passes (or similar) must be achieved before a 'goal' can be scored. You can decide how a goal is scored for example, by knocking a cone over with a ball, by dribbling/passing the ball out of the area, or by passing to a teammate through a small goal created from two cones. Once again after five attempts to score a 'goal' have been taken the defender is changed.

Rationale: Now the pupils will have to show progression in their decision making, from simply keeping possession to keeping possession for a purpose (to score a goal). This requires the pupils to not only think about when to keep possession but also when to make the decision to 'go for it'.

See this activity 'in action' at www.sport-IQ.com

Activity four: Finally, in this example direction is added. The defender plays out a pass to the attackers who have to attack the line/goal/cones behind the defender. If they are successful in a set number of attempts (e.g. three), then one of the attackers joins the defender to make a 3 v 2 situation. If the attackers are unsuccessful, then the defender is changed.

Rationale: By adding a set direction, decisions will need to be made about going forward with the ball or whether going backward at times may be better to keep possession. In turn, pupils can be challenged to consider where they should provide support and they should also take into account how support offered by other players may impact the support position they take up.

See this activity 'in action' at www.sport-IQ.com

Reflect

- What aspects of the key concepts of physical education are covered here?
- Consider how you would support the learning of your pupils while these activities are taking place, what would your role as the teacher be? For example, if you want the pupils to make and apply decisions, will you or the pupils be responsible for finding the answers? Consider how your use of questions will facilitate this process.

Developing physical and mental capacity

Pupils should be able to:

a) Develop their physical strength, stamina, speed and flexibility to cope with the demands of different activities;
b) Develop their mental determination to succeed.

(QCA, 2007a: 192)

The ability to shoot and score goals is a fundamental component of many games. Some pupils love scoring goals and will shoot all day while others will try and avoid the opportunity and literally pass responsibility over to another pupil. Therefore, it is a good vehicle to highlight the key processes of 'developing physical and mental capacity'. In this example we use the basketball set shot to show how this key process may be developed.

Reflect

Could you teach shooting without focusing on technique? (Probably not!). However, is the following teaching and learning activity actually focusing on the techniques of shooting, or rather developing confidence?

Here the lesson objective is 'to develop pupils' confidence to have a go at shooting and to increase their understanding of the benefits of being quick to react to a shooting opportunity'.

Sample teaching episodes for 'developing physical and mental capacity'

Activity: In pairs pupils have one ball and one basket between them. They also have five 'shooting mats' that are worth different points. When the music begins pupil A chooses which mat he or she will shoot from; if it goes in the basket then that pair score that number of points. Pupil B rebounds the ball, dribbles to a mat of their choice and shoots to try and add to their score. They continue until the music (one minute) stops.

Rationale: By working in pairs pupils are less likely to feel 'pressure' in terms of competing against others in the group. Also, the 'rules' of the activity mean that everybody in the group should have experienced 'having a go'. The lesson objectives will have been explained to the pupils and that the focus is on increasing confidence rather than improving technique.

The following quote is from Michael Jordan and was written on the whiteboard and discussed after the warm-up:

> I've missed about 9000 shots in my career, I've lost almost 300 games, 26 times I've been trusted to take the game winning shot, and missed, I've failed over and over again. And that is why I succeed.

The pupils have also been told to record their score but that it will not be announced to the rest of the group. It is hoped that the music will also encourage the pupils to complete the activity quickly and get as many shots as possible.

See this activity 'in action' at www.sport-IQ.com

Activity: On this occasion the teacher demonstrates sample quick movement patterns between each shot (moving backwards, forwards and sideways). The challenge for the pupils is to step on each shooting mat twice (not on the same mat twice in a row) in a time as fast as they can (recorded by their partner). The pupils have the choice of shooting a ball between each mat or simulating a set shot before moving to another shooting mat.

Rationale: As with the previous scores, the pupils' times are not disclosed. What follows is a set period of time in which the pairs work together to try and improve the number of shots they can take within the minute. The class finish this section of the lesson by trying to beat a) the number of shots they take in a minute and b) their score from the first activity.

Activity: A 4 v 4 game in which usual basketball scoring exists but pupils can also score one point by failing to score a basket but hitting the backboard or the rim of the basket.

Rationale: By increasing the 'target' and reducing the likelihood of missing the shot, the pupils should have more confidence to shoot in the game. Speed and quickness can be encouraged by emphasizing the need to gain rebounds and to shoot before defenders can slow down the shot.

Reflect

- What aspects of the key concepts of physical education are covered here?
- Do you think competition helps or hinders pupils to develop their 'mental determination to succeed'?

Evaluating and improving

Pupils should be able to:

a) analyse performances, identifying strengths and weaknesses;
b) make decisions about what to do to improve their performance and the performance of others;
c) act on these decisions in future performances;
d) be clear about what they want to achieve in their own work and what they have actually achieved;

(QCA, 2007a: 193)

Once again it is important not to view the key processes in isolation and instead make the connections between them. It is likely that pupils' evaluating and improving skills will be evident in the majority of well-planned lessons. However, the following example of designing a quarterback move from a 'play' in tag American football will focus specifically on these skills. Therefore, the lesson objective here is 'to improve the pupils' ability to analyse their own and others' strengths and weaknesses and to use this analysis to improve the performance of their group's attacking play'.

Sample teaching episodes for 'evaluating and improving'

Activity: Pupils are put into groups and design and practise a couple of plays to try and outwit their opposing defence and gain ground (they practise without an actual defence).

Rationale: In the changing room pupils are shown some video clips of different successful plays and the criteria for success discussed (e.g. disguise, decision making, accuracy of throw/catch, speed of run, remembering the play). Pupils are provided with brief information on the role of specialist positions in American football (e.g. effective decision making and good throwing technique for the quarterback, strength and agility for blockers). The pupils then assign each others' positions and design and practise an effective play.

See this activity 'in action' at www.sport-IQ.com

Activity: Pupils join another group and now have to perform their play under pressure from defenders who try and tag the ball handler to stop the play being successful. After a few attempts the groups swap over.

Rationale: Now the pupils can begin to evaluate their strengths and weaknesses both in terms of the design of the play and their own effectiveness in carrying it out. Knowing that they will be trying again soon, the discussion could also include the strengths and weaknesses of their opponents' defence. The next activity will encourage the pupils to further practise any changes suggested and improve on their performance.

Reflect

- What aspects of the key concepts of physical education are covered here?
- How in the activities shown could you as the teacher help your pupils develop their evaluating skills?

Making informed choices about healthy active lifestyles

Pupils should be able to:

    a)   identify the types of activity they are best suited to;
    b)   identify the types of role they would like to take on;
    c)   make choices about their involvement in healthy physical activity.

(QCA, 2007a: 193)

Occasionally adopting different types of role within PE lessons has been left for the pupils unable to take part due to illness or injury, or for pupils who have not enjoyed 'taking part' in the lessons. These particular key processes identify that participation in PE should enable all pupils to experience a broad and balanced range of activities and experience a diverse range of roles in addition to being the performer. The lesson objective of 'introduce the pupils to some of the roles other than performer associated with invasion games' could be applied to any invasion game.

Sample teaching episode for 'making informed choices about healthy, active lifestyles'

Activity: A 4 v 4 game will take place with additional four pupils providing the following roles; two referees/officials (they will be in charge of half the game each, as in basketball), one scorer/match analyst (they will record important information such as the number of shots on goal) and one coach (they will be able to call one 'time out' for each team and suggest tactical changes). After a set period of time the scorer and coach will swap and become the referees/officials. This can also be an opportunity for the performers to swap playing positions.

Rationale: Once again the need to evaluate and improve is necessary for the pupils undertaking 'other types of role' and this feedback can come from the pupils who were playing the game. Although perhaps not always possible in one lesson, if this key process (or part of it) was the focus of the unit of work, then all pupils should experience these 'other roles' over the series of lessons.

Reflect

- What aspects of the key concepts of PE are covered here?
- How would you plan for progression of pupils undergoing 'other roles' within a lesson or over a series of lessons?
- How would you enable pupils to 'identify' and make choices about their involvement in healthy and active lifestyles beyond performing?

Beyond the key processes

As already stated, your lesson objectives will be planned after you have taken into account a number of different considerations. Whether your department's schemes of work are based around the subject's key concepts, key processes or its importance statement and curriculum opportunities, your lesson objectives may also focus on aspects such as the cross-curriculum dimensions, personal learning and thinking skills or functional skills required for pupils to achieve the aims of the curriculum (QCA, 2007a). These aspects are explored further in other chapters in this book but perhaps it is important at this stage to emphasize that PE can be a great subject in which to successfully contribute to many of these dimensions and skills.

Reflect

Read the following Year 9 basketball lesson observation (Ofsted, 2005: 7). With regard to the lesson plan, what do you think may have contributed to the 'weak individual skills', 'little understanding of how to exploit space' and 'poor progression'? What would be your lesson objectives for the following lesson and how would you plan to achieve these?

Year 9 basketball lesson observation

Pupils generally had weak individual skills, except in passing over short distances and showing little understanding of how to exploit space with a numerical advantage. In the warm-up, boys were passing and receiving consistently, accurately and effectively over short distances. In the fast break practice on the basket to lay up, passing over longer distances and on the move lacked consistency in accuracy and length. Movement on to the ball was hesitant. Only two boys could do a lay up.

As the lesson progressed, a small number of boys improved in passing accurately over the distance. In the conditioned games, 3 against 2 and 2 against 1, pupils had little understanding of how to exploit space with a numerical advantage. Progress was poor, even though pupils had experienced three long units of work and were a more able group.

Summary

The major arguments in this chapter so far have been that it is important for you as the teacher to think about how your lessons will contribute to the aims of the curriculum and how they will help pupils develop the concepts, processes and skills required to achieve these aims. It has also emphasized that the traditional focus upon skill development does not provide pupils with a holistic experience or a broad understanding of the concepts, processes and skills required to be truly 'physically educated'.

It has also stressed that links and connections within and between key processes are vital across a PE curriculum and this may even be achieved at the lesson level. For example, pupils' evaluating and improving skills are arguably vital to the development of any concept, process or skill. Although this chapter uses the range and content of 'outwitting opponents (through invasion games) as its stimulus, the principles of adopting challenging (both cognitively and as well as physically), motivating, enjoyable and progressive teaching activities are hopefully clear beyond the examples provided.

Reflect

Read the following 'soccer sports coaching' articles and assess their value for your own teaching of physical education (not just in soccer or other invasion games):

Holt, J.E., Ward, P. and Wallhead, T.L. (2006) The transfer of learning from play practices to game play in young adult soccer players, *Physical Education and Sport Pedagogy, 11*(2): 101 18.

Williams, M.A. and Hodges, N.J. (2005) Practice, instruction and skill acquisition in soccer: challenging tradition, *Journal of Sports Sciences, 23*(6): 637–50.

Reflect

What value do you think a sport education model would bring to teaching the key concepts processes and skills to your pupils?

This chapter has attempted to show that your planning in PE should be process-driven rather than activity-driven. It recognizes that your lesson will fit into schemes and units of work that have already been planned. However, like your lesson, they will hopefully have been planned with the learner's needs at the forefront of the planning process. A focused and clearly defined lesson objective will enable you to plan everything else effectively (from how you plan to assess learning within the lesson, to how you will organize groups). All learners are motivated by progress (QCA, 2008c) so plan how you aim to help your pupils achieve and recognize this.

The programme of study in PE provides great opportunity for teachers to plan and teach motivating, creative, challenging, active and enjoyable lessons for all pupils. It is your challenge as a trainee teacher to take the framework provided by the national curriculum and use it to develop:

- successful learners who enjoy learning, make progress and achieve;
- confident individuals who are able to live safe, healthy and fulfilling lives;
- responsible citizens who make a positive contribution to society.

(QCA, 2007: 189)

What next?

The lesson plan is not a 'straightjacket' but rather a framework with which you work from. In this chapter you will have begun to focus upon what you need to teach as well as how you plan to teach it. The following chapters seek to provide you with other information crucial to planning and teaching your PE lesson including:

- how you will assess the learning outcomes of your lesson;
- how you will manage the lesson and plan for positive behaviour;
- how you will ensure that the lesson is safe;
- how you will promote an inclusive 'classroom' through differentiation;
- how you may teach personal learning, thinking skills and functional skills;
- how you may successfully incorporate information and communications technology (ICT) into your lessons.

A trainee teacher's lesson observation notes

I would now like you to fully maximize your teaching activities to encourage the girls to think about 'why and where' the skills are important. In this lesson they were unable to incorporate the lay-up when placed in a 3 v 3 game, why? Could your teaching activities have had a more realistic relation to the game, for example a defender chasing, a defender alongside, beating a defender? Could the game have 'forced' the use of the lay–up? 5 v 3? A 'free lay–up' zone? A 'no defender' zone?

Sample interview questions and developing a personal philosophy for teaching

Interview questions

- Describe a sequence of lessons you have taught in which you felt pupil learning levels were high. What were the success factors?
- Can you explain the process that you go through when planning a lesson?
- Argue against or for the statement that 'football should be in every school's PE curriculum'.

Is this you? Do you agree?

Could you describe what you think makes a good PE teacher?

Someone who is enthusiastic and competent at sport so they can perform accurate demonstrations. Also, someone who is patient and open to new ideas.

Sue Smith, Women's football

www.sportingchampions.org.uk

Further reading

DfES (2004) *High Quality PE and Sport for Young People.* Nottinghamshire: Department for Education and Skills.

Ellis, V., Butler, R. and Simpson, D. (2005) Planning for learning, in V. Ellis (ed.), *Learning and Teaching in Secondary Schools*, pp. 19–32. Exeter: Learning Matters.

OfSTED (2005a) *Ofsted Subject Reports*: 2003/04: *Physical Education in Secondary Schools.* HMI.

QCA (December 2005b) *Physical Education: 2004/05 Annual Report on Curriculum and Assessment.* London: Qualifications and Curriculum Authority.

QCA (2007) *Physical Education Programme of Study* accessed 2 July 2008 from Qualifications and Curriculum Authority (www.curriculum.qca.org).

Name:

Subject: **PE: Outwitting opponents through street soccer**

Trainee Target(s):	Standards
Design effective learning sequences within lessons ... demonstrating secure subject/curriculum knowledge	Q22

Pupil preparation for next lesson (homework)

Pupils are asked to do one thing which puts them out of their 'comfort zone'

Date & time	Class & attainment range	Lesson sequence	Curriculum references: (KS3/KS4/Post 16)
	Year 8 (4–6)	1 of 8	Key concepts: 1.1a, 1.3a, b Key processes: 2.1a, 2.3b Range and content: 3a, b Curriculum opportunities: 4a, c

Points from previous learning that need reinforcement e.g. misconceptions.

Already in Year 8 pupils have explored outwitting opponents through table tennis and hockey. A lot of pupils in the group seem reluctant to make mistakes and instead 'play safe'.

Learning objectives

By the end of the lesson pupils will:

• know the importance of individual technique and strategy in outwitting an opponent in street soccer. They will also understand the mental determination required to be creative in performing 1 v 1 skills.

The big picture

This unit will look at the pupils developing skills and use them creatively to outwit opponents.
It will also develop the mental determination required to succeed.
The PLT skills of creative thinking and becoming effective participators are particularly encouraged throughout this unit.

Learning outcomes

All pupils will:

- know 2 street soccer moves used to outwit an opponent;
- understand the need for mental determination (confidence) to be prepared to try these moves.

Most pupils will:

- have applied at least 2 stree soccer moves in a 1 v 1 and small game context;
- demonstrated confidence by attempting creative attack and escape moves.

Some pupils will:

- have applied a range of creative street soccer moves in a 1 v 1 and small game contexts;
- demonstrated confidence by attempting their own creative attack and escape moves.

Addressing the needs of individual= – strategies you will use to ensure inclusion:

- setting suitable learning challenges – differentiate learning outcomes for the lesson.
- different equipment is available far different pupils.
- use of continuous video loop to help learning.

How I will assess the learning objective/s (HIWALO):

- through teacher observation of pupils' involvement levels and their willingness to take risks.
- pupils' self-perceptions of their own confidence will be assessed via the plenary.

Cross curricular links (with specific curriculum references)		
PLTS	Functional skills and Key skills	Other links
Creative thinkers – use imagination and own ideas for creative improvisation.	N/A	ECM – use their imagination and creativity to develop new ideas, insights and new ways of doing things.
Effective participators – active participation and engagement of pupils.		Cross curriculum dimensions – Creativity and critical thinking.

Resources (including ICT)
24 pupils
24 balls, cones, bibs, street soccer DVD, TV and projector

ORGANIZATION & EQUIPMENT	TEACHING POINTS	DIFFERENTIATION
In the changing rooms a video of street soccer is shown and pupils are told that they will be learning these moves over the duration of this unit of work.	The 'big picture' is shown at the start of the lesson to provide the pupils with understanding of the unit of work.	
Pupils are told in the changing room that the first activity will require them to get a partner. Pupil A collects a ball from behind the bench and rejoins pupil B.		
The following explanation of street soccer has been written on the board: **What is street soccer?** 'Street soccer has many different styles from all over the world, but what we consider street soccer to be is fluid play, **feints, deception**, and extensive use of groundwork, as well as goals, pannas and **creative moves** to **beat your opponent. Technique and strategy** are the key elements to play a good game. Each move in street soccer becomes a way to show a **creative attack and escape technique**, rather than a simple way to go round your opponent, the aim is to **play beautifully**'.	The philosophy of street soccer is outlined to show that the focus will be on creativity and deception to outwit an opponent.	
The lessons objectives are outlined and then the teacher quickly uses a pupil to		

demonstrate a panna (a nutmeg)	'Lots of touches and movement on the ball'. 'Keep at a fast pace'.	Teacher can move pupils to provide even competition. Tennis balls are available to make control even harder. 'Can you get a panna on another pupil'?
Pupils then begin their 1 v 1 and attempt to gain a panna over their opponent. Change opponents frequently. (Play music)		
The teacher leads the pupils in a warm-up in which the development of rhythm is important; • opposites • knee taps • foot taps • elbow taps • cap dance • cap wiggle dance (Music)	Explained that this is a type of warm-up common in Brazil	*The focus is not on formations or team strategy at this stage but instead the emphasis is the pupils having the confidence to try things.* *Reinforcing the need for rhythm in street soccer and a different approach to traditional football.*
When the warm-up is finished the teacher puts the pupils into teams of 3s. One small pitch is set up and shown and the pupils then set up their pitch and play.	None at this stage but pupils are reminded about the panna and what is written on the board. 'Try things' 'Be positive' 'Be confident to try to take on a player'	Goals can be made bigger or smaller for a team. Teams can be changed and adjusted.
The skill (flipping an opponent) is played on a loop and projected onto the sports hall wall.	Disguise Quick feet Confidence Getting	Pupils practise without an opponent and then challenge another pupil when they think they are ready. A variety of balls are available.

Pupils are encouraged to put into the practice the skill/principles learned.

This lesson is not about one team winning a 'tournament'.

Pupils are mixed up and now play for a different team. A goal can also be scored by creating a panna.	Again the focus is on trying as many skills as they can to attack and escape from an opponent	Goals can be made bigger or smaller for a team. Teams can be changed and adjusted.
In their 3s pupils have a ball each. They perform the following routine: a) All pass with their hands the ball to their right – put the ball on the floor b) Now pass the ball with the feet on the floor to the right – pick it up and c) Volley from a self-feed to the right, catch it and d) Head it to the right.	'Here's a challenge for your team' 'Concentrate and work as a team to complete the challenge'	Use only one/two balls Speed up/change direction Use a tennis ball
After the balls have been returned to the bench, pupils sit down in front of the whiteboard. 'When I say go I want you to put up your right hand up if you now feel more confident in trying to beat/outwit your opponent and put your left hand if you still worry when you are given the ball … go'. 'Before the next lesson I would like you to do one thing that puts you out of your comfort zone e.g. answering a question in class, volunteering for something'.	No pupil is 'singled out' and the teacher can quickly assess how the pupils felt during the lesson. The target is not PE-specific in an attempt to relate the lesson's objectives to the pupils' school life.	

2   Assessment and reflection within the physical education lesson

Ian Luke

A teacher's story

> We were asked to map the National Curriculum key processes against the content in the activities and units of work that we follow in the PE department. It soon became very obvious to us that all our units focused almost completely on skill development, and that there was significant overlap between units in what we were trying to achieve with regard to the key processes. It was a big slap in the face for the design of our curriculum but also for us as teachers in how we were limiting learning opportunities for pupils within individual lessons. If we could not defend what we were trying to achieve, how could we argue that pupils were progressing?
>
> Paul, PE Teacher, age 37

The learning outcomes for this chapter are:

☑ To understand the principles of assessment for learning
☑ To understand the impact that assessment can have on the learning of your pupils
☑ To relate assessment principles to the programme of study in PE
☑ To consider how strategies such as questioning and providing feedback relate to assessment

The professional standards for Qualified Teacher Status (QTS) addressed in this chapter

Q4:	Communicate effectively with children, young people, colleagues, parents and carers.
Q10:	Have a knowledge and understanding of a range of teaching, learning and behaviour management strategies and know how to use and adapt them, including how to personalize learning and provide opportunities for all learners to achieve their potential.
Q12:	Know a range of approaches to assessment, including the importance of formative assessment.
Q22:	Plan for progression across the age and ability for which they are trained, designing effective learning sequences within lessons and across series of lessons and demonstrating secure subject/curriculum knowledge.
Q25:	Teach lessons and sequences of lessons across the age and abilty range for which they are trained in which they: **(b)** build on prior knowledge, develop concepts and processes, enable learners to apply new knowledge, understanding and skills and meet learning objectives; **(d)** Teach lessons ... in which they manage the learning of individuals, groups and whole classes, modifying their teaching to suit the stage of the lesson.
Q26(a):	Make effective use of a range of assessment, monitoring and recording strategies.
Q26(b):	Assess the learning needs of those they teach in order to set challenging learning objectives.
Q27:	Provide timely, accurate and constructive feedback on learners' attainment, progress and areas for development.
Q28:	Support and guide learners to reflect on their learning, identify the progress they have made and identify their emerging learning needs.

Starting point

'All types of assessment, of any degree of formality, involve interpretation of a pupil's response against some standard of expectation' (Harlen et al., 1994: 273). As such, assessment involves choices and decisions about what is appropriate evidence for a particular purpose (Harlen, 2005), and how to interpret that evidence. Assessment is about encouraging progress, improvement and achievement, and is integral to the learning and teaching processes.

Reflect

Imagine yourself standing in front of five hoops, four of which are the same colour and one a different colour. You have five bean bags in your hands. You are asked to throw the bean bags one at a time to try and hit the odd colour hoop. Unfortunately, you are blindfolded and therefore you do not know which of the five hoops you are aiming for (Figure 2.1).

Figure 2.1 Blindfolded target task
Source: adapted from a workshop task developed by Andy Frapwell

Consider the following sequential scenarios and the effect each would have on your actions and on your emotions. The position of the odd hoop is changed after each scenario.

1   After every throw you receive no feedback, not a noise.
2   After every throw you receive great praise, regardless of where each bean bag lands.
3   After every throw you receive feedback on your result (e.g. too long).
4   After every throw, you receive feedback on your result and suggestions to improve the throw (e.g. too long, try releasing the bean bag earlier).
5   After every throw, you return to the scenario whereby you receive no feedback as in scenario (1).

What would your reaction be to each scenario? In scenario (1) you are likely to throw one bean bag in roughly the direction of each hoop, although you may be a little frustrated that you will only get 20 per cent success at maximum, assuming you are accurate – emotionally, you may feel left out in the cold. In scenario (2), therefore, the praise initially will be welcomed, although it could actually limit progress as you try and replicate the action that got praise (which, unbeknown to you, could have actually been unsuccessful). Scenario (3), however, provides some corrective feedback. You may become frustrated if you keep receiving exactly the same feedback even though you are trying different things, or when you do not know what to try in order to correct the mistake. Scenario (4) gives you that desired feedback, stating where you are, what you need and how to get there in terms of strategy. Emotionally, you are likely to feel supported and therefore be more willing to keep practising. Yet, scenario (5) returns to no feedback, at which point you are likely to be even more frustrated and annoyed than when you first encountered the situation in scenario (1), and possibly more likely to 'not bother' and throw the bean bags anywhere.

In a nutshell, that is assessment – assessment *for* improvement, progress and achievement. Assessment needs to inform, guide and provide steps for progression. Assessment is, quite simply, integral to effective teaching and significantly influences pupils' learning *and* behaviour in a lesson. Focusing at 'lesson-based' assessment, the majority of key principles can be discussed under the umbrella concept of *assessment for learning* (Casbon and Spackman, 2005).

Assessment for learning principles and strategies will be discussed, but initially it is important to take a wider focus of assessment; there is a need to examine what assessment in PE is all about, to consider some of the fundamental principles of assessment and to highlight some of the most common mistakes in undertaking assessment in PE.

PE and assessment

In general, PE suffers from a misunderstanding of assessment. Obviously, there is not universal unawareness of principles underpinning assessment; indeed, it could be argued that these are articulated both in departmental policies and by teachers. However, true understanding would imply that these principles are consistently and effectively applied, and this is simply not the case.

It is imperative that teachers understand the effects that a well-considered approach to assessment can have on pupils' learning (DfES, 2007). 'Teaching to the test' should be avoided as such requirements are not conducive to good formative practices (Black et al., 2003) but it should be acknowledged that learning is strongly guided by assessment and the nature of pupils' understanding is enmeshed in the learning tasks, activities and opportunities provided (DfES, 2007). Thus, while assessment is not the 'master' of what is taught, it should not be viewed as a bolt-on addition; it needs to be included analytically into learning and teaching processes (Lambert, 1995). Indeed, assessment has to be an integral aspect of good teaching in physical education (Piotrowski and Capel, 2000; OfSTED, 2003).

Reminder

To lay down the foundations and context for lesson-based assessment, there are some important points to remember:

- Attainment Target Levels in the National Curriculum for PE are based on the content of the 'key processes' of the Curriculum.
- There are five key processes (developing skills in physical activity; making and applying decisions; developing physical and mental capacity; evaluating and improving; making informed choices about healthy, active lifestyles).
- The five key processes are subdivided, with the subdivisions totalling 16.
- Some subdivisions contain more than one point or factor to consider.
- Attainment Target Levels are a 'best-fit', 'pen portrait' of pupils working at that particular level.

The purpose of assessment

Most teachers would concur that the overriding purpose of assessment in PE should be to encourage improvement, progress, achievement, confidence and feelings of competence, and better attitudes to learning (Casbon and Spackman, 2005). The problems start emerging in the interpretation of these purposes, and how they are translated into specific contexts (e.g. different teachers may have different views on what is 'progress' in a specific gymnastics lesson). 'Purpose' is context-bound depending on pupils' stage of learning and the 'direction' in which you would like pupils to progress. In short, assessment can be used for a range of purposes and, therefore, choices need to be made in order to fit an appropriate assessment strategy for the purpose to which the assessment is to be put (Lambert, 1995). Teachers have to make choices, and underpinning these choices are what Carroll (1994) referred to as the 'why' questions of assessment (Why assess pupils? What use is made of it?). Carroll continued to neatly summarize the choices as formative (feedback; diagnostic; motivation) and summative (certification; recognition of achievement; motivation).

While teachers may not always like to admit it, from a historical perspective the purpose of assessment has often been selection; 'We need to see who will be in the district athletics' for example. The implications of this are numerous and significant. For example, it may be that the tasks selected are likely to be 'final-event' structured, so whole-action or full-sized games/activities are introduced earlier than would be desired or, more significantly, the feedback that has most impact will become product- rather than process-oriented. Taking the latter point, consider the following scenario:

> *A lesson has focused on sprinting technique and pupils have practised the pumping action of the arms and the clawing action of the legs – yet the lesson finishes with timed races or races purely to identify the rank order of pupils in speed. The praise, feedback and impact lies then with speed and not technique. Assuming that learning a new skill can sometimes lead to an initial dip in performance during*

> *transitional periods from old to new technique, and when under pressure pupils are likely to resort to previously learned technique, the teacher may not really be creating a learning environment conducive to progressive learning.*

Obviously, this is an extreme example, with 'high-stakes' assessment in terms of public peer pressure being emphasized, and it is accepted that the gradual application of 'pressurized' lower stake situations may be necessary in certain activities. However, the point is that the purpose of assessment has a significant impact upon the learning that takes place in PE. Thus, as there is obvious scope in purpose, each purpose has to be kept in mind when the arrangements for assessment are designed (Task Group on Assessment & Testing (TGAT), 2007).

Referencing systems

At this point, it is worth considering and comparing the different reference systems that form the foundations of assessment (Table 2.1), which, in turn, can also highlight some of the incongruity of common assessment practices in PE departments.

Table 2.1 A comparison of different reference systems using an example of PE

	Ipsative-reference	Norm-reference	Criterion-reference
Example	Pupils' educational gymnastics sequence of own creation	Pupil's fitness test score	Pupil's attempts at scoring a number of baskets from a set position
Ideology	Child centred	Group centred	Activity centred
Purpose	Comparison with pupil's own previous sequence. To assess progress	Comparison with group fitness scores. To assess how fit pupil is in relation to other pupils of same age	Comparison with a standard (scoring baskets). To assess how much pupil has mastered skill of scoring baskets from a set position

Note: This section of table taken from Carroll (1994: 12).

The National Curriculum for PE is *criterion-referenced*. Attainment target levels form the criteria and pupils are judged against these. The key point to make here is that the criteria relates to the 'key processes' (QCA, 2007b) or previously the 'aspects/strands' (DfES/QCA, 1999) in the National Curriculum, and not activities or individual sports.

If and when pupils are directly compared to each other (e.g. rank order), or against wider, more generalized data (e.g. age-related fitness levels), assessment is deemed to be *norm-* (or nomothetic-) *referenced* (Rowntree, 1977; Carroll, 1994).

Taking a more child-centred philosophy, assessment is *ipsative-* (or ideographic-) *referenced* when the focus is on individual progress and development, and any comparisons made are purely against a pupil's previous work.

It could be argued, therefore, that when we return to the overall aims of assessment (i.e. to encourage improvement, progress, achievement, confidence and feelings of competence in PE, and better attitudes to learning), most assessment should be a combination of criterion- and ipsative-referenced; this is not to ignore norm-referenced assessment but clearly, a more mastery-oriented focus would, in theory, be more desirable.

Referencing systems in practice

Criterion-referencing

Even though the assessment criteria for the National Curriculum is based on 'key processes', PE departments prefer to level, or even sublevel, pupils with regards to 'activity', providing them with an attainment target level for their performance in each and every unit of work. The National Curriculum for PE has never required this and, more importantly, was never designed for this. Each activity is simply a vehicle, a context, for pupils to progress in their learning of the 'key processes'. The assumption that you can 'level' at the end of a unit of work, or worse still, that 'levelling' can take place in individual lessons (Greenwell, 2006), wraps assessment firmly into task completion and content, rather than quality and process. In addition, QCA (2008a) noted, 'there should be sufficient time between level-related judgements to allow a pupil to show progress'. Moreover, each attainment target level is an amalgamation of all the key processes, thereby creating a 'pen portrait' of a pupil who is working at that level. As such, to say a child has 'attained' that level within a lesson or unit would suggest that a teacher has assessed all 16 subdivisions to the five key processes in the National Curriculum, for every pupil in the class, in anything between one and six hours! The problem is often magnified as the levels gained for each unit are then usually 'averaged' to provide the 'final' level for each pupil – potentially resulting in a new level altogether (e.g. Level 6 for football and Level 4 for hockey would provide the average result of Level 5). Clearly this is wrong; the key aim should be to 'best-fit' each pupil to a 'pen portrait' level. Interestingly, as Harlen et al. (1994: 273–74) noted:

> the usefulness of criterion-referenced assessment depends on the way in which the criteria are defined. Too tightly defined criteria, while facilitating easy judgement of mastery, require an extensive list which fragments the curriculum.

Levelling and sublevelling in every unit, creating an almost endless list of 'statement banks' for every activity clearly, will fragment judgement against the key processes. As such, while PE departments have defended their practices in levelling and sublevelling activities (Cunningham and Smith, 2003; Greenwell, 2006), the effectiveness of the practice has to be questioned.

Norm-referencing

Comparing pupils can, and indeed, will happen in PE lessons. While the issues surrounding this can be debated, the intention here is to state that as a 'rule of thumb', open or overt comparisons do not need to be emphasized – pupils will do enough of it themselves! Teachers may argue that they do not openly emphasize comparisons; yet, in reality, it is integrated into common practice. Consider the practice of sublevelling pupils in activities (e.g. following a football unit Billy is awarded 4c, James 4a and Sam 4b); to make this 'criterion-referenced' the PE department must have created large statement banks for every aim in every unit or activity; PE departments have tried this. Greenwell argued that on a lesson focusing on 'straight and square passing in hockey', then it would be 'good practice' to state objectives such as:

> By the end of today's lesson you should understand how to complete straight and square passing which is a level 4b skill. If you are able to apply the straight and square passing in the game situation you will achieve a level 5c. Some of you will be able to control the game by using the straight and square passing effectively and therefore start to work at level 6.

(2006: 28)

Without even questioning whether all pupils will have the same opportunity in a single lesson to show all of these things, and not even asking what levels 4a, 4c, 5a and 5b would look like, such comments are far from useful – in reality, pupils will probably be compared to each other and will be graded on 'ability' (e.g. James has scraped 4a, Sam is not a 5 but is better than James so we need to give him 4b and clearly Billy is the best out of the three but again is not a 5 – level 4c then). Immediately, this questions reliability of assessment, as Harlen (2005: 213) noted, bias in teachers' assessments is, 'generally due to teachers taking into account information about non-relevant aspects of students' behaviour or the ... [general] ability of a student in judging performance in a particular task'.

Ipsative-referencing

For effective ipsative-referencing, effective planning and recording of pupils' progress is required, especially when it is likely that pupils will have different teachers for different units throughout the year. In addition, the focus needs to be on pupils' learning and not simply on task completion or behaviour (Casbon and Spackman, 2005). As such, we are moving into the realms of assessment for learning that is discussed later.

Profiling

The previous section seems to highlight problems and mistakes without offering solutions. However, pupils' individual needs can be planned for, which in turn can be 'tracked' to language that exists in attainment target levels. There is a natural link between focusing on pupils' learning and being able to track to 'levels' (e.g. in the context of gymnastics, pupil may be trying improve the *consistency* by which they perform movements efficiently, which would track across to language in attainment target level 5)

Notably, it has been argued that assessment should be learning-focused. A key benefit of de-emphasizing the levelling function of assessment and re-emphasizing the learning function is that teachers and pupils are encouraged to make links between physical education activities and their learning (DfES, 2007). As such, levels are not ignored but the focus is on learning, and not simply on content. The important point here is that a teacher would be *profiling* the development of a pupil and assessing 'achievement' as opposed to 'attainment'.

Frapwell et al. (2002) argued the need to consider the difference between the terms 'attainment' and 'achievement'; 'achievement' being a term also encouraged by Casbon and Spackman (2005). The distinction is very useful when we wish to consider how to integrate assessment into day-to-day teaching. It means teachers can consider *profiling* pupils' progress, and therefore plan, teach and review for improvement and progress. In short, not every subdivision of the key processes is focused on at a single time or lesson – a pupil could show that they are 'achieving' at a 'level' with regard to specific subdivisions of key processes, which over a period of time, and in coordination with other lessons and units of work, could add to an overall profile of all the subdivisions.

So how do we start profiling?

When focusing on lesson content, it may be useful first to consider learning outcomes. It is crucial that learning outcomes are both precise and assessable. Without precision, pupils may struggle to understand what is being asked of them and, inevitably, the teacher will find it harder to identify progress. From a cynical perspective, if the learning outcome is not precise, it may be that the teacher does not actually know what they are looking for. The key to both precision and assessability is to focus on pupils' learning needs which can then be tracked to language found in the attainment target levels in the National Curriculum; for example, 'consistently', 'with accuracy' and 'with precision'.

Consider the importance of language within the following three statements:

1   Billy did a forward roll.
2   Billy can do a forward roll.
3   Billy can do a forward roll consistently.

(adapted from examples cited in Carroll, 1994)

The implications of each statement are clearly evident; Billy doing a forward roll could mean that he did it once and was never successful again, Billy being able to do a forward roll suggests a greater element of consistency, but the word 'consistently' removes doubt. Interestingly, none of these statements indicate how well Billy performs the forward roll; to put it bluntly, the quality of Billy's performance could be awful. However, if we add 'and with fluency', or 'and with precision', the implications of the final statement ('Billy can do a forward roll consistently, and with fluency') are very much different. It could be argued that this point is just one of semantics, but is it is far from that. Once the outcome is both precise and assessable, the development of a 'core' task for the lesson is more easily designed and effective teaching practice is encouraged. That is, Billy needs the opportunity to learn the forward roll but also needs several attempts to demonstrate that he can perform it with consistency and with fluency. However, almost built automatically into this requirement is the learning opportunity for both self- and peer assessment. Thus, a 'core task' may be working in pairs, teaching each other a forward roll with the aid of task cards or Information and Communications Technology (ICT) mechanisms; importantly, this process also encourages the design of clear success criteria that can be shared with pupils, encouraging them to become more independent learners. As OfSTED (2003: 1) noted, 'where on-going assessment is effective, teachers ensure precise, shared, learning objectives are used to check pupils' progress at different stages throughout lessons'. It is also worth noting that this approach focuses on the key processes in the National Curriculum but helps put 'meat on the bones' with regard to appropriate content and context.

Moreover, 'profiling' will ensure that assessment will not become burdensome, but instead will become, something that is manageable and beneficial for everyone involved in the learning and teaching processes. It will mean that lessons will have 'flexibility' to focus on the needs of pupils because you are not trying to compress 16 subdivisions of key processes into every one lesson. Crucially, this flexibility also means that teachers may be more likely to spot that occasion when an individual pupil does something special, when that individual achieves something they have not before; as QCA (2008a) noted:

> occasionally, learners will demonstrate progress in their skills and understanding when this was not expected' and teachers need to be in a position to grasp these moments. As a result, lessons are more likely to become 'exhibitions of learning'.
>
> (DfES, 2007).

The added benefit of using precise learning outcomes, and the emerging 'core tasks' from these outcomes, is the natural sense of ecological validity and authenticity to the assessment. Such curriculum-integrated assessment will maximize validity, linking 'learning activities' with 'assessment opportunities' (Shepard, 1993, cited in Black, 1993). Assessment will integrate with 'pedagogy to maximise its formative potential in promoting learning (Torrance and Pryor, 2001: 616).

Importantly, teachers already have a raft of resources to help them with their planning of core tasks. Once we accept that individual needs can then be tracked to attainment target language, the attainment target level identified from that language can guide teachers to QCA guidance material and schemes of work for example.

Having planned to individual needs (and tracked them to 'levels'), assessment becomes a process of acknowledging whether pupils achieved intended learning outcomes or not. Pupils may have struggled with a core task and therefore need to keep working towards the intended learning outcomes or, indeed, they may have exceeded them – useful information for planning future lessons! In short, assessment becomes an integral part of the learning and teaching processes, providing both 'feedback' and 'feedforward' (Lambert, 1995) and the focus is in terms of what to do to help further learning, not what level a pupil has reached (Harlen, 2005).

Profiling at lesson level easily builds up to profiling at unit level. If curriculum design is well constructed (rather than the practice whereby experts in a department design the unit of work for 'their sport' that often results in a content focus and overlap in key processes taught), and teachers are required to focus on specific processes within specific units, it is a relatively simple process to expand profiling to years and key stages and thus provide an easy means by which to examine the 'best fit' level for a pupil. As OfSTED (2003: 2) noted, 'the very best departments use assessment information as a means of reflecting upon curriculum planning and programme design'.

Reflect

It is the end of a Year 7 unit of work, which the department has labelled 'football – control and passing', and the teachers of two groups decide they need to assess the pupils. A series of small-sided games are established in a form of a round-robin tournament. The teachers stand on the sidelines ready to assess the pupils and ready to place an attainment level to each pupil's performance.

Is the assessment task an appropriate one? Will all the children have an equal opportunity to demonstrate their ability? Can an attainment target level be stated for each pupil? What problems will the teachers face in their assessment? What issues are there for the pupils with regard to this assessment task?

Considering the scene in the above scenario, for example, it is possible that without 'clear performance criteria' pupils and teachers may have different perceptions of what is required, and, thus, immediately placing doubt on the reliability of the assessment task. Unfortunately, the teacher will drift into a system of assessment whereby they are left hoping that pupils will show them what they want to see and pupils are left guessing whether they are demonstrating what the teacher wants to see. It is likely, as a result, that teachers focus on 'how good' they think pupils are in terms of general ability rather than assess them for improvement, progress or achievement.

Assessment for learning

Assessment for learning is about process. It is about interpreting evidence, for the use of learners as well as teachers, in deciding how to progress learning, deciding where learners are in their learning; identifying the intended learning outcomes; and planning how best to get to those outcomes.

(Assessment Reform Group, 2002: 1).

Assessment for learning has been well documented both in a generic educational sense (e.g. Black et al., 2003) and also with specific reference to PE (e.g. Casbon and Spackman, 2005). As such, the review here focuses on basic principles and suggests some useful strategies to encourage learning and possible ways to avoid assessment pitfalls.

Formative, summative and progressive assessment

Discussions surrounding assessment for learning often include a distinction between the terms 'formative' and 'summative' assessment; formative being the main focus undertaken as it refers to assessments that are used in the process of interaction in the learning and teaching processes of PE including 'diagnosis, feedback, correction or confirmation' (Carroll, 1994: 13). However, summative assessment, the overall summary of performance, can also provide useful feedback that can aid the learning processes. As a result, there have been calls for a more holistic view of 'progressive assessment' (Maxwell, 2004, cited in Harlen, 2005) acknowledging that if there is a focus on the learning processes, then the boundaries between 'formative assessment' and 'summative assessment' converge.

Day-to-day, periodic and transitional assessment

While the focus remains at the individual lesson level, it should be acknowledged that assessing pupils' progress (APP) requires an integrated and well-considered approach to day-to-day, periodic and transitional assessment (QCA, 2008a). Assessment at all these points requires that assessment criteria are 'grounded in the national curriculum programmes of study and level descriptions' and have 'the potential both to offer a profile of pupils' current achievement as well as formative outcomes' (QCA, 2008a). Clearly, the profiling mechanism suggested would encourage a coordinated approach across lessons, units, years and key stages; assessment for learning (or progressive assessment) would require this.

Effective assessment for learning

It is argued that the cyclic, three key processes involved in effective assessment for learning are:

1   planning for improvement, progress and achievement;
2   teaching and assessing for improvement, progress and achievement;
3   reviewing improvement, progress and achievement.

The planning aspect with regard to specific and assessable learning outcomes has been addressed, and from a lesson-level perspective the reviewing aspect can be absorbed into a focus on the learning, teaching and assessing. Such a focus requires teachers and pupils to be engaged in a learning dialogue. It would appear that in order to develop this dialogue teachers need to clarify and share success criteria, develop effective questioning strategies to prompt pupils' knowledge, skills and understanding (and listen to what pupils say); and provide feedback that summarizes where pupils are in their learning, where they need to go and suggest ways to improve, make progress and achieve. In addition, these aspects are all 'wrapped up' in the development of pupils' ability to self- and peer assess (Assessment Reform Group, 2002; Casbon and Spackman, 2005).

Clarifying and sharing success criteria

At a superficial level, this point may seem the most obvious, and indeed, assuming earlier guidance with regard to establishing specific and assessable learning outcomes is followed, it is relatively straightforward to share these outcomes (and therefore the assessment criteria) with pupils. The common mnemonic here for teachers is the acronym 'W.I.L.F.' – referring to the stem phrase to utilize in lessons, 'What I'm Looking For ...'. Other stem phrases include 'What I expect from everyone is ...' and 'To be successful you ...' (DfES, 2004a). However, importantly, the teacher must have good pedagogical content knowledge to ensure that this aspect of assessment for learning is effective; without it, 'teachers will struggle to plan effectively or build their conversations with pupils around key ideas in order to move student learning forward' (Jones and Moreland, 2005: 157). Thus, teachers must have a 'baseline' understanding of pupils' present knowledge, skills and understanding, and must understand what they would like the pupils to achieve and what this 'looks' like. Finally, it is worth pointing out that sharing learning outcomes requires teachers to focus on what pupils are going to *learn* and not what they are going to *do*; that is, teachers need to be learning-focused as opposed to content-focused (DfES, 2004a). To clarify, 'to know the characteristics of an effective bounce pass' is a learning outcome, whereas 'to do a bounce pass' is simply an activity that will occur in the lesson.

Questioning

Questioning can have several purposes; it can focus thinking, it can develop interest, it can challenge; it can encourage speculation; it can direct and guide reasoning. Importantly, from an assessment perspective, questioning can directly link to either *convergent* or *divergent assessment*; the former assessing *if* the pupil knows, understands or can do a predetermined thing and would therefore be characterized by closed questioning and tasks, the latter assessing *what* a pupil knows, understands and can do, and would therefore be characterized by more open questioning and tasks (Torrance and Prior, 2001). Bloom and Krathwohl (1956) considered questions according to cognitive complexity, ranging from the cognitive objective of 'knowledge' through to the cognitive objective of 'evaluation' (Table 2.2) which can be useful in designing questions.

Table 2.2 Bloom's taxonomy

Cognitive objective	What pupils need to do. Possible question stems
Knowledge	Define; Recall; Describe; Label; Identify; Match
Comprehension	Explain; Translate; Illustrate; Summarize; Extend
Application	Demonstrate; Predict; Employ; Solve; Use
Analysis	Analyse; Infer; Relate; Explore; Support
Synthesis	Design; Create; Compose; Reorganize; Combine
Evaluation	Assess; Evaluate; Appraise; Defend; Justify

Source: adapted from DfES (2004b: 13).

Nevertheless, however you wish to differentiate the types of question, the important point to make is that questioning is powerful and therefore cannot be an afterthought in planning or assessment. As OfSTED (2003) noted, well-focused questioning of pupils' knowledge and understanding can reinforce pupils' practical responses and teachers can use the resulting information to redefine tasks for pupils of differing abilities. Thus, depending on intended learning outcomes, key questions and prompts must be included in any lesson plan, and these must be backed up by careful observations during the lesson: 'Observation should guide questioning, with teachers' interventions then being more informed and better focused' (Torrance and Pryor, 2001: 628). Indeed, one of the most common mistakes teachers can make is to stop a group, having observed something is not working, but not preparing the key questions and prompts to encourage a change.

Reflect

You are in the middle of a question-and-answer session focusing upon rotation in gymnastics. You perceive that, at the very least, pupils should appreciate that during rotation, moving from a large to a small shape will result in faster rotation. However, you are aware that some in the group may need to be challenged. What questions and prompts would you plan for? What order should the questions be in?

Prior to examining common pitfalls in questioning (Table 2.3), it is worth considering pupils' focus in lessons. It has been argued that pupils can be more concerned with getting the correct answer than understanding the answer that they provide (Woods, 1980; Luke, 1998), and can use strategies such as referring to items previously articulated in teacher dialogue. In short, correct answers to questions, especially to closed questions, are not necessarily accompanied by understanding. As such, a teacher needs to consider 'expected answers' and to look for indicators of misunderstanding. Misunderstanding, and poor answers to questions, can potentially be incredibly illuminating with regard to evaluating the effectiveness of a lesson and how to differentiate for particular pupils. Thus, while a teacher may not want to 'embarrass' a pupil who provides an incorrect answer, that pupil should be the first person that the teacher goes to at the beginning of the next task – someone else getting the 'correct' answer does not mean that the first pupil will now understand the 'mistake' in their original answer. A teacher must follow through with misunderstanding and find the cause even though this may not be in the whole group scenario in the first instance.

Reflect

DfES (2004b) highlighted several examples of common pitfalls in questioning, and possible questioning strategies to consider (Table 2.3). Examine the table and reflect on a particular lesson you have taught. How many of the pitfalls did you fall into? Did you use any of the possible strategies for effective questioning?

Table 2.3 Pitfalls in questioning and strategies for effective questioning

Pitfalls	Strategies for effective questioning
Not being clear about why you are asking the question	Building in 'wait time' before requiring an answer; the aim is to encourage longer answers, encourage variety in answers, encourage pupils to ask questions in return and take more 'risks'
Asking too many closed questions that need only a short answer	Use the 'no-hands' rule to allow you to distribute and direct questions and pitch them appropriately to individuals
Asking too many questions at once	'Hands-up' rule, and slowly offer more 'cues' to the answer until majority of class have their hand up; the aim is to encourage engagement and potentially identify where there are gaps in understanding

Asking difficult questions without building up to them	Use of 'small whiteboards' so all pupils have to provide an answer at the same time; the aim is to get a quick overview of the group's understanding
Asking superficial questions	Give pupils the 'big question' in advance for pupils to prepare for a question as they work through a lesson
Asking a question and then answering it yourself	Probing for clarification; the aim is to encourage pupils to extend their answers
Asking bogus 'guess what is in my head' questions	Allowing time for collaboration before answering
Focusing on a small number of pupils	Avoiding effusive praise for correct answers but highlight why answers were good, or which parts were good
Dealing ineffectively with wrong answers or misconceptions	
Not treating pupils' answers seriously	

Source: adapted from DfES (2003)

Feedback

> At best, teachers carefully observe pupils' responses to tasks, identifying strengths, errors and misconceptions. They use this information to intervene and provide specific feedback to guide pupils towards improvement.
>
> (OfSTED, 2003: 1)

Feedback can have several purposes: it can acknowledge what has been learned, it can encourage reflection and speculation, it can encourage and motivate; it can guide progression; and it can encourage independent learning. Importantly, teachers 'should always be positive – recognising pupils' efforts and achievements to date, and developmental – offering specific details of ways forward' (DfES, 2004a: 12). From an assessment for learning perspective, it is crucial that teachers provide feedback that helps pupils know where they are in relation to learning goals (Harlen, 2005), and feedback that helps pupils understand where they need to go with their learning and how to get there (Assessment Reform Group, 2002).

Understandably, feedback is effective when it is personalized. However, in structuring how feedback is provided, it is worth remembering that assessment in integral to the learning and teaching processes and does not stand in isolation. Thus, there are several options that teachers can consider when providing feedback, depending on the context faced (Figure 2.2); the options being a combination of individual, small- or whole-group feedback that occurs 'within tasks' or 'between tasks'.

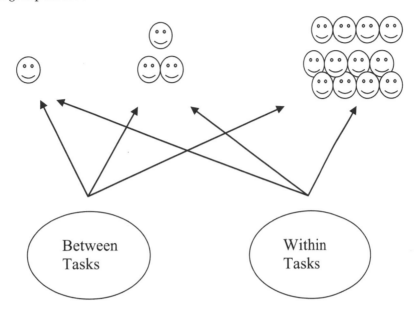

Figure 2.2 Options in how feedback is provided

Reflect

Consider the options in Figure 2.2. Why would you select a specific option? What would be the advantages and disadvantages of selecting each option? What implications does each option have for other aspects of pedagogy such as pace of lesson, behaviour management, motivation, and so on? As an example, the *small-group/within-task feedback* option is common in PE lessons but picture the scenario: a teacher sets a task to five groups and one by one moves through the groups. Group One are immediately engaged and their work 'corrected' to encourage progress in their learning. As the teacher moves through the groups, potentially 'correcting' the same mistakes, Group One are becoming a little bored – the challenge has gone. However, Group Five are still continuing, but inefficiently, as they have received no feedback yet. The teacher finally gets to Group Five, struggles to give them feedback because Group One are now being disruptive. However, the teacher finally completes the feedback, only to then stop the task because it has been going for 15 minutes and it is time to move on. Group Five have less than a minute in practising the work efficiently.

Self- and peer assessment

> Pupils do not become self-evaluative overnight. The development of peer- and self-assessment takes planning, time, patience and commitment ... By planning and using a range of techniques and by dedicating time to allow pupils to reflect on and discuss their learning, teachers can develop pupils' assessment skills.
>
> (DfES, 2004a: 10)

If it is accepted that assessment should be a continuous part of the teaching–learning process and involve pupils, wherever possible, as well as teachers in identifying next steps for progression (Harlen et al., 1994), then the key focus must be how to engage pupils in self- and peer assessment. It is more than 'marking' each other; it is about encouraging pupils to examine the quality of their work and their learning processes (QCA, 2008a). QCA (2008a) offered several strategies to encourage self- and peer assessment although DfES (2004a) suggested that 'thinking aloud' and 'teacher modelling' are useful in developing the necessary language and understanding of the self- and peer-assessment processes. Teachers must go beyond instructions; they must explain the intended learning outcomes, clarify the success criteria, make explicit what the pupils ordinarily cannot see, that is, the thoughts, ideas, strategies, reflections and feelings that go with decisions (Nisbet and Shucksmith, 1986; Luke and Hardy, 1999). It is worth noting though that physical actions can be difficult to describe and explain and this can become even more difficult as task complexity increases (Luke and Hardy, 1999), thus, the development of self- and peer assessment has to be a gradual and progressive process, becoming part of every lesson.

Conclusion

Assessment is integral to pedagogy – it has an impact on learning, emotion and behaviour; as such, it must be planned. Lesson-based assessment must be 'progressive' in that is has to combine features of both formative and summative assessment in order to encourage progress, improvement and achievement. To ensure that lesson-based assessment can feed into day-to-day, periodic and transitional assessment, intended learning outcomes (while focusing on individual needs) need to be tracked to language found in attainment target level 'pen portraits' – this has the added benefit of guiding the development of authentic, ecologically valid core tasks. Finally, to ensure assessment for learning takes place, teachers need to reflect and develop their practice in the effective sharing of success criteria, effective questioning, effective provision of feedback and the effective development of pupils' ability to self- and peer assess.

A trainee teacher's lesson observation notes

There is now a lot more thought to your own actions and behaviour. Your variety of questioning is now beginning to move beyond just recapping 'how can we make our dance more interesting?' and other strategies such as 'stand up and show us'. This can be further developed by thinking about how you can help students with the answers and assessing the group, for example extend thinking time or those who haven't got their hand up go and sit with someone who has and discuss answers. In addition to your improved range of questioning techniques you now 'show' what you expect and model ideas for the students to extend.

Sample interview questions and developing a personal philosophy for teaching

---

Interview questions

- What part does assessment play in the development of pupil learning in PE?
- How do you involve pupils in their own and others' assessment?
- How do you provide feedback to pupils within your lessons?

Is this you? Do you agree?

Could you describe what you think makes a good PE teacher?

A: A good PE teacher listens and is able to help adjust sporting needs to every individual.

Courtney Fry, Boxing

www.sportingchampions.org.uk

Addressing the needs of individuals: strategies you will use to ensure inclusion.
1) Setting suitable learning challenges: differentiation through outcomes and levelled questioning.
2) Responding to pupils' diverse learning needs: holistic/ analytic and verbalizer/imager cognitive-style dimensions considered in delivery. Provision learning resources to support communication of desired outcomes.
3) Overcoming potential barriers to learning and assessment for individuals: ICT 'video analysis software and task cards to aid in self- and peer assessment

Cross-curricular links (with specific curriculum references)

PLTs	Functional and key skills
• Effective participators	
• Reflective learners	

Resources (including ICT)	ICT: use of video analysis 'delay' software to aid self-and peer assessment. Task cards: to reinforce 'preparation skills' and 'ways of linking'. 25 mats; action grids and coordinates; whiteboard; whiteboard marker; 25 pencils and paper.
Health & Safety	People: (pupils) appropriate dress code. Ensure skills practised and introduced into personal sequence are within capabilities. Context: building on prior understanding of 'preparatory skills' – need to reinforce these in warm-up. Organization: mat layout to ensure adequate spacing but also to guide 'pathways' of sequences.

ACTIVITY	ORGANIZATION & EQUIPMENT	TEACHING POINTS	DIFFERENTIATION
	Pre-organization: Action grids on the walls. Coordinates placed on benches under each action grid. Pupils require paper and pencil.		
(1) Registration and resource distribution	As pupils enter, in pairs mats laid out around the gymnasium. Establish 'Freeze' as classroom management tool for pupils to return to mats and sit the pike position.		
(2) Warm-up: Recapitulation of step patterns and introduction to basic compositional principles of sequencing	Instructions: Jog, chassé or gallop in and out of mats. No contact with mats or each other. When changing from one to another alter speed and direction. On the signal 'go' move to an action grid, collect a coordinate, locate the relevant action and record on paper. Repeat 4 times.	Jog: 'on your toes' Chassé: 'extend the arms', 'drive through the legs', 'point your toes'. Gallop: 'drive through the legs', 'point your toes', 'swing the arms'.	Individual feedback on whether pupil should concentrate on one or more of the teaching cues
	Transition: After recording four actions pencil and paper to the side of the gymnasium. Process smoother if pupils are asked during the activity, especially those who are a concern with regard to behavioural management.		Different assessment strategies utilized throughout.
(3) Stretch sequence Recapitulation of preparatory skills and introduction to basic compositional principles of sequencing	Preparatory skills: front and back support, shapes (straddle, pike, stretch), arch and dish, all linked in a stretch sequence. ICT analysis software ('delay') running to help with self- and peer assessment. Success criteria noted on task cards.	Front and back support: 'hips high', 'hands flat, fingers spread', 'legs straight', 'toes pointed' Straddle, pike and stretch: 'Straight legs', 'toes pointed' Arch and Dish: 'Straight legs', 'toes pointed'.	Individual feedback on whether pupil should concentrate on one or more of the teaching cues. Opportunity for peer-assessment and coaching/alternative role.
(4) Introduction to tip: Static to rotation	Statics: arabesque, stretch, shoulder stand Rotation: Rocking, forward roll. Each movement taught one at a time.	Arabesque: 'Chest up', 'back leg straight', 'toes pointed'. Stretch: 'chest sucked in', 'hips under/tilted'.	Individual feedback on whether pupil should concentrate on one or more of the teaching cues. Opportunity for peer assessment and

	ICT analysis software ('delay') running to help with self and peer assessment. Success criteria noted on task cards.	Shoulder stand: 'hips high and in line with feet', 'toes pointed', 'legs straight'. Rocking: 'hands on shins' Forward roll: 'hands flat', 'weight on shoulders', 'extend through the legs'. Implications for control of movement and ability to replicate?	coaching/alternative role.
Linking movements	Linking movements: (a) stretch to rock; (b) shoulder stand to stand rotational task (spin in pike, spin in tuck, spin in pike for quarter turn and then tuck. What happens?); (c) stretch to rock, to shoulder stand, to stand; (d) arabesque into forward roll. ICT analysis software ('delay') running to help with self- and peer assessment. Success criteria noted on task cards.	(a) 'curl the back' (b) 'lead with the heels', 'tuck in at the last moment'. Question: why do we tuck at the last moment? Following rotational task answer 'big to small to speed up rotation'. Question: As we are static in the shoulder stand we need to create momentum before rotation. How do we do this? Following experimentation, 'tip' and/or 'moving our centre of gravity'. (c) 'tip and curl', 'lead with heels to tip', 'tuck at the last moment'; (d) 'lift the heel', 'lift and tip', 'extend'. Implications for control of movement and ability to replicate?	Individual pupils can be asked about the movement of their centre of gravity and how to control this movement. (d) extension task
Opportunities for accurate self-and peer-assessment.	Transition: pupils collect their paper with their four movements. 'Freeze' command. 'Face whiteboard'.		
(5) Language of movement	Comparing sequencing to handwriting: 'fluent and joined up', 'end of one letter/movement is the beginning of the next', 'as sentences have linking words sequences have linking movements'. On sequence sheet (from activity 2) add the word 'and' in between each action word. Each 'and' needs to be considered as a movement.	Question: What are your 'and' movements and why have you selected these?	Opportunity for peer assessment and coaching/alternative role.

(6) Short sequences	Use movements from the sequence sheet to create a sequence. The start and finish positions should be a stretch shape.	'End of one movement is the beginning of the next', 'tip', 'move your Centre of Gravity'. Implications for control of movement and ability to replicate?	Individual feedback and questions. Variety in number of movements and desired fluency depending on each individual's need.
	Transition: teacher to view small number of performances at one time. Once viewed these pupils can return their mats and sit around whiteboard.		
(7) Plenary	Around whiteboard.	Questions: 'How can we encourage fluency in a sequence?', 'Why does the tip help link statics to rotational movements?', 'How can we control our centre of gravity?' Implications for control of movement and ability to replicate?	Specific groups of pupils to be asked specific questions. 'No-hands' strategy to be utilized.

Planned questioning strategy to support assessment is evident.

3 Lesson organization and managing behaviour for learning

Harvey Grout and Gareth Long

A Teacher's story

This particular Year 8 group had annoyed me in their previous lesson; they had been a bit restless and the quality of their work had not been as good as I wanted. I made the decision as I walked into the gym that I may need to be stricter with them this lesson to get them focused again. I was pleased that the group was sat where they should be and seemed ready to go!

As I started the register two of the group walked in late and sat down, I continued with the register thinking I would find out their reasons for being late later. Halfway through the register I realized that the two lads were trying really hard to stifle a laugh. Soon they could not contain their laugh and they began to giggle. Initially I gave them a "stop laughing", look and tried to continue with the register, this did not work and the rest of the class were clearly looking at me to see how I would react. 'Stop laughing please', although they were clearly trying to stop, this just increased their laughter.

I decided I needed to put a stop to this otherwise the class would think that I didn't have control, so with my planner in my hand I decided to show how annoyed I was by slamming my planner to the floor and anticipated that the noise echoing around the gym would shock the lads into silence. Unfortunately, on impact with the gym floor, my planner literally exploded and instead of quiet I now had a whole class laughing; and my lesson plans, registers, excuse notes floating all over the gym!

Gavin, Key Stage 4 Coordinator of PE, age 30

Reflect

Read the teacher's story again and consider how you would handle the same situation differently. Justify your decisions. What strategies could you have had in place for pupils who arrive late? What else could you have done if pupils are laughing uncontrollably?

The learning outcomes of the chapter are:

☑ To develop detailed planning skills to ensure 'classroom' management creates a successful lesson
☑ To understand that by creating a purposeful learning environment, which is stimulating and challenging, misbehaviour will be less likely
☑ To understand that misbehaviour can occur in any lesson so a range of management strategies are necessary.
☑ To understand that learning and managing behaviour should be intertwined and not separate.

The professional standards for qualified teacher status (QTS) addressed in this chapter

Q30: Establish a purposeful and safe learning environment conducive to learning and identify opportunities for learners to learn in out-of-school contexts

Q31: Establish a clear framework for classroom discipline to manage learners' behaviour constructively and promote their self-control and independence

Introduction

Every teacher has taught a lesson where the lesson plan looked great on paper but the lesson itself did not go as well as they had thought it would. There are also many situations when pupil behaviour was not exactly how we wanted it to be. So, now we have accepted that we are not perfect teachers (all of the time!) and that perhaps the perfect lesson is never achieved, we can now move on and consider the following objectives:

● Well thought out and detailed planning of 'classroom' management will increase the 'smoothness' of your lessons and reduce opportunities for pupil misbehaviour to occur.
● By adopting a range of strategies and applying them appropriately you may be able to limit misbehaviour that can disrupt pupils' learning.

As with all aspects of your teaching, it is important to reflect on your own practice and question whether you could do something different in the future. For example, what was it that 'caused' the misbehaviour? Were the pupils off task because of your own classroom management? When misbehaviour was evident did you deal with it in the best way? Perhaps too often conclusions such as 'they are just a poorly behaved group' or 'nothing will work with this pupil' are drawn. While the authors of this chapter have certainly felt like this at times, it is important to continue to critically analyse your lessons and arrive at decisions that will assist in the planning of future lessons.

Lesson organization

The perfect group!

Wouldn't it be great if all your pupils arrived on time? If they all had the correct kit? If they all sat down quietly with keen interest while you took the register and outlined the lesson objectives? Wouldn't it be easy if they could follow your instructions to the letter and set up the activity you had just demonstrated? It would be great if your pupils worked together as a team and asked for help when a problem arose. Unless you are very lucky, this doesn't normally happen all by itself!

In reality, 'managing' 30 pupils in a crowded changing room, on a windy sports field, or in a sports hall with poor acoustics is usually a totally different matter with a multitude of factors that need to be planned for. This chapter highlights what you need to consider and provides some ideas and examples of ways in which you may put these considerations into practice.

What do PE teachers need to manage?

Although the following list is indicative rather than exhaustive, it may be useful to use it as a 'checklist' to see whether your lesson plan has considered everything; therefore, in your lesson plan you need to consider how you will manage and plan for:

- the teaching space/environment;
- time;
- equipment;
- people;
- learning activities.

Let us take a chronological approach to your PE lesson and consider each area and plan for these circumstances. By adopting this approach, it will help you in your lesson planning and also enable to you consider circumstances that could arise during the lesson.

Before your lesson consider these following questions:

- How many pupils are in the lesson?

- What equipment will be required?
- Will there be support staff in the lesson?
- What additional information about the pupils do I need to know; for example, special educational needs, gifted and talented, English as an additional language?
- What are the schools rewards and sanction policies?

Lesson organization

The changing rooms

Unfortunately, a poor start to a lesson can set a negative tone for the remainder of it. The start of a PE lesson is clearly very different to a classroom lesson and as a result problems can potentially begin in the changing room. Whenever possible try and arrive at the changing rooms before the pupils as this enables you to establish your expectations as a teacher. You will be amazed how much disruption unsupervised pupils can cause in the changing room! Arriving before the pupils is not always as easy as it sounds; you may have been caught by a colleague on the way to your lesson, your lunchtime club may have slightly overrun, or you were teaching another class on the third floor of the building furthest away from the changing rooms. However, the rule remains that, when and wherever possible, be the first to the changing rooms to 'meet and greet' your pupils, monitor their entry and deal with potential problems (e.g. the pupil who has forgotten kit). You may also use this opportunity to establish want you want to happen next: *'in three minutes time I would like you to be sat on the first badminton court's service line with a partner'*. You can also ensure they are getting changed quietly and responsibly.

A reoccurring theme throughout this chapter is the importance of establishing rules and routines to help your classroom management. It is not the place of this book to tell you which ones you should use as every school, PE department, teacher, PE group and pupil is different. However, by finding the routines that suit you and your group, an effective start to the lesson can be achieved.

Reflect

Below are some of the decisions you will need to consider during the first few weeks of teaching a new group (of course, many of these will probably have already been considered by your school and department, so it will be important to find out what happens early on in your school-based training placement):

- Do you want the pupils to enter the changing room and get changed quickly or line up until you arrive?
- Where will the registration take place?
- Will you be in or outside of the changing rooms?

- What are the systems for pupils who have forgotten their kit or have an injury/illness?
- Will you collect valuables?
- How will you absorb any latecomers?
- Who will lock the changing rooms?
- What are the rules and routines you wish to establish? Are they common across your department?

The start of the lesson

Within your lesson plan you must consider how your 'classroom management' will help facilitate the first teaching activity. Consider the usefulness of the following instructions:

'Come in and sit behind a partner on the black basketball sideline'.

This would be a good clear instruction if you knew that your first activity was in pairs, and that the basketball sideline was a good place for pupils to view the demonstration (and that the pupils knew where the basketball sideline was!).

'Can you three please cone off the basketball courts while I take the register'.

This recognizes that the class will mainly be working on the basketball courts and by marking them out while you take the register, it will save time later when you have planned some 'cross-court' games.

'Collect a basketball and practice your lay-ups from last week'.

Here, you clearly trust the group to remain on task while you organize the first activity, which will develop from the previous lesson. The key point here is not to judge which of the above statements is 'better' but to realize that the management of the pupils' needs is to be planned alongside and correspond with the content of the lesson plan. Consequently, the rules and routines for the start of the lesson are not rigid and will evolve depending on what you are teaching and how well you know your group.

Reflect

Consider how you would incorporate for the following pupils in your lesson:

- pupils who arrive late;
- pupils who have forgotten their kit;
- pupils who have an injury;
- pupils who have an injury and cannot take part physically;
- pupils who missed the previous lesson;
- pupils who are new to the group.

Organizing groups

Strategies

Reflect

You have 28 pupils in your class and your practice requires them to be in groups of four for the next activity – how will you organize it?

Example: *'Get yourself in groups of four'*

The above scenario does not always happen (remember that perfect group!), but asking pupils to get into groups of four can lead to a major disruption as pupils 'fight' to establish the best group that contains their best friends! Without proper organization a task that you would think pupils could do quickly and quietly can lead to arguments and tears! Considerable time can be wasted while pupils organize themselves into their groups and also some pupils may find it difficult to approach other pupils to ask them to be in their group. In this situation pupils are likely to go with their friends; is this what you wanted? Do pupils seek out other pupils of similar ability? Again, ask yourself whether this is what you wanted. One strategy that can speed this process up is by making it a competition; for example, 'which will be the first group to be lined up on the end line in groups of four? Go'.

Now consider this example:

'You're number 1, you're number 2, and you're number 3, number 4, 5, 6, 7, all number 1s get together ...'

Once again, if we have the perfect group this would work every time! However, with a bit more clarity you can save yourself time. Consider the following scenario

again and imagine if seven pupils were already sat down on a line with the first pupil holding up one finger to indicate they are 'number 1', the second pupil along the line holding up two fingers (nicely!) to indicate they are number two and so on. Or you can place cones with numbers written on them along the line or laminate numbers 1–7 and place them on the wall around the sports hall.

Reflect

What do you think about the following suggestions?

'You four sit behind the blue cone please, you four behind the red cone ...'

'You will jog down to the field with a partner, when you get to the centre circle, join up with another pair and begin stretching in your 4s'.

'Jog around the circle and when I call out a number I want you to get into groups of that number as quickly as possible, 3..5..2..4, OK in your groups of 4 come and sit down here'.

'I have placed a variety of coloured bibs around the grid (7 sets of 4 bibs), when I say go you must run and grab a bib and come back to this line, GO ... now please sit with the people who have the same coloured bib as you'.

Indoor lessons only:

'Run to this line, take a shoe off and hop back to the line, GO' (you then place shoes in groups of 4).

'Find your shoe and sit down with the people who own the other 3 shoes'.

You could even have the names of the class on individual cards and then shuffle and deal out groups of 4!

You will certainly see other strategies within your school placement that teachers use to form groups quickly and effectively and it is worth considering what method would be most suitable for the group you are teaching and the environment you are teaching in.

Reflect

Consider why you are putting pupils into groups; is it purely because you need a certain number for a teaching activity to work? Alternatively, do you want 'fair teams'? Maybe you want to differentiate your groups so the pupils are working with classmates of similar ability? It may be you just want them to work with different people than they usually do?

Whatever your objective, this may have an influence on the strategy you plan to employ.

Organizing space

Demonstrations

Demonstrations explain to your pupils clearly what they will be doing, why they will be doing it and how they should be doing it, yet it is often an area of teaching that is not always fully outlined in the lesson plan. Teachers should not assume that a verbal explanation will suffice. Not only can management issues arise when this happens but also the full potential for learning can be restricted. Therefore, this next section looks at some of the considerations required for an effective and purposeful demonstration, beyond making sure the pupils are not staring into the sun!

In the lesson plan it is worthwhile planning the following factors:

- Who is the demonstration for? Will you show it to the whole class or will you show it to small groups at different times?
- Who will perform the demonstration? You? Pupils? Experts featured on a DVD?
- Will the pupils performing the demonstration understand and practise it before performing it in front of the class?
- Where will the pupils sit/stand to watch the demonstration?
- What do you want the pupils to understand after the demonstration?

Let us take some of these points and explore them further. The visual demonstration is an important method to show pupils what they are going to be doing and how they should be doing it. Therefore, it is usually a good idea to simply show the demonstration once or twice without too much talking: *'Have a look at the next activity we will be doing'*. Think about how the demonstration should be performed; will it help the students to see the action/activity in slow motion or at full pace? It is useful to explain if and why you are doing it in slow motion so that this is not replaced by the pupils reproducing it lazily and casually.

In your lesson plan consideration should also be given to where your pupils will observe the demonstration, where will they see the focus of the demonstration clearly?

Reflect

Where would you position the pupils if you wanted to demonstrate the following concepts?

- The correct point of contact for the smash in badminton.
- The follow-through of the trial leg in hurdling.

Often a demonstration is solely used to show what the teacher wants the pupils to replicate; this is a shame as it can be used more effectively to help pupil learning. An option is for the teacher to give pupils a focus when watching the demonstration. For instance, the following instructions would enable the pupils to not only see what they have to do but also engage them in analysing the skill:

> 'Watch the overhead clear two times … now this time I would like this group to watch my feet position when the shuttle is hit, this group to watch where the point of contact is, this group to watch the angle of the face of the racket on contact, and this group to watch any follow through after the shot. I'll ask you for your comments after two more shots'.

An active demonstration where the pupils do more than simply watch will help the pupils achieve the lesson's objectives. This may involve them analysing a technique, shadowing a movement or having to guess why you are asking them to do a certain practice. Another common example of 'pitfalls' in teacher demonstrations is a tendency to overload teaching points and give the pupils all the 'answers'.

Reflect

Read the following teacher's demonstration instructions. Do you think it is effective? What may you change and do differently?

> 'In a minute you will practise the smash with your partner; one of you will be the feeder and stand on one side of the net and the person smashing on the other side of the net. After 5 attempts at the smash you will swap over. After a high serve, you have to try and get the shuttle to land on the other side of the court, your partner will try and catch the shuttle to stop it hitting the floor. Watch me have a couple of goes and see if you can guess which teaching points are the same as last week's overhead clear and which ones are different (the teacher now performs the smash). You have 5 minutes to play and when I call you back in I want you to tell me how to play a successful smash. Any questions? Go'.

In this example the pupils should now be clear about the organization of the activity and the purpose of the activity (to understand how to play a smash) but the teacher did not give any teaching points as this can be done when the pupils are called in later. The idea is that the pupils will be more engaged in analysing and observing the demonstration; that is, it is a method to focus learning, not just a management tool.

Monitoring the class

Two common problems that teachers can exhibit when they monitor a group working on an activity are: (1) 'diving' in straight away to help the pupils and/or (2) feeling at a 'loose end' and perceiving this time as an opportunity to organize their next activity rather than actually teaching.

Your first consideration should be to check that the pupils have understood the demonstration and are on task. Therefore, simply step to a corner where you can see the whole group; this will help you check understanding and begin to identify those pupils who will need your attention sooner than others. From a classroom management perspective, it is sometimes a good idea to let the pupils know that you are observing them (sometimes simply praising the group furthest away from you can be enough for this to happen).

Reflect

You identify a group/student that clearly understands the task but is having difficulty completing it. Think about the factors that you need to consider to help the pupils improve.

- How can you help the group/student while seeing the rest of the class (it is important to know what might be going on behind your back!)?
- How will you manage the feedback you wish to provide?
- After providing feedback what will you do next?

Providing feedback

The provision of feedback will require you to again assess why you are actually providing the feedback and how you can provide effective feedback to the pupils to enhance learning.

Reflect

Do any of these common 'pitfalls' apply to your current teaching?

- Overuse of vague praise –'that was good'.
- Overly critical feedback – 'you are doing it wrong'.
- Only using whole-class feedback – 'we are struggling with gaining distance so we will now work on ...'.
- Overreliance on teacher-delivered feedback.

Questions that you will need to reflect upon when providing feedback to the class or individual pupil will include: should you provide public or private feedback? How should you provide the feedback? And who should provide the feedback? Although not wishing to appear 'robotic', the sequence as shown in Table 3.1 might be useful as a framework.

Table 3.1 A framework for providing individual feedback to a pupil

Make a positive statement (not just 'good')	'That was a good overhead drop shot as the shuttle passed close to the net and followed a steep trajectory'
Identify an error	'However, your partner could tell that you were playing the overhead drop shot and could have got to it'
Offer advice on how to correct it	'When you approach the shuttle try to make it look the same as an overhead clear'
Stay close to acknowledge a successful attempt at the correction	'That's better, I thought you were going to hit it to the back of the court'

Reflect

The above sequence is fine and avoids most of the 'pitfalls' identified earlier. However, how does the following example, as shown in Table 3.2, of the same situation differ?

Table 3.2 An alternative framework for providing feedback to pupils

To the pupil who has just attempted an overhead drop shot	'Tell me why your drop shot was similar to the demonstration we watched on the DVD'
To the pupil's partner	'You got to the shuttle, how did you know that a drop shot was being played?'

Back to the original pupil	*'How could you better disguise your shot?'* Prompt: *'What other shot could the overhead drop shot look like?'*
To both pupils	*'After your high serve, as the shuttle is about to be hit back to you I would like you to shout "front" or "back" and try and guess which area of the court the shuttle is going to be hit to'*

With a class of 30 pupils, it can be a useful strategy to prepare pupils to be in charge of their own and others' feedback; it will save you time and is an important process in pupils taking responsibility for their own learning through the process of self- and peer observation and evaluation.

Bringing pupils back in and sending them away again

In any lesson, time always seems to be limited and therefore the less time spent on 'management' tasks the better. Bringing the pupils in for a new demonstration or at the end of the lesson is perhaps an area of teaching that can benefit from a routine. If you have had situations where you have spent valuable time repeating your instructions, or had pupils moving before you have finished all your instructions, or been left scratching your head wondering whether you had just spoken a different language, the following routine may prove useful.

Reflect

Read the following instructions and see if you can apply a similar routine to your next lesson plan:

'Stop, stand still and look this way (pause and look around to check). When I say "go" (a very important phrase!), one of you will carry the ball and place it in this bag; can that person who will be doing that hold the ball up so I can see who will be doing it?... thank you. When I say "go" the other person will grab one bib from this pile. Both of you need to be sat one behind the other on this yellow line in 30 seconds. Any questions? ... Go'.

Reflect

Would a whistle be just as effective in stopping a group? Eventually, what would you want the pupils to do when you say *'stop'* to save you having to say a whole list of instructions?

So, the pupils have come in perfectly and you have demonstrated what they will be doing next; now you just need to send them away, what could go wrong? Well, probably not too much if you have considered the following:

- Do the pupils know the location they will be working? For example, *'You will be working on half a court'*.
- Do they know the group size? For example, *'You will be working in your group of three, with one person waiting at the side of the court until it is their turn'*.
- Do they know the duration of the task? For example, *'You will be working for one minute before I tell you to change partners'*.
- Do they understand? For example, *'Are there any questions about this next activity?'*.
- Do they know when to start? For example, *'You can start as soon as you get to your court'*.

Reflect

1   When you are setting the duration for a task, what are the advantages of the following?

'You will do the task 5 times each'

'You will work for 2 minutes'

'You will carry on until I say stop'

2   Consider which sentence is better in assessing whether the pupils have understood your instructions.

'Does anybody not understand?'

'Are there any questions about the activity?'

Managing equipment

Whether the school you are working in only has a few footballs or they have enough for two per pupil, it is important that the lesson plan considers how you intend to manage the equipment required. As much as we would love to expect the pupils to sensibly walk over to the bag of balls, form a line and one by one collect a ball, the reality is the simple words of *'go collect a ball'* can cause a mass stampede towards the bag with a mass brawl for their favourite ball, which happens to be at the bottom and so heads clash and tears start!

Reflect

How could you overcome the following potential problems?.
- Queues of pupils collecting/returning equipment.
- Pupils setting out equipment incorrectly.
- Extra equipment getting in the way of the activity/being left in the playing area.
- Losing equipment.

CASE STUDY

Let us take the following example of how a teacher had planned to manage equipment; during the register two pupils are asked to help collect equipment and where to put it:

'Please could you two collect a bag of balls each and carry them to the field?'

Evidence of routines could be seen by the fact that two pupils were waiting to count how many balls were brought to the lesson. During the warm-up the teacher had organized one area consisting of four cones, two bibs and two balls. The pupils were brought in to the area in groups of four and sat in a line.

'The pupil at the front of the queue put your hand up and when I say go you will collect four cones. The next pupil in line put your hand up and when I say go you will collect two bibs. The third pupil in line put your hand up and when I say go you will collect two balls. The pupil at the back of the line put your hand up and when I say go you will find a space away from the other groups and call your group to you. Any questions? ... Go'

Later in the lesson groups of four were combined to make groups of eight and only one ball was needed. For this the teacher had put the bags in the middle of the groups and pupils were asked to carry and place the spare balls in. Towards the end of the lesson the teacher had placed the spare cones, balls and bibs beside each other and the pupils were then asked to carry the equipment in, and when no equipment was left to sit back in their groups. The pupils responsible for counting the balls did so and groups were then assigned to take equipment back to the store cupboard.

In the above paragraph two important points stand out. First, it was clear that the teacher had planned for the management of equipment and, second, that routines had been established over previous lessons.

Another important factor to consider is the safety implication. What equipment are you using and where can it be stored while it is not being used? Do the pupils know where to store the equipment? If the practice progresses from two balls to one ball, pupils given half a chance will just put the spare ball on the floor and carry on with the game. Of course, now we have a major health and safety issue. Also, if you ask pupils to *'put the ball in the corner of the sports hall'*, many will roll it or throw it towards the corner and so asking the pupils to place the ball behind the bench or in the storage box is always an advisable option.

Managing behaviour

By considering and applying the classroom management strategies explored so far in this chapter, pupils in your lesson will spend less time off task. This, combined with your planning of a stimulating and challenging lesson, will lead to less opportunities for misbehavior. However, PE teaching is not simply the application of management rules and routines, and as you know children are complex individuals so misbehaviour can occur in any teacher's lesson and therefore all teachers need strategies to apply when poor behaviour occurs. Bleach and McLachlen (2000) also recognize that differences occur in what teachers perceive misbehaviour to be and therefore it is vital to consider how your perceptions match those of the school and department that you are working in.

Reflect

Write down examples of what you consider to be low-level disruption, for example, a pupil talking while you are explaining the next activity.

The rest of this chapter focuses on strategies for reducing 'low-level disruptive' behaviour. At this point in your career, you may be unfortunate enough to witness aggressive and more serious forms of behaviour, but although it is important that you continue to evaluate your own role in these scenarios, your subject mentors will deal with the sanctions regarding this. Causes of misbehaviour are varied and too diverse to fully do justice here. However, it is useful to think of the potential causes as belonging to two categories – long-term causes and short-term triggers. An example of a long-term cause could be a pupil's lack of self-confidence while a short-term trigger could be a pupil who is distracted by another pupil.

Reflect

What other long-term causes and short-term triggers may influence poor pupil behaviour in a PE lesson?

The 'list' that you have made in response to the above is important as you will recognize that many of the causes of pupil misbehaviour are not 'solved' by you simply adopting strategies and methods. Clearly, in these cases schools need to care for the cause of the problem rather then just focusing on the 'symptoms'.

Reflect

- When on school placements, what information about your group would help you prepare to manage behaviour?
- Who in the school would be useful people to speak to about pupils with long-term behaviour problems?

The traditional view of the PE teacher has often been one of a strict teacher adopting military-style discipline to a fearful group of pupils. Recent trends in education have attempted to move away from this image, even to a point where shouting is seen as unnecessary. Although this chapter does not rule out 'raising the voice' as a behaviour-management strategy (it can be very effective), it does advocate that it should not need to be used frequently or too quickly. Already by applying some of the previous strategies discussed in the early chapters of this book, 'preventative' action can be used. For example, being organized and on time and having a lively, exciting start to the lesson can have a positive influence on pupil behaviour. By offering pupils learning activities and challenges that are stimulating, enjoyable and create a positive climate, they are more likely to want to participate in the lesson and stay on task. The idea that misbehaviour may lead to missing out on these activities is often a powerful tool.

So, before we take a look at what to do when unwanted behaviour occurs in your lesson, let us focus on establishing positive relationships and learning environments with your classes.

The use of rewards

Reflect

- What do you reward pupils for in your lessons? Good work? Talent? Good behaviour? Compliance?
- How do you currently acknowledge and reward good behaviour?

The use of rewards in PE lessons should not be an onerous task. Incorporating informal rewards into your own teaching behaviour can be very effective. The key here is catching pupils being good! Imagine you have asked the group to run in and sit in groups of five; rather than reprimanding the slow disorganized group, it is good practice to praise the group who arrived first. This action will still show the class your expectations without (a) wasting time and (b) potentially escalating a minor situation into a bigger one. Simple informal rewards to use in your teaching can include smiling (you are allowed!), verbal praise (delivered with the correct tone of voice – mean it!), putting your thumbs up and showing your pupils trust. Typical (and useful) advice given to a trainee teacher starting their placement is *'don't go in too soft, you can always lighten up later with a group but it is harder to get stricter'*.

Reflect

Do you think that a teacher who uses informal rewards could be described as a 'soft' teacher?

When you begin a school-based training placement, it is important to find out the school and PE department's formal rewards policy. If pupils are well versed to these systems, you can use them effectively in your own teaching. These may include 'house points' or certificates; some pupils will even like having responsibilities such as being the equipment monitor! Either way, consider what you are awarding the reward for; try to use them to promote pupils' good behaviour as well as their performance and effort.

Teacher language

Reflect

A pupil (Richard) arrives late to the sports hall while you are already taking the register. What do you say to him?

While this chapter does not suggest that teachers can actually plan what they will say in all situations, it does advocate that there are certain communication strategies that can help you manage pupil behaviour and, at times, avoid unhelpful situations from arising. Take the scenario above of Richard arriving late while you take the register; consider the following responses:

Response 1: Say nothing and ignore it.

This will send out a wrong signal to the class that it is OK to be late for the lesson. If a group knows you well and is aware that you do not accept lateness a frown may be enough at times.

Response 2: 'Richard, what time do you call this?'

A problem with this teacher response is that the pupil is now required to reply and an unnecessary conversation will interrupt the register. There is also the chance that the pupil will reply '11.15 Sir/Miss' and how do you respond to that!

Response 3: 'I'm sure you have a good reason for being late Richard, sit down and I'll come and ask you for it later'.

Here the class are aware that you have recognized the lateness and will deal with it, but it is less likely that the pupil in question will react in a negative way. They have not been 'embarrassed' in front of their peers and do not have to publicly say why they have been late (which, of course, may be a personal and very valid reason).

While observing experienced teachers, try to notice the following strategies used for dealing with low-level disruption.

The Problem Scenario

In a basketball lesson Richard is bouncing a ball while the teacher is trying to talk.

- Does the teacher use non-verbal messages to tackle low-level disruption? For example, the teacher carries on with their instructions but holds out a hand to signal to Richard that he should stop bouncing the ball, or simply moves into Richard's space to highlight that the disruption has been noted.
- Does the teacher tactically ignore the situation? For example, the teacher perhaps feels that Richard is seeking a response in front of the class and will mention it later on in private.
- Does the teacher try to divert and rechannel the behaviour? *'OK, the next time I say stop I would like to see who can quickly get into the triple threat position'.*
- Does the teacher show politeness to the pupil? *'Richard, stop bouncing the ball – thank you'.*
- Does the teacher use role models? *'Richard, look how quickly other members of the class get the ball under control'.*
- Does the teacher use humour (or try to!)? *'Richard, your memory is as poor as mine and I'm old – keep the ball under control'.*
- Does the teacher remind the pupil of the rules? *'Richard, remember that when I say stop that also means keep the ball still'.*
- Does the teacher involve the pupil in the resolution of the problem? *'Richard, how will it help me if you keep the ball still?'.*
- Does the teacher provide a choice for the pupil? *'Richard, if you stop bouncing the ball we will be able to move on quicker'.*
- Does the teacher outline a consequence if the behaviour is not changed? *'Richard, if you can't stop bouncing the ball I'll have to take it off you whenever I say stop'.*
- Does the teacher provide any exit procedures? *'Richard, I've asked you a few times to stop bouncing the ball, please go and sit down on the bench and I'll come and talk to you in a minute'.*

A trainee teacher's lesson observation notes

The classroom management that you have planned (and some others that are becoming 'natural') is evident throughout. This definitely increases teaching and learning time for you and your students. There will always be ways of improving this and it is important that you continue to reflect on this during and after the lesson; for example, you try to introduce a lot of things at once (canon, finishing position, change of speed and partner interaction). This combined with the 'six concepts' you want to emphasize may not result in the quality and attention to each that you may want. So, may it have been better to have had the six concepts already on the board and introduced the other aspects one at a time? For instance, this may have been introduced by observing a pair demonstrating good partner interaction and showing the rest of the group their work

Sample interview questions and developing a personal philosophy for teaching

Interview questions

- In what ways would you expect to act as a role model for your pupils?
- What strategies do you use to encourage pupils, especially those resistant to PE, to enjoy the subject and participate fully?
- How do you reward pupils within your lessons?
- What would you do if in your first year of teaching you were teaching a class and struggling to maintain control?

Is this you? Do you agree?

Could you describe what you think makes a good PE teacher?

Someone who has a passion for what they are doing, they are planned, organized and knowledgeable enough to teach it!

Jared Deacon, Athletics, 400m

www.sportingchampions.org.uk

Further Reading

Bleach, K. and McLachlan, K. (2000) Managing behaviour and discipline in *The Newly Qualified Secondary Teacher's Handbook: Meeting the Standards in Secondary and Middle Schools*, pp. 18–26. London: David Fulton Publishers.

Cowley, S. (2006) *Getting the Buggers to Behave* (3rd edn). London: Continuum.

DfES (2004) *Pedagogy and Practice: Teaching and Learning in Secondary Schools, Unit 20: Classroom Management*. London: Her Majesty's Stationery Office.

Garner, P. (2005) Behaviour for learning: a positive approach to managing classroom behaviour, in S. Capel, M. Leask and T. Turner (eds) *Learning to Teach in the Secondary School* (4th edn), pp. 136–50. Abingdon: Routledge.

Powell, S. and Tod, J. (2004) *A Systematic Review of How Theories Explain Learning Behaviour in School Contexts* (accessed 21 July 2008 from behaviour4learning: www.behaviour4learning.ac.uk).

Wood, P. (2008) Classroom management, in S. Dymoke and J. Harrison (eds) *Reflective Teaching and Learning: A Guide to Professional Issues for Beginning Secondary Teachers*, pp. 109–54. London: Sage Publications.

Wright, D. (2005) *There's No Need to Shout: The Secondary Teacher's Guide to Successful Behaviour Management*. Cheltenham: Nelson Thornes.

Name:

Subject: **PE: (Outwitting opponents – badminton)**

Trainee target(s):		Standards	Pupil preparation for next lesson (homework)
Establish a purposeful and safe learning environment conducive to learning and identify opportunities for learners to learn in and out of school contexts		Q30	To be prepared to discuss the fitness components required for an elite badminton player.

Date & Time	Class & attainment range	Lesson sequence	Curriculum references: (KS3/KS4/Post 16)
	Yr 10 GCSE AQA Levels 6–10	3 of 8	Key concepts: 1.1b Key processes: 2.1c, 2.2a, b, 2.4a, b Range and content: 3a Curriculum opportunities: 4a

Points from previous learning that need reinforcement e.g. misconceptions:

- In the last practical GCSE lesson pupils struggled with recognizing the correct time and place to play a particular shot and how their opponents,' strenghs and weaknesses could influence the shot they play.
- In the last theory lesson there remained some misunderstanding of the different types of strength.

Learning objectives
By the end of the lesson pupils will:

- appreciate when to play an attacking overhead shot (i.e. the smash);
- understand and improve the techniques of a successful smash;
- develop strategies to stop their opponent from playing the smash.

The big picture

Pupils are working towards achieving a high practical grade for their GCSE coursework mark.

Learning outcomes	How I will assess the learning objective/s (*HIWALO*):
All pupils will: • appreciate when it is appropriate to play an attacking overhead shot; • understand the key teaching points required for this shot and the similarities and differences between this and the overhead clear. **Most pupils will:** • be successful in playing attacking shots when the shuttle is high and short on their side of the net; • Be able to recognize another pupil's strengths and weaknesses in performing the smash; • Devise strategies to stop their opponent from achieving 'smashing opportunities'. **Some pupils will:** • be able to play more difficult attacking shots (e.g. backhand smash and shots nearer the rear of the court); • practise more advanced techniques (e.g. jump smash, experiment with different shot placement, faster speeds); • devise strategies to 'force' their opponents to create a opportunity from them to smash.	• observation of practical performance in 'the win game', 'smash and catch' and 'smash analysis game'; • observation of 'pupil teaching' in 'smash and catch' and 'smash analysis game'; • Q and A through the activities covered and via the plenary.
Addressing the needs of individuals – strategies you will use to ensure inclusion: • suitable learning activities, differentiation by task and outcome, opportunities provided to take on different roles; questions 'levelled'; number of teaching cues provided varied.	

Cross-curricular links (with specific curriculum references)

PLTS	Functional skills and key skills	Other links
Developing critical thinkers and reflective learners	N/A	Citizenship and responsibilities of an umpire

Resources (including ICT)
4 badminton courts
16 badminton rackets (plus a few short handled rackets if needed)
30 shuttles
Whiteboard markers
'Smash analysis' sheets.

ACTIVITY	ORGANIZATION & EQUIPMENT	Teaching points	Differentiation
Warm-up activity 'Get Off My Court' followed by individual stretching	Pupils are told in the changing room that the first activity will require groups of 3 or 4 and to sit on court 1 (after they have set up the nets) in their groups to watch the demonstration on court 2. 3 v 3/4 v 4 game Each pupil starts with a shuttle in their hand. On the command 'go' the pupils must throw the shuttle overarm to land over the net on their opponents side. This continues until the whistle to stop is blown. Which team has the least shuttles on their side of the net? Staying on court pupils use a series of dynamic/static stretches covered in previous weeks.	'Throw the shuttle the way you would play an overhead clear shot'. 'Throw into space'. All pupils will start together and stop together on the whistle, therefore the teacher can control the start of the next activity.	Stronger throwers are encouraged to throw from further back.

	In this stage ask two pupils whether they are prepared to help demonstrate the first activity. Rackets have been laid out in 2s away from the courts. *[Callout:* Equipment has safely been stored ready for a smooth transition to the next activity.*]*		
Introductory game 'The Win Game'	'Stop, (pause), when I say go your team will leave their shuttles and come and sit on court one, any questions? Go'. Two pupils demonstrate the game while the teacher explains the rules and explains the management of the game. 'When I say go, the person at the front of the queue will go and collect 2 rackets for your group and return to your original court. The second person will collect the shuttles off your court and place them at the side of your court. Person 3 and 4 you will get ready to umpire the first game. Go'.	*Rules (no teaching points at this stage)* Play rally point. Half court singles. Whoever has the shuttle serves. A 'normal' win = 1 point. If a player shouts 'WIN' before playing a winning shot they get 3 points. If they fail to win the rally (on that shot) after shouting 'WIN' their opponent gets 2 points. Play to 5 points and rotate players fairly.	
'The Win Game'	Observe that the game is taking place correctly. Observe that the umpires are doing their job correctly and safely (e.g. away from the nets). Work around the group observing which pupils are correctly identifying opportunities to smash, which pupils are still weak on their overhead clear and observe the techniques being used. *[Callout:* A period of observation to assess that pupils have understood the task.*]*		*Extend* Only give points if the opponent cannot get their racket on the shuttle. *Enable* Observe the pupils that may benefit from a short handle racket. Award higher points for pupils reluctant to attempt the smash.

Discussion of 'The Win Game'	'Stop, when I say go come back into the same place as last time. Go'.	'When did you shout win?' – when should we attempt a smash? 'When did you shout win but not win the rally' – poor technique? Wrong decision? Position of opponent?
'Smash and Catch' demonstration and observation	Select a pupil (A) who is good at the high serve. Pupil A serves high and short (middle of court). Teacher plays a smash. Pupil A puts down racket after serve and attempts to catch the shuttle. Repeat × 3 (pupils are told that they would swap over at this point). Watching pupils are asked to observe and comment on the points on the board (the 5 points listed in the next column). Their answers are written next to the points listed.	Pupils to observe the following 5 points: 1) Preparatory body position 2) Point of contact of shuttle; 3) Angle of racket face; 4) Flight of shuttle after contact; 5) Follow through. Pupils are encouraged to recognize the difference between this shot and the overhead clear and overhead drop shot.
'Smash and catch' practice	Observe that the practice is being performed correctly – e.g. all smashes coming from one side of the net, the rackets are being placed down rather than thrown. Observe that the waiting pupils are giving feedback to the 'smasher'. Observe and intervene when technique can be improved.	See above. Waiting pupil to use teaching points on the board to 'teach' the other pupils in their group. *Extend* Demonstrate and encourage those doing well to attempt the backhand smash jump smash. Can they 'catch' the shuttle on their racket? *Enable* The shuttle can be thrown or 'illegally' served (like a tennis serve) if the feeder is struggling to get height.

> Pupils are engaged throughout the demonstration and have a focus to maintain their concentration.

Demonstration of 'smash analysis' Game	'Stop, when I say go come back into the same place as last time. Go'. Recap the tactics (win game) and the technique (smash and catch) of the smash. Explain how to complete the 'smash analysis' sheet (only 3 boxes to tick).	How many smashes did player A and B attempt? How many smashes resulted in that player winning the point? How many opportunities to smash were not taken?	
'Smash analysis' Game	Play to a set number (5 points) and rotate players and observers. Observer to show and use the statistics to help 'teach' the pupils they watched. Intervene when appropriate.		*Enable* Bring the pupils who are 'struggling' onto court 4 and work with them on a separate practice. *Extend* Set a target % of smashes played and smashes won.
Plenary	'Stop, when I say go one person from your group will sensibly bring in the equipment while the other two will pack away the courts. When there is nothing else to pack away come and sit down in front of the board. Go'.	Ask what the pupils thought today's lesson objectives were. What do they think will be covered next lesson? (return of smash)	

> Pupils were not given the lesson objectives at the beginning of the lesson to 'force' them to think about the lesson content. They are also encouraged to look ahead to next week's lesson.

4   Maintaining a safe teaching and learning environment

Gill Golder

A teacher's story

As a newly qualified teacher of PE, my primary concern was focused on keeping pupils under control and teaching lessons that were clearly structured so pupils were kept safe. For example, in game-based activities I would plan a lesson with specific progressive activities where I would manage the learning of pupils with fairly tight control, moving all pupils on to the next progression. As I reflect upon this, I would say that pupils were generally on task and doing what I wanted and when I wanted them to do it, but they were rarely challenged or engaged in any independent learning that required them to makes choices. I was teaching safely but not providing appropriate levels of challenge to really motivate pupils and stretch them. Perhaps I was too concerned about young people's safety, and not concerned enough about encouraging children to be physically active and enjoy challenge.

I now plan lessons differently, starting with the level of challenge, making sure that my lessons include elements of risk, as without this they may cease to be exciting or stimulating. That is not to say that I ask pupils to take part in a series of high-risk activities that will put them in danger; rather, I manage the risk effectively by using a range of differentiated learning activities, group management strategies and a variety of teaching and learning resources that are suitable for the pupils' level of development, the context of the learning and the environment in which the lesson is taking place.

Rachel, PE Teacher, age 29

The learning outcomes of this chapter are:

☑   To develop an awareness of the legal responsibilities of a teacher in PE
☑   To understand how to complete a detailed risk assessment for PE
☑   To explore how to plan effectively to set suitable challenge and manage risk

> **Reflect**
>
> - What effect has the responsibility of ensuring the pupils are 'safe' in your lesson had on the activities you teach?
> - Have you tended to be overcautious?
> - Have you devised unsuitable activities that were deemed unsafe?

The professional standards for qualified teacher status (QTS) addressed in this chapter

Q3(a): Be aware of the professional duties of teachers and the statutory framework within which they work.

Q3(b): Be aware of the policies and practices of the workplace and share in collective responsibility for their implementation.

Q21(a): Be aware of the current legal requirements, national policies and guidance on the safeguarding and promotion of the well-being of children and young people.

Q30: Establish a purposeful and safe learning environment conducive to learning and identify opportunities for learners to learn in out-of-school contexts.

Introduction

Preventable accidents in PE are usually the cause of inadequate planning or failure to take necessary precautions. Severs (2006) identified injuries reported to the Health and Safety Executive (HSA). Here, many fractures, dislocations, bruises, cuts and sprains are attributed to negligence as the majority of reported cases were in activities that have lower risks, whereas teachers are generally alert to higher risk hazards.

This chapter explores key considerations to ensure pupils learn safely and about safety. An understanding of the management of risk in PE is essential if a teacher is to create a challenging, engaging, interactive and safe learning environment. A key criterion in maintaining a safe teaching and learning environment, according to Beaumont (2006), is ensuring that lessons are effectively organized and orderly. However, according to Whitlam (2006), there is a delicate balance between setting appropriate levels of challenge and acceptable risk; get this right and you can create

Raising awareness of your legal duties and responsibilities in relation to safe practice is essential as school staff have a legal duty to work in a system that anticipates and reduces foreseeable risks (BAALPE, 2004). Long-established requirements exist in common law for those acting *in loco parentis* that forms the basis of duty of care. Raymond (1999) describes the responsibility of a teacher towards the pupil literally meaning taking the place of the parent. BAALPE (1995) suggests that a teacher must exercise the same duty of care as would a reasonable parent. BAALPE (2004) also states the duty of care in PE applies to school staff when carrying out their duties whether in school hours, during out-of-hours learning (OSHL) both on and off site. This duty of care is defined as:

> those involved in Physical Education [have] the duty of care to:
>
> a) identify foreseeable risks that may result in injury;
>
> b) take reasonably practicable steps to reduce the risk to an acceptable level.
>
> (BAALPE, 2004: 10)

Assessing risk in PE

The HSE applies a no-nonsense approach to risk assessment suggesting that risk assessment should involve a careful examination of what could cause harm to people so that you can decide if you have taken enough precautions to prevent it. HSE (1999) advocate a five-step approach to risk assessment, which is illustrated in Figure 4.1.

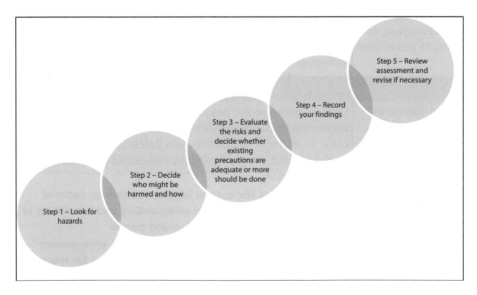

Figure 4.1 Five steps to risk assessment

Safe practice in PE is, in part, a matter of common sense; risk assessment is the process of identifying what could cause harm to people and deciding upon appropriate precautions that could be taken to minimize harm. According to Whitlam (2006), risk is simply the likelihood of injury occurring, therefore it stands to reason that if you identify when risks are present you can reduce the possibility of injury by managing risk. Figure 4.2 (courtesy of Beaumont et al., 2008) illustrates the key issues that should be considered when carrying out risk assessment. This figure clearly shows that the risk assessment process is threefold, finding the balance between appropriate challenge and acceptable risk involves exploring issues relating to people, context and organization. Claims of negligence can be made against the school or staff where the complainant demonstrates that their injury or loss occurred as a direct result of the school of staff being negligent in their duty of care. BAALPE (2004) argues that school staff are far more greatly protected if good regular practice is followed and the level of competence usually associated with the teaching profession used; specifically, risk assessment in terms of people, context and organization.

Figure 4.2 indicates that within the area of context, you would need to consider what facilities are to be used in the lesson, what procedures are in place and what equipment might be involved in the lesson. Risks associated with people relate not just to the pupils but also to the teaching staff or other adults supporting learning. Finally, risks associated with organization concern themselves with planning and preparation, class management and teaching strategies. As an example of this, we can explore a certain scenario: a teacher is delivering a unit of work to a Year 8 class with key learning outcomes relating to three areas of the key processes: (1) making and applying decisions; (2) evaluating and improving; and (3) making informed choices about healthy, active lifestyles through problem-solving activities. The teacher might be looking to develop pupils' performance and competence in these and therefore assess pupils in lesson objectives relating to them being able to (a) recognize hazards and make decisions about how to control any risks to themselves and others; (b) make decisions about what to do to improve their performance; and (c) the performance of others and identifying the types of role they would like to take on. Each lesson would set learning objectives and challenges that enable pupils to show progress in these areas.

Managing risk in this *context* therefore would need the teacher to consider what *equipment* you were allowing pupils to use to meet the challenge and potentially how pupils might choose to use it; the environment (*facilities*) in which the challenge was taking place, for example, you might have a water-based problem for pupils to solve that may have very different potential risks to a high ropes-based problem or a gymnasium-based problem; the *procedures* you set for pupils to respond to the challenge would also need managing in that you might put conditions on activities to restrict or extend possible solutions. A consideration of *people* would need to be made when managing risk; for example, you would need to consider issues such as *staff expertise* in supporting learning, for example, for the high ropes-based context, *pupils'* prior knowledge would need to be taken into consideration; their clothing, group sizes, particular need of individuals or the group in addition to how you would teach pupils to develop an awareness of personal and group safety.

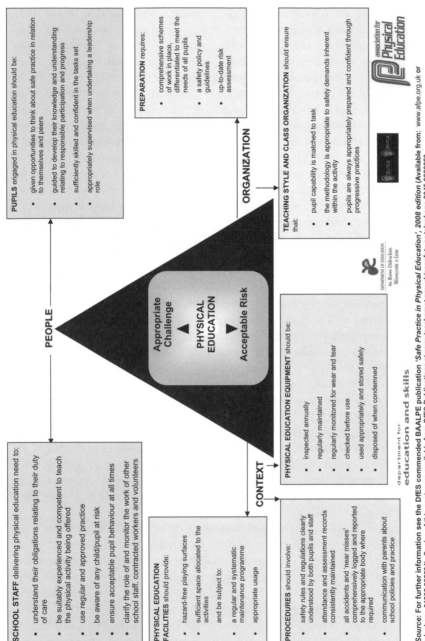

Figure 4.2: Safe practice in PE

Finally the *organization* of the activity would need to be planned carefully to ensure that prior planning (*preparation*) for example, schemes of work, showed progressive differentiated learning opportunities and a clear risk assessment associated with them; finally, that the *teaching and learning approaches* used to deliver the learning objectives were appropriate for the activities and the pupils and that class management strategies suited the demands of the challenge.

Reflect

Consider a unit of work that you are teaching in school-based training or that you have seen being taught – try to apply the same thought process for that unit as has been discussed above. To help you with this refer to the generic risk assessment for PE (Table 4.2).

Recording this information on a formal risk assessment is essential in that it shows that you have taken all precautions to minimize the potential risk and injuries for all those involved. As can be seen from Table 4.1 risk assessment is a legal requirement under the Management of Health and Safety at Work Regulations (1999). Risk assessments should be used to identify hazards that may cause injury. BAALPE (2004) identify a hazard as anything that might cause harm and a risk as the chance of that hazard causing harm, therefore a risk assessment assesses the likelihood of people coming to harm. The role of the PE teacher is, therefore, to decide whether a risk is significant and, if so, decide on necessary precautions and implement them to eliminate and minimize that risk. A risk assessment record should be regularly reviewed and amended; by doing so you are ensuring that you are doing all that is reasonably practicable to safeguard the health, safety and welfare of pupils, recognizing hazards and minimizing risks. By completing and reviewing a risk assessment you are able to demonstrate knowledge and understanding of the risks involved in the activities you teach and take precautions appropriate to that knowledge and understanding (BAALPE, 2004). Beaumont suggests that effective risk management not only involves the teachers but also the pupils, therefore you should teach pupils to understand safety and work safely: 'the development of pupil understanding and knowledge as to why a particular safety policy exists remains critical, going beyond the relatively simple imposition of do's and don'ts' (2006: 52).

Developing pupils' knowledge and understanding of safety and safe practice is echoed in the National Curriculum (QCA, 2007: 192), where in the key processes pupils should be able 'recognise hazards and make decisions about how to control any risks to themselves and others'. In addition, two of the six *range and content* explicitly relate to pupils developing knowledge and understanding of safety, *identifying and solving problems* to overcome challenges uses personal survival and outdoor activities to exemplify ideas, whereas *exercising safely and effectively* uses fitness and health activities to illustrate the point.

Table 4.2 Generic Risk Assessment For PE: Some Issues to Consider

People	Context	Organization	Controlling Risks
1. Pupils:	**1. Facility:**	**1. Class organization:**	**1. Ensuring that the people work safely:**
• Group sizes	• Hazard free	• Numbers known/register check	• Provide protective equipment/clothing
• Teacher/pupil ratio	• Clean, non-slip floor/water clarity	• Regular scanning/head counts	• Provide necessary CPD
• Additional supervision required?	• Sufficient space for group size/activity	• Group organization/management procedures	• Devise appropriate procedures
• Control/discipline/behaviour	• Any shared use issues?	• Warm-up/preparation/safe exercise	• Set appropriate discipline and control standards
• Individual and group abilities	• Access issues for those with disabilities	• Demonstrations accurate	• Develop observation skills
• Needs match demands of activity	• Operating procedures known/ applied	• Involvement of pupils with visual, hearing, motor or cognitive impairment	**2. Ensuring the context is safe:**
• Clothing /personal effects	• Fire regulations applied	• Other aspects?	• Inspect facility periodically
• Clothing appropriate for activity	• Safety signs in place	**2. Teaching style:**	• Place warning notices/protective devices where risks exist
• Jewellery	• Other aspects?	• Planned sessions	• Buy quality equipment
• Safety equipment/personal protection	**2. Procedures/routines:**	• Appropriate teaching style used	• Inspect the equipment
• Medical conditions known	• Orderly movement to work area	• Rules consistently applied	• Repair/service the equipment
• Policy on physical contact/substantial access applied	• Access to facility	• Regular and approved practice used	
• Disability Act requirements re access and involvement in PE for those with cognitive, visual, hearing or motor impairment	• First-aid equipment/procedures /responsibilities	• Support techniques known and applied	

Table 4.2 Cont.

• Pupils/performers know routines and procedures • Other aspects? **2. Staff:** • Qualifications/experience/confidence • CPD needed? • Supervision at all times • Knowledge of individuals and group • Observation and analysis skills adequate • Teaching position in relation to performers • Assistants know limits of role/responsibility • Effective communication between teacher and support staff • Insurance cover where needed? • Disclosure certificates seen • Parents informed and involved as necessary • Other aspects?	• Notices • Other aspects? **3. Equipment:** • Used for purpose designed • Suitable for the activity • Handling/carrying/siting issues • Accessibility/storage • Safety/rescue equipment present • Annual/periodic inspection check • Checked before use by performers • No improvisation • Routines for collection/retrieval/changing • Other aspects? **4. Transport:** • Roadworthiness • Safe embarkation • Seat belts used • Driver requirements/responsibilities • Passenger lists • Other aspects?	• Intervention appropriate • Tasks differentiated • Other aspects? **3. Preparation:** • Written scheme of work sets out safety issues to be followed • Equipment – size/type/quality/suitability • Carrying/ moving/placing equipment • Storage • Safety policy applied • Other aspects? **4. Progression:** • Progressive practices known/applied • Appropriate activities **5. Emergency action:** • Emergency/accident procedures/contingency plans known and applied • Other aspects?	• Modify the equipment • Teach how to use the equipment/facility • Amend how the equipment is used **3. Ensuring the organization is safe:** • Teach progressive practices thoroughly • Explain any inherent risks • Emphasize playing within the rules • Change the way the activity is carried out • Stop the activity • Avoid the area • Use a safer alternative

Source: From Beaumont et al. (2008). Reprinted with kind permission.

Recent initiatives and developments in education and sport (such as the Physical Education, School Sport and Club Links Strategy (PESSCL; DfES and DCMS 2002) 'Every Child Matters: Change for Children' (DfES, 2004f) 'Working Together to Safeguard Children' (2006); 'National Strategy for Safeguarding and Protecting Children in Sport 2006–2012'), have combined to impose a wider remit for the PE teacher and those working with children in schools. Rather than the PE teacher being the only facilitator for PE, a network of individuals/groups may now be involved in providing opportunities for pupils to experience and learn from high quality PE and school sport. A key agenda in the development of multi-agency work is identifying the principles underpinning work to safeguard and promote the welfare of children. Central to this is the focus on 'people' in the risk assessment procedure. Whitlam explores the idea that the level of risk is relative to the expertise of the staff and participants involved and that the risk increases when staff lack the required competence. In support of this, Skills Active and DCSF (2007: 7) define competence as a 'demonstration of acquired skills and knowledge'. In order to be deemed competent Whitlam suggests that competence is made up of expertise in a range of activities, for example, technical knowledge, progressions, safety, rules; knowledge of the needs of individuals in the group, observation and analysis skills, class management and control skills and professional relationships.

To enable easier identification of staff who hold competencies suitable to support PE and school sport, Skills Active and DCSF (2007) have developed four categories of staff working with children and competences they should have. An example of this is category 2, which may include the following: coach (level 2+ where the qualification enables them to take sole charge or overall responsibility for the children they are working with), teacher, instructor and community sports development officer. It is important to reiterate that as a trainee teacher you are deemed to be a volunteer and should therefore not be left unsupervised; however, as with many trainee teachers you may hold NBG qualifications at level 2+ in a variety of sports and therefore could be asked to run OSHL activities (e.g. a basketball club). In this case the school may ask you to become a 'contracted' employee which would enable you to take activities on your own. If this is the case, you need to be very sure of the school policies, practice and procedures with regard to safeguarding children and safe practice.

Reflect

Consider what you would need to do to ensure the safety and well-being of a group in the following scenario:

> You have been working alongside an experienced teacher with extra curricular activities and have been asked to take on 'coaching' the under-14 rugby team. The under-15 team is being coached at the same time by the experienced member of staff. You hold a RFU Level 2 coaching award. The following week there is a home fixture planned, but the u-15 team has an away fixture so the member of staff will be taking them to a different school.

Simple steps to ensuring that pupils progress in a learning environment that is both challenging and safe should always be close to hand. Whitlam (2006) outlines what a qualifying or newly qualified teacher should consider to become a safe teacher, suggesting that good practice is in fact safe practice. Lesson planning is at the forefront, ensuring that the lesson format includes a warm-up, technical development and cool-down. At the start of the lesson you should check personal effects, the teaching space and equipment; while teaching you should consider your teaching position to ensure that you can regularly scan the class and maximize observation; as you teach you should use approved practice; for example, in a swimming lesson use ASA-approved practice; the activities planned should progress according to the ability of the group and be flexible enough to change based upon your observations; the learning activities should match pupil size, physical maturation, experience, ability and confidence to set appropriate challenge; you as a teacher should not take a full participation role in a game as this reduces your ability to scan the class and observe; within game activities you should ensure clear and concise application of rules; you should involve pupils in managing their own safety, checking their understanding. If you do as Whitlam (2006: 48) suggests then you should enjoy teaching and pupils learning in a safe environment: 'Think logically through a lesson – what could cause harm? – have I covered the likelihood?'

Planning and preparation play a big part in developing and maintaining a safe teaching and learning environment where teachers teach safely and pupils learn safety. The lesson plan that appears at the end of this chapter exemplifies the planning process for a single lesson, highlighted areas and notes illustrate the triangular model of risk assessment. The accompanying risk assessment document provides greater detail of identification and elimination or reduction of risk.

Reflect

Having read this chapter and additional reading suggested in this chapter, work with your mentor in school to draw up a checklist for safe practice in PE – you will need to consider the following: relevant documents, risk assessment, risk management, routines and planning.

A trainee teacher's lesson observation notes

A difficulty being a female teacher of a male group is that of the changing facility issue. What strategies could you employ to make sure the students are on time and safe in the changing area? Maybe this is something that you discuss as a department? During the register you could have checked for safety of the students' equipment, especially with regard to the nature of your lesson content, for example, safe studs and gum shields.

Sample interview questions and developing a personal philosophy for teaching

---

Interview questions

- How would you deal with an asthma attack in one of your lessons?
- How do you think PE can contribute to the *Every Child Matters* outcome of the pupils' right to 'be safe'?
- How do you teach pupils to recognize hazards and make decisions about how to control any risks to themselves and others?

Is this you? Do you agree?

Could you describe what you think makes a good PE teacher?

Someone who is enthusiastic, passionate, fun and has good teaching methods.

Shelly Woods, Wheelchair Racing, 1500m, 5000m, Marathon
www.sportingchampions.org.uk

Further reading

AALA (2004) *Adventure Activities Licensing Regulations*. Cardiff: Adventure Activities Licensing Authority.

Association for Physical Education (2008) *Safe Practice in Physical Education and School Sport*. Leeds: Coachwise Business Solutions.

BAALPE (1995) *Safe Practice in Physical Education*. Dudley: British Association of Advisers and Lecturers in Physical Education.

BAALPE (2004) *Safe Practice in Physical Education*. Dudley: British Association of Advisers and Lecturers in Physical Education.

Beaumont, G. (2006) Health and safety: safety education, *Physical Education Matters*, 1(2): 56.

Beaumont, E.G., Kirkby, G.N. and Whitlam, P. (2008) Association for Physical Education (2008) *Safe Practice in Physical Education and School Sport*. Leeds: Coachwise Business Solutions.

Edmonson, G. (2006) Physical education and the law: risk management of the trainee teachers, *Physical Education Matters*, 1(2): 56.

GTC (2006) *The Statement of Professional Values and Practice for Teachers*. London: General Teaching Council.

HMSO (1974) *Health and Safety at Work etc Act. SI1974/1439*. London: Her Majesty's Stationery Office.

HMSO (1984) *The Occupiers Liability Act*. London: Her Majesty's Stationery Office.

HMSO (1999) *Management of Health and Safety at Work Regulations* (MHSWR). SI1999/3242. London: Her Majesty's Stationery Office.

HSE (1999) *5 Steps to Risk Assessment*. Sheffield: Health and Safety Executive.

QCA (2007) *Physical Education: Programme of Study for Key Stage 3 and Attainment Target*. London: QCA.

Raymond, C. (1999) *Safety Across the Curriculum*. London: Falmer Press.

Severs (2006) Accidents in physical education: an analysis of injuries reported to the Health and Safety Executive (HSE), *Physical Education Matters*, 1(1): 19–21.

Skills Active and DCSF (2007) *Guidance Document: Roles, Skills, Knowledge & Competencies for Safeguarding & Protecting Children in the Sports Sector*. London: DCSF.

Teacher Development Agency (2007) *Professional Standards for Teachers in England* (QTS). London: TDA.

Whitlam, P. (2006) Health and safety: avoiding risk + avoiding challenge = avoiding high quality: understanding the management of risk in physical education and school sport, *Physical Education Matters*, 1(3): 48.

Whitlam, P. (2007) Health and safety, *Physical Education Matters*, 2(2): 32.

Whitlam, P. (2008) Health and safety: best practice guidance on the effective use of individual and agency coaches in physical education and school sport, *Physical Education Matters*, 2(4): 47.

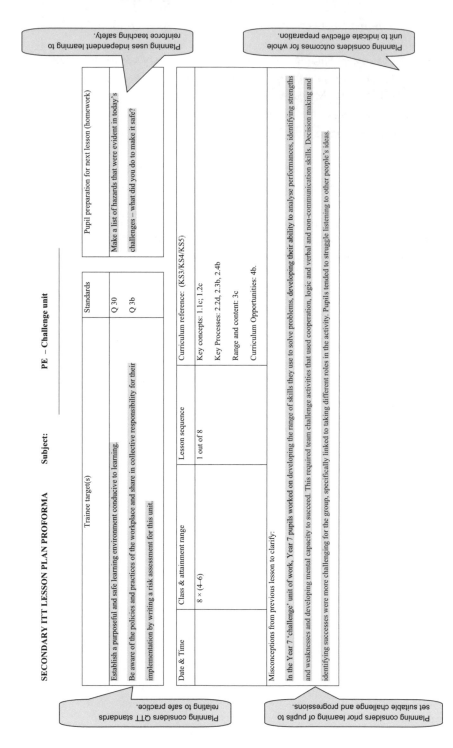

Planning uses independent learning to reinforce teaching safety.

Planning considers outcomes for whole unit to indicate effective preparation.

Planning considers QTT standards relating to safe practice.

Planning considers prior learning of pupils to set suitable challenge and progressions.

SECONDARY ITT LESSON PLAN PROFORMA   Subject: **PE – Challenge unit**

Trainee target(s)	Standards	Pupil preparation for next lesson (homework)
Establish a purposeful and safe learning environment conducive to learning.	Q 30	Make a list of hazards that were evident in today's challenges – what did you do to make it safe?
Be aware of the policies and practices of the workplace and share in collective responsibility for their implementation by writing a risk assessment for this unit.	Q 3b	

Date & Time	Class & attainment range	Lesson sequence	Curriculum reference: (KS3/KS4/KS5)
	8 × (4–6)	1 out of 8	Key concepts: 1.1c; 1.2c
			Key Processes: 2.2d, 2.3b, 2.4b
			Range and content: 3c
			Curriculum Opportunities: 4b.

Misconceptions from previous lesson to clarify:

In the Year 7 'challenge' unit of work, Year 7 pupils worked on developing the range of skills they use to solve problems, developing their ability to analyse performances, identifying strengths and weaknesses and developing mental capacity to succeed. This required team challenge activities that used cooperation, logic and verbal and non-communication skills. Decision making and identifying successes were more challenging for the group, specifically linked to taking different roles in the activity. Pupils tended to struggle listening to other people's ideas.

1

Learning objectives (*This is what the pupils are going to learn by the end of the lesson – what the pupils should know, understand and do. It should be presented to pupils as 'We are learning to: WALT'*) By the end of this lesson pupils will know how important team work and communication are in solving challenges. They will be able to understand how to recognize hazards in relation to the challenge and they will experience different roles in each activity.	The big picture – unit outcomes – linked to key processes relating to them being able to: a) recognize hazards and make decisions about how to control any risks to themselves and others; b) make decisions about what to do to improve their performance and the performance of others; c) identify the types of role they would like to take on.
Learning outcome (*This is what the results of the teaching will look like – the success criteria. It should be presented to pupils as 'What I'm looking for: WILF'*) **All pupils will:** • work as part of a team to solve different challenges; • be able to identify three hazards in the challenges; • act in two different roles in the challenges. **Most pupils will:** • work as a team to solves challenges using verbal communication to help the team reach decisions; • be able to identify three hazards and what they can do to overcome them; • act in two different roles deciding which role they work best in. **Some pupils will:** • work as a team using effective communication skills and identifying what the strengths of the team were; • be able to identify a range of hazards, suggest ways of overcoming them; • act in two different roles, one of which being group leader, listening to ideas and making decisions.	*How I will assess the learning objective/s* (**HIWALO**): • Questioning strategies to bring out ideas of teamwork, roles and safety (groups). • Challenge 1 – set activity and observe pupils working to identify different roles they take on. • Challenge 2 – assign particular roles to individuals in groups and observe how they carry out the roles. • Challenge 3 – allow pupils to give roles to different people in the group based on reflection of previous challenges. Between each challenge listen to pupil evaluation of activity successes and shortcomings.

Addressing the needs of individuals – strategies you will use to ensure inclusion:

1. Setting suitable learning challenges – differentiate learning outcomes for the lesson, opportunity to take on different roles in activity, modifying the challenges.

2. Responding to pupils' diverse learning needs – set specific targets for individual in the roles they take, provide learning resources to support communication of objectives, pupil × (EBD) – deploy TA to work with group, give specific responsibility to pupil.

3. Overcoming potential barriers to learning and assessment for individuals and groups of students – deploy TA for pupil X to refocus learning, use different equipment, uses mini video cameras per group to enable recall of activity. Complete RA to manage environment.

> Planning considers pupils' learning needs that might impact on safe practice.

Cross-curricular links (with specific curriculum references)

PHSE	Citizenship	National strategy	Skills PLTS – team workers
N/A	N/A	Literacy – oracy and listening – use verbal communication effectively to share ideas and solve challenges.	• collaborate with others to work towards common goals; • adapt behaviour to suit different roles and situations, including leadership roles.

Resources (including ICT)	
Mini video camera per group	
Challenge instruction cards	
Ropes, hopes, spot markers, blindfolds	
Flip chart paper and pens, blue-tack	
Stop watch, whistle	

3

	Challenge evaluation prompt sheets
Health & Safety	People – staff – prepare challenges in advance, provide mini plan for TA to work with one group; pupils – appropriate clothing and footwear; in addition support for pupil X, maximum group size of 10.
	Context – build on prior learning in Year 7, sports hall RA completed.
	Organization – guided learning teaching style adopted, prompts and observation for safe completion of challenges, groups mixed ability with more able pupil in each; challenges progressive building on skills each time, resources preplanned.

Planning considers health and safety for specific issues involved with the learning activities to be addressed in this lesson relating to the triangle model of risk assessment.

> Planning included deployment of TA to support EDB pupil.

> LO – enable pupils to know focus for learning esp. safe practice.

TIME	ACTIVITY	ORGANIZATION & EQUIPMENT *Please use diagrams to illustrate*	TEACHING POINTS	DIFFERENTIATION
0–10	Icebreaker activity to unit	Meet group outside changing room – set changing room challenge – with the person you are changing next to try and come up with the range of activities you did in Year 7 and skills you developed through them.	State title of new unit; ask to reflect on what they did in unit in Year 7 – give a maximum of 6 minutes changing time, giving time to move from changing room to sports hall.	In changing room use whiteboard to write prompts up if needed: • Indoor – outdoor • Individual – team • Physical – mental
10–18	Introduce learning outcomes of unit and lesson	Sit class in groups they will work in for next two lesson – give them two minutes to draw together what they were asked to discuss in changing rooms – in the group create a diagram – stick diagrams on walls and ask pupils to read through one other group's diagram. Use whiteboard to show outcomes for the unit and specifically for lesson – explain what they will know do and understand by the end of the lesson.	Pre-plan groups using experience teachers advise. Provide template on flip charts for diagrams (e.g.): 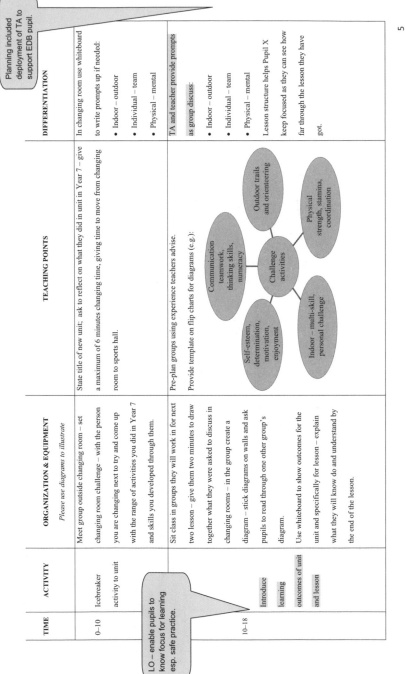	TA and teacher provide prompts as group discuss: • Indoor – outdoor • Individual – team • Physical – mental Lesson structure helps Pupil X keep focused as they can see how far through the lesson they have got.

Callout: Planned group management strategies keep organization safe.

Callout: 'Think safe' information on challenge cards highlight teaching safely and safety.

			Have LOs on white board as well as lesson structure	Planned group management strategies
18–28	Challenge one – human knots	Human 'knots' card will be in the centre of their area, they have 10 minutes to complete the task. A group of 8 people forms a circle. Each person puts their right hand into the centre of the circle and clasps hands with one other person who is not standing next to them. They should be holding two different people's hands. The goal is to untangle the knot without letting go of anyone's hand. *Think safe: what do you need to make sure you do so that people do not get hurt?*	Assign each group a work area in the sports hall – that is their area and they are responsible for managing the equipment in that area. (Set out sports hall space prior to start of lesson with 4 sets of equipment in each corner and 'Human Knots' card in centre of each area.) Start stop watch. Safety prompts – think about the people in the group; how you clasp hands, what positions they might get into; think about how you communicate your ideas. As groups work rotate round group and observe different roles being taken by each group member. If they break grip start again. At the end of the time limit consider how many pupils were untangled.	TA goes to support one group specifically but can oversee second group as well so not to pressurize pupil X. Teacher and TA checks that pupils understand instructions on the card. Provide prompts for solution if needed. Provide prompts for communication speaking and listening if needed e.g. What did Y just say?
28–45	Challenge 2 – ring on a string Part one	Pupils are responsible for setting up equipment with leader taking charge.	Call all groups into the centre of the sports hall; as a group think of one thing that worked well in your team – teacher nominates a leader – ask that person to say what it was that went well – let that person know that they will be the leader for the next challenge – give that person the challenge card. They are not to show others in the team the card but use communication skills to	30 - second discussion time Choose leader for each group based of observation e.g. someone

6

	Place the markers randomly around the play area about 3 or 4 feet apart.	explain the task.	who came up with good ideas but was not listened to, someone who played minimal role in ideas in first challenge.
	Place the pile of rope in about the centre of the area, within reach of at least 1 marker.	Teacher and TA check that leader understands the task. Safety prompts – think about the people in the group; how to send and receive the rope, what positions they might get into; think about how you communicate your ideas.	Provide support for the leader if they need it e.g. how is it easiest to throw a rope, how can you be sure it is safe?
	Everyone, except the leader takes position on a marker. Tell everyone that they cannot move their feet for the rest of the challenge.	As groups work teacher to rotate round group and observe different roles being taken by each group member.	
	Everyone must have two hands on the rope and the rope cannot cross over itself. The rope cannot be touched by the leader, THINK safety – how can you pass the rope safely between the team?	Provide prompts for solution if needed.	
Challenge 2 – ring on a string Part two	Put the blindfold on the leader, give them the hula hoop, and guide them to one end of the rope.		
	The challenge is for the hula hoop to be passed from one end of the rope to the other without touching the rope or anyone standing on a marker. The team members		

Teaching strategies employed ensure pupils are aware of hazards and kept out of harm's way.

7

must give exact instructions of how they can move if the hoop touches the rope the leader must go back to the last team player.

THINK safety – how can you give exact instructions to the leader so that they do not injure themselves or the rest of the team?

45–55	Evaluate challenges 1 and 2 4-way tug-of-war	Pupils use evaluation prompt cards to decide how effective their team work was, what could have been done better and how different people's roles worked - use this to decide upon who will be leading the final challenge 4-way tug-of-war – pupils decide who the group leader is and therefore who will give instructions. THINK safety – only hold the	Stop groups in their area – ask them to sit down and give each group an evaluation prompt sheet. Set up equipment with hoop in the centre of the sports hall and spot markers for team positions.	Teacher and TA provide more or less support for discussion as needed – use direct questioning or focus attention of particular pupils' ideas. Teacher and TA may prompt some team leader about different tactics to use.

8

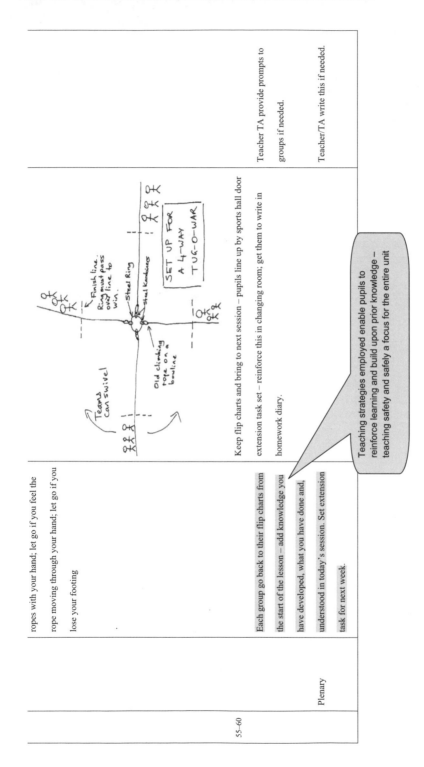

55–60	ropes with your hand; let go if you feel the rope moving through your hand; let go if you lose your footing
Plenary	Each group go back to their flip charts from the start of the lesson – add knowledge you have developed, what you have done and, understood in today's session. Set extension task for next week.

Keep flip charts and bring to next session – pupils line up by sports hall door extension task set – reinforce this in changing room; get them to write in homework diary.

Teacher TA provide prompts to groups if needed.

Teacher/TA write this if needed.

Teaching strategies employed enable pupils to reinforce learning and build upon prior knowledge – teaching safety and safely a focus for the entire unit

RISK ASSESSMENT IN PHYSICAL EDUCATION – SECONDARY SCHOOL EXAMPLE

School:............. Any place Community College............. Work area:............. Sports Hall.............

ASPECTS TO CONSIDER (List only actual hazards)	SATISFACTORY? (tick Y)		WHO IS AFFECTED? Pupils (P), Staff (S), Visitors (V)	IS FURTHER ACTION NECESSARY? RISK CONTROL (Comment)		Completed?
	Yes	No		What?	By when?	
1. PEOPLE: **1.1 Pupils:** **1.2 Staff:** • TA with limited PE experience required to support challenge activities		Y	P	• Support through shared planning, provide TA prompt sheet for different challenge sheets with explicit reference to managing risk	Ongoing	
2. CONTEXT: **2.1 Facility:** • Equipment in open storage area at times spills out into sports hall space		Y	P	• Notice to be placed on wall re storing equipment in area • Notice via staff meeting • Emphasize in handbook – procedures	1/4	disk updated
2.2 Procedures: • Orderly movement into work area – pupils follow departmental procedure for movement in area	Y					
2.3 Equipment: • Condemned mats not removed from store room – still available for use • Ropes and karabiners BS EN standards		Y	P.V.	• Condemned mats removed and disposed of immediately – firm doing annual inspection; asked to remove in future and check ropes	23/3	√ checked 23/5 + letter 15/6
2.4 Transport:	N/A					

10

ASPECTS TO CONSIDER (List only actual hazards)	SATISFACTORY? (tick Y)		WHO IS AFFECTED? Pupils (P), Staff (S), Visitors (V)	IS FURTHER ACTION NECESSARY? RISK CONTROL. (Comment)		
	Yes	No		What?	By When?	Completed?
3. ORGANIZATION:						
3.1 Class organization:						
• Variable groups sizes require different group management procedures per lesson	Y					
• SEN pupil need greater support to access learning						
3.2 Teaching style:				P			
• Guided discovery approach to learning – use group and independent study prompts	Y	Y				
• Rules to class clear (B4L) – challenges have 'think safety' links	Y			• Request TA support in class and use		
3.3 Preparation:				IEP for target setting and monitoring	21/7	Y checked
• Written unit of work	Y					20/5
• Equipment planned for	Y					
• Pupil challenge cards planned	Y					
3.4 Progression:	Y					
• Challenges increase in risk – Appropriate progressions planned in unit including extension and easier options	Y					
3.5 Emergency action:						

Signed: Headteacher ....

Subject leader..................................

Date of assessment:..................................

Review 1............................. .... **(date and initial)**

Review 2............................. .... **(date and initial)**

Review 3............................. ....**(date and initial)**

11

5   Inclusion in physical education lessons through differentiated teaching approaches and removing barriers to learning

Harvey Grout, Gareth Long and Paul Marshallsay

A teacher's story

When I was training to become a PE teacher, I was petrified of the word 'differentiation'. I had enough trouble spelling the word, never mind implementing it! It just seemed as if every lesson observation feedback I received had 'differentiation' on it and whatever I tried the word would keep appearing.

I thought I knew what it meant but I did struggle to implement it into my lessons. One badminton lesson I taught had such a mixed ability it seemed that I was effectively teaching a completely different lesson on each court. I don't know about the pupils but I was exhausted by the end of the lesson!

One of the most effective ways I observed was for the pupils to be working at their own level of ability. For example, while pupils were developing skills through learning the basketball lay-up I introduced '6 Stages' Stage 1 – walk the 2 steps and shoot the lay-up; Stage 2 – one bounce, 2 steps and shoot the lay-up; Stage 3 – walking pace, dribble the ball and shoot the lay-up; Stage 4 – jogging pace and shoot the lay-up; Stage 5 – introduced a passive defender; and then Stage 6 – introduced an active defender. Pupils could only progress to the next stage when they felt that they had achieved success at that stage. As a result I could assess who was at what stage and offer suitable guidance and help the pupil develop the precision of their skill and technique under increasingly difficult contexts.

However, my differentiation story focuses on a lesson in which the focus had been on developing cardiovascular stamina to cope with endurance running. In my Year 7 class I had the second best cross-country runner in the county through to pupils who struggled with their aerobic fitness.

During the previous lesson the class had run a 'fitness trail course' and measured heart rates along the route. My problem was that everyone had run the same distance and it was apparent that it took some pupils twice as long as others. For the next lesson the pupils were put into teams and they had to place themselves at different start points based on their best time and where they felt it would take 10 minutes to get to the finish line. Although points were to be awarded for finishing positions, there were more points 'up for grabs' for those pupils who were crossing the line as close to 10 minutes as possible.

Sometimes things just seemed to come together, and not only was the finish of the race the most dramatic I had ever seen (pupils from all levels of ability) but, more importantly, the challenge for all pupils had enabled them to achieve success (the pupils and me were convinced it was the highest standard they had produced so far).

Lee, PE Teacher, age 31

The learning outcomes of the chapter are:

☑ To understand and respond to the diverse learning needs of pupils within a PE lesson
☑ To develop suitable and effective learning challenges for pupils in a PE lesson
☑ To explore a range of practical strategies to overcome potential barriers to pupils' learning in physical education

The professional standards for qualified teacher status (QTS) addressed in this chapter

Q10: Have a knowledge and understanding of a range of teaching, learning and behaviour management strategies and know how to use and adapt them, including how to personalize learning and provide opportunities for all learners to achieve their potential.

Q18: Understand how children and young people develop and that the progress and well-being of learners are affected by a range of developmental, social, religious, ethnic, cultural and linguistic influences.

Q19: Know how to make effective personalized provision for those they teach, including those for whom English is an additional language or who have special educational needs or disabilities, and how to take practical account of diversity and promote equality and inclusion in their teaching.

Q20: Know and understand the roles of colleagues with specific responsibilities, including those with responsibility for learners with special educational needs and disabilities and other individual learning needs.

Introduction

Here are some definitions that will help to explain some of the content of this chapter:

> Personalisation is the process of making what is taught and learnt and how it is taught and learnt match as closely as possible to the needs of the learner.

> (QCA, 2008a)

> Inclusion is about acceptance and supporting all learners to achieve their maximum potential within a context where they are equally valued and their individual rights and freedoms are respected.

> (Dymoke, 2008: 74)

> The best way to meet pupils' different learning needs is to deliver the curriculum in a number of different ways; to differentiate the vehicle by which the skills, knowledge and concepts arrive, as well as presenting a range of tasks.

> (McNamara, 1999: 30)

Clearly, all three terms are inevitable linked. Within every class you teach there is an understanding that a diverse range of needs exists and that a variety of teaching methods are required to ensure all pupils within your lesson are learning within a modern, relevant and engaging curriculum.

Within your class the pupils' learning can be affected by a whole range of important factors such as their

- physical development;
- intellectual development;
- linguistic development;
- social development;
- cultural development;
- emotional development.

Reflect

Think of one class that you have taught. Look at the various development factors listed here and consider what differences exist in that class.

When teachers provide information it only becomes knowledge when learners can process and apply it (O'Brien and Guiney, 2001). As a result, it is imperative that as a trainee teacher you 'differentiate' your teaching to ensure the individual needs of the pupils in your class are met. Differentiation therefore is not about maintaining difference, but about ensuring that each pupil has the same learning opportunities as every other pupil. In effect, it is about ensuring inclusion for all.

The three principles of inclusion in the National Curriculum (QCA, 2008a) underpin how individual needs should be met:

- setting suitable learning challenges;
- responding to pupils' diverse needs;
- overcoming potential barriers in learning and assessment for individuals and groups of pupils.

This statutory inclusion statement sets out these three principles for developing an inclusive curriculum that provides all pupils with relevant and challenging learning. The first part of this chapter focuses on how the PE teacher can set suitable learning challenges through differentiation.

Planning to set suitable learning challenges through differentiation

Capel (1997: 308) provides the following definition of differentiation as 'the matching of work to the differing capabilities of individuals or groups of pupils in order to extend their learning'. If we accept that no two pupils are identical, nor do they learn in exactly the same ways, then we can probably agree that differentiation is necessary for setting suitable learning challenges for all.

Here is a 'story' that we hope highlights the need for successful differentiation and takes place from three different perspectives. This is a true story about the first time the three authors of this chapter went skiing together.

The learners' story

For one of the authors it was only their second time on the snow (the learner) while the other two were experienced skiers. At first the learner was growing increasingly frustrated as everyone around him was making it seem so easy, and despite trying to analyse what these skiers were doing, it didn't help him improve. Along with his aching legs and increasing annoyance, he felt that the best part of the morning was the hot chocolate break!

One teacher's story

One of the friends (teacher 1) could see that his mate was becoming frustrated, so he decided to show him some drills that he had used when he had learned how to ski. Every few attempts down the slope the friend would adapt and refine the drill depending on what he felt his friend needed to work on. This helped a bit but the beginner skier was still getting frustrated and his friend secretly was getting frustrated as well and began to wonder how his mate could call himself a PE teacher as he was rubbish!

The other teacher's story

The other friend (teacher 2) knew the beginner skier longer than their other friend. He knew that his friend would have expected to pick up skiing easily and although he was doing what was expected for his experience, he would not believe this. He also had a good idea of how his friend learned, so every so often (quite rarely) he would tell his friend a short snappy sentence of something to concentrate on and repeat in his head as he skied. This, coupled with genuine praise and some short 'races', seemed to do the trick and the learner was much happier and very soon better at skiing than his friends (ok, that last bit may not be true!).

Reflect

Which principles of differentiation can be seen in this story?

What is perhaps clear is that it will not just be *what* you plan to do (organization and content) that will need to be considered when trying to differentiate but also *how* you as the teacher present the information (presentation). Also important is that having an understanding of the learner's needs is extremely useful when selecting the appropriate methods of differentiation.

When you first start teaching, planning for differentiation can seem quite daunting. Although the programmes of study stipulate what should be taught at each key stage, it does allow for flexibility in that knowledge, skills and understanding can be used from earlier or later key stages (QCA, 2008a). Therefore, different curriculum experiences should be personalized so that pupils can have differentiated goals and targets with shared and agreed success criteria. As such then, it is important that your planning focuses more on 'where the pupils are' as opposed to 'what needs to be covered'.

This section of the chapter largely focuses on how differentiation can occur within the PE lesson.

Differentiation by outcome

In differentiation by outcome, all pupils receive the same stimulus and task, therefore various different outcomes are expected. For example, a class may be set the challenge of finding out how many ways they can incorporate partner balances into a gymnastics routine. The 'danger' of this form of differentiation is that the only difference could be with regard to the volume of outcomes; for example, group A came up with six partner balances while group C could only think of two.

Reflect

Consider the point of view that 'differentiation by outcome' is not really differentiation at all.

A problem with this approach is that a teacher may 'teach to the middle' and that the level of the lesson will be too high or too low for most pupils (probably two-thirds of the class). In essence, if we always teach the same thing, in the same way, to all the pupils, we will not be addressing the learning of all pupils.

Differentiation by task

Differentiation by task at its most basic level means setting different tasks (or different versions of the same task) for individuals or groups within the class. In its simplest form, it might be that one pupil has to score 10 points in two minutes and another is aiming for 5 points. It is obviously very difficult to set different tasks for *all* pupils within our classes. A sensible idea would be to set different learning outcomes for different groups of pupils and consider how each group would best succeed in these. Although this can be represented in the lesson plan by:

- all pupils will ...
- most pupils will ...
- some pupils will ...

It is worth remembering that the needs of *all* individuals will not fit into these groups and therefore more targets and support may well be required for some pupils. In this case learning outcomes would be appropriate for the teacher's predicted levels of ability.

Differentiation by task may also involve providing the class with a choice of tasks for the pupils to experience and therefore a range of outcomes would be observed. For example, pupils wishing to develop their physical capacity (e.g. speed over hurdles) may choose a task they feel is best suited for them. This could be a range of tasks working on different aspects of hurdling, for example, working on developing reaction time to the first hurdle, improving lead leg technique or trail leg technique, or discovering the ideal stride patterns between hurdles.

Alternatively, tasks may be graded and pupils progress along the different parts of the tasks (see the basketball lay up example in 'a teacher's story'). With graded tasks not all pupils are expected to complete all parts of the task (therefore a range of outcomes will once again be evident).

Reflect

Will you or the pupils decide which task they begin with? When/how will they progress to the next grade?

> **Reflect**
>
> How could you differentiate by the 'roles' you may give to individual pupils working in a group?

Differentiation by resource

Here the task may be the same but various resources are provided to differentiate the task. So, for example, if students were 'analysing performances, identifying strengths and weaknesses' some pupils may be provided with an analysis 'checklist' sheet with success criteria already listed. Another version may have images identifying what sample strengths and weaknesses may look like. Other sheets may just have 'headings' on, while another requires the pupil to find pupils with similar strengths and weaknesses.

> **Reflect**
>
> - How would you 'handle' pupils who wonder why they have different work to their classmates?
> - How could the equipment you choose for your next lesson help with differentiation?

> **Reflect**
>
> Take three of the key processes from the programme of study, for example:
>
> - refine and adapt skills into techniques;
> - develop their mental determination to succeed;
> - make decisions about what to do to improve their performance and the performance of others.
>
> Think about a particular group you have taught and consider how you would differentiate within your lessons. What strategies would you plan to use?
>
> Was this harder than if you had been asked to consider how you would differentiate within the range and content (e.g. outwitting opponents)? If so why?

Differentiation by grouping

The department in which you work will already have made decisions on how they group the pupils into classes (e.g. gender, mixed ability). However, even in 'same-ability' PE classes there will remain plenty of differences between the pupils and their learning needs.

Reflect

- What are you views on 'same-gender' classes in PE?
- What about 'same-ability' classes?

With this in mind, there may be times in your lesson when you do group pupils by their ability, enabling you to differentiate more effectively by setting suitable learning challenges for each group. For example, if pupils are working towards choreographing a dance routine, it may be easier *for you* to use some of the differentiation methods already discussed if they are working in ability groups. However, the reason behind putting pupils into groups should not always be based on ability; if low-ability pupils are always 'put together', then where will their new ideas come from? In turn, by using these groupings, it is likely that pupils will begin to perceive themselves in terms of which group they are in and pupils may become demotivated if they see themselves as 'low attainers' (QCA, 2008a). In this sense differentiation by grouping has the potential to lead to a 'self-fulfilling prophecy' in which pupils respond to the level of the group they are in.

Reflect

Picture what you imagine by the term 'a low-ability pupil in PE'.

It is also important that if you decide to group pupils in your class according to their ability in PE, this is not based on a mental picture dominated by their skill and physical development. If this is the case, you would be ignoring ability in other key processes (e.g. evaluating and improving); identifying ability in PE should therefore consider a more holistic approach.

Example scenario: differentiation within a 'game/challenge'

You will already be getting the impression that planning for differentiation is hard! As already outlined, the teacher can adapt the same task, provide a range of tasks or 'grade' the tasks. Alongside this the teacher has to consider how they will group the pupils; for example, will it be by ability, friendship groups or done randomly? This can often be an issue when pupils are about to experience a competitive environment. In this situation the usual strategy by the teacher may be to ensure the teams are 'fair'.

So, in a 1 v 1 game (e.g. tennis), the teacher may pair pupils off against someone of a similar ability. In a small-sided team game (e.g. tag rugby) the teacher may do the same (e.g. good players v good players, weak players v weak players), or they may mix the teams so that each team has 'even teams'. Clearly, there is nothing wrong with the above strategies but the issues discussed in the 'differentiation by groupings' section would need to be considered by the teacher, as would the potential organizational issues (selecting 'even teams' can take time!).

Another option is to ensure that the rules of the game provide a level of differentiation. This can then have the same result as other forms of differentiation but (a) reduce organizational time for the teacher and (b) be less 'obvious' that different tasks are provided for different pupils, thus reducing the potential 'labelling' effect. Here are some examples:

Example 1: Refine and adapt skills into techniques (shooting in football).

The rules of this 3 v 3 game used in this lesson are very simple; if a team scores a goal (marked by cones) the goal that they scored in is made smaller while the goal they are defending is made bigger. This happens every time a goal is scored.

The advantage here is that even with randomly selected teams, the side that is less able at shooting will have a bigger target to aim for, while challenging the side that have already scored goals, yet this is determined by the rules of the game rather than the teacher.

Example 2: Select and use tactics and strategies effectively in competitive contexts (attacking serves in table tennis).

In this lesson a pupil plays against another pupil and every time they get to 11 points they win 'a medal' and begin the next game. However, whenever the teacher stops the game both pupils take their existing number of points to the next game (e.g. if the score was pupil A 5, pupil B 10 then both pupils start their next game against a different pupil on that number of points). The benefit of this format is that after even if a pupil loses a game 11–5 they start the next game against the same pupil 5–0 up and a differentiated task is in place without the pupils realizing it. In this format it is likely that every pupil will win at least 'one medal'.

Example 3: Plan and implement what needs practising to be more effective in performance (identifying and solving problems through team-building activities).

The group is faced with the challenge of getting each member of the group through the spider's web (a rope obstacle suspended from the ceiling). The challenge is to get all members of the group through the web to the other side. The rules state that no two members of the group can go through the same gap (the gaps are varying shapes and sizes).

Once again the differentiation here will be decided by the group and the task. The group will decide together which pupil will pass through which gap and it is likely that each pupil will experience a challenge relevant to their level without it being highlighted by the teacher.

Reflect: Can you think of other similar examples that you have seen or use in your teaching?

Differentiation by support

As already indicated, support for pupils within a lesson does not always come from the teacher and can, if appropriate, involve other pupils (e.g. peer assessment). On your school-based training you are likely to work with teaching and learning assistants (TLAs) who may be supporting individual pupils within your class. Although the differentiation that occurs in your lesson is still your responsibility, communication with the TLA is vital. Not only is the TLA likely to know the pupil well, they will have witnessed lots of different strategies that have been successful with the pupil. Furthermore, prior discussion of your lesson plan with the TLA will enable the two of you to work closely to ensure that suitable learning challenges are set and to identify how the support provided may be gradually withdrawn.

Reflect

What information from your department would be helpful so that you could plan to differentiate for a class that you were meeting for the first time?

Thinking on your feet! The STTEP framework

The key message so far in this chapter is that it is vital to plan for differentiation in your lessons and to adopt a variety of strategies. However, things do not always go to plan so it is useful to have a framework that you (and the pupils) can use within the lesson to prompt you to adapt and refine things. The following example of the STTEP (space, time, task, equipment, people) framework (Table 5.1) shows an example of adaptations that can be made quickly within a lesson (in this case developing the range of skills (shooting) in basketball). Imagine for this example that when you had planned your lesson, you had expected all your pupils to be able to shoot successfully, but now you have noticed that some were finding it easy (and becoming bored) while others were finding it too hard (and becoming frustrated).

Table 5.1 The STTEP framework

Space	Move the pupils further/closer away from the basket to enable or extend the challenge. Use different shooting angles to enable the backboard to be used
Time	Ask some pupils to shoot directly when receiving a pass (open skill) and others to prepare themselves to think about their technique before shooting as in a free throw (closed skill)
Task	After 10 shots each you can set the following rules: for pupils who scored between 6–10 baskets their next 10 shots only count if they score without the ball touching the rim (swoosh shot!). Those pupils who scored 3–5 baskets can carry on as before with the target of beating their score, while those who scored less than three baskets now score if their ball touches the rim even if it does not go through the hoop
Equipment	You provide some of the pupils with the basketballs that have the 'shooting hand positions' imprinted on them. With others you use a lower basket, and for some pupils you ask them to use a variety of balls to see if the same techniques apply to the different equipment
People	In mixed pairings the more able pupil must shoot while being put under pressure by the less able pupils. When it is the less able pupil's turn their partner analyses and improves their technique

Reflect

Consider how you could have used the STTEP framework to adapt a lesson you recently taught.

Although useful, the STTEP framework is not meant to cover every possible differentiation option; it can be useful to consider when you need to be adaptable and make changes within the lesson. However, it does not include other important changes that can be made and in particular does not consider the *presentation* of the learning activities; for example, the teaching styles used or the levels of questioning.

Responding to pupils' diverse learning needs and motivating them to progress

The statutory inclusion statement outlines the principle that schools must 'respond to pupils' diverse learning needs' and in particular that teachers should take specific action to respond to these needs by:

(a) creating effective learning environments;

(b) securing their motivation and concentration;

(c)   providing equality of opportunity through teaching approaches;

(d)   using appropriate assessment approaches;

(e)   setting targets for learning.

(QCA, 2008a)

This particular section of the chapter focuses on 'providing equality of opportunity through teaching approaches' and illustrates how an inclusive lesson can demonstrate a variety of different teaching and learning styles. Although differentiation through the teacher's use of questioning was covered in Chapter 2, it remains an important consideration when thinking how to differentiate and support learning.

Teaching and learning styles

McCormick and Leask (2005) provide a good overview of individual styles and how you as a teacher can analyse your own teaching style. The purpose of this chapter is not to claim that one style is favourable over another or that you can even plan which style you will teach in for the duration of the lesson. Conversely, it proposes that your teaching style should be influenced by the lesson objective that your pupils are working towards, the pupils themselves, and the activities being taught. Salvara et al. (2006: 66) argue that the trend of PE teachers to limit their teaching styles largely to the more direct ones reflects a desire to 'keep control' and 'teach motor skill performance'. Thus, it seems that if you want to teach your pupils all the concepts, processes and skills inherent to physical education, and provide for the diverse range of learning styles evident in your class, you will need to use different styles as appropriate.

Reflect

Table 5.2 will familiarize you with Mosston's continuum of teaching styles (Mosston and Ashworth, 2002). By using this book's lesson plans, identify which of the styles listed would be most appropriate to teach the lesson's objectives and specific learning activities.

Table 5.2 Mosston and Ashworth's (2002) continuum of teaching styles

The command style
Within this style the teacher makes all of the decisions. Often described as teacher directed and autocratic
The practice style
Pupils carry out teacher-prescribed tasks, enabling the teacher to work with individuals

Table 5.2 cont.

The reciprocal style
Pupils will work with a partner and while one works the other provides feedback.
Criteria are often provided to help the partner to supply feedback

The self-check style
The pupil evaluates their own performance against set criteria. New goals and targets
can be set in conjunction with the teacher

The inclusion style
The teacher sets differentiated tasks to ensure that all pupils gain success. Pupils can
often decide at what level they start

Guided discovery
The teacher will guide and assist the pupil to discover the answer to the problem

Convergent discovery style
As above, there is a desired outcome but this time the pupils can control the process to
find the conclusion. The teacher may provide feedback to assist the process

Divergent discovery style
In this instance pupils are encouraged to find different solutions to one particular
question. More than one solution is possible. Again this process operates with support
from the teacher

Individual programme
The teacher sets and plans the framework and content but the pupil will plan their own
programme

Learner-initiated style
As above, but the initial stimulus and request for learning also come from the pupil

Self-teaching style
This is independent learning where the pupil takes full responsibility for the learning
process

Reflect

Think of examples of when you have used or observed the different teaching
styles in PE. Why do you think that style was used at that time?

Careful consideration and planning should also go into the learning styles of
your pupils. Although it is beyond the scope of this chapter to outline the multitude
of learning theories, it is important that you acknowledge that although all pupils
will have common and similar learning needs, they will also have individual ones. As
a result, your pupils all have different learning styles and therefore learning should be
personlized.

Reflect

Take two of the learning theories you have studied as part of your course (e.g. Kolb's (1984) four learning styles, or Gardner's (1999) multiple intelligences) and consider an understanding of how these could impact upon your planning of including diverse learning needs in your class.

The message here is that it is beneficial for your learners to experience learning through a variety of mediums, and that a teacher who adopts a wide range of styles will be more likely to succeed in this.

Reflect

Would the following concept of differentiation be useful in helping you plan for learner's diverse needs and setting suitable learning challenges?

- Organization – e.g. grouping of students and effective use of available space.
- Presentation – e.g. the teaching style, resources and support used.
- Content – e.g. the selection of tasks and the pace that the tasks are covered.

(Bailey, 2001)

Overcoming barriers to learning

The principles and methods of differentiation discussed are relevant to all learners, but some pupils will have particular learning requirements that are specific to them. These will include supporting inclusion for gifted and talented pupils, those with learning difficulties and disabilities, and pupils for whom English is an additional language (EAL). Although this chapter is not detailed enough to explore the intricacies of supporting the inclusion of all these pupils in your PE lessons, it does provide a couple of case studies to highlight some important factors.

Inclusion case study: gifted and talented pupils

The 2005 White Paper, *Higher Standards: Better Schools for All* (DfES, 2005) sets out the government's ambition that every pupil should have the right personalized support to reach the limits of their capability. One of the Physical Education Sport Strategy and Young people (PESSYP) strategies is to improve the range and quality of teaching and learning for talented pupils in PE and sport in order to raise their attainment, aspirations, motivation and self-esteem.

What do you imagine by a talented learner in PE?

The Youth Sport Trust describe that talented learners in PE and sport are likely to:

- think quickly and accurately;
- work systematically;
- generate creative working solutions;
- work flexibly, processing in familiar information and applying knowledge, experience and insight to unfamiliar situations;
- communicate their thoughts and ideas well;
- be determined, diligent and interested in uncovering patterns;
- achieve, or show potential, in a wide range of contexts;
- be particularly creative;
- demonstrate particular physical dexterity or skill;
- make sound judgements;
- be outstanding leaders or team members;
- demonstrate high levels of attainment in PE or a particular sport.

Sounds great doesn't it? However, what is not mentioned is that they are only likely to do the above successfully if supported by the curriculum and teacher to do so!

A gifted and talented pupil in PE may demonstrate all or some of the following abilities:

- physical ability;
- social ability;
- personal ability;
- cognitive ability;
- creative ability.

(Bailey and Morley, 2008)

- How do these abilities link with PE's key concepts and processes?
- What about personal, learning and thinking skills (discussed in the next chapter)?

Although Bailey and Morley (2008: 7) recommend that within PE 'mainstream curricular provision is adapted, modified or replaced to meet the distinctive needs of talented pupils in PE' this is out of the remit of the trainee teacher. However, it should be the aim of the trainee teacher to ensure that 'differentiated practice is adapted to meet the distinctive needs of talented pupils in PE' (Bailey and Morley, 2008: 7). What appears clear is that the five abilities indicative of gifted and talented pupils in PE are indeed firmly embedded in the PE programme of study. What is important is that while a gifted and talented pupil may require extending challenges in one of the abilities, they may need extra support in one of the others.

> ### Reflect
>
> How does your department/school identify and provide support for its gifted and talented pupils in PE?

> ### Reflect
>
> How would you differentiate one of your previous lesson plans for these three pupils (pupil A, pupil B and pupil C) identified as gifted and talented? Pupil A is particularly talented in their physical ability; pupil B is particularly talented in their cognitive ability and pupil C in their creative ability.

Pupils with special educational needs (SEN)

The programme of study in PE is driven by the needs of the learner and therefore pupils with learning difficulties or disabilities should not be prevented from taking part in lessons, and teaching and learning should be designed to match the needs and interests of all. In the past a focus on content (e.g. "today we are doing rugby") instead of process ("today we are looking to develop our skills into techniques") may have resulted in pupils' learning needs being ineffectively addressed. One model that may provide a useful structure for the design of the inclusive PE curriculum (but also useful within your own lessons) is the inclusion spectrum (Pickup et al., 2008; Figure 5.1).

> ### Reflect
>
> Consider how the inclusion spectrum demonstrates the principles and methods of differentiation already discussed.

> ### Reflect
>
> Where and how do sports and activities such as boccia, goalball, sitting volleyball, table cricket, polybat and wheelchair slalom 'fit' into the national curriculum for PE?

Figure 5.1 The inclusion spectrum

(Pickup et al. 2008)

Inclusion case study: pupils with autism spectrum disorders (ASD)

Pupils with an ASD (e.g. autism, Asperger's syndrome) face great challenges when accessing learning alongside their peers. Their range of ability is as great as the learning difficulties they face (DfES, 2003). Aspects of challenge for pupils with ASD include:

- social interaction e.g. turn taking/sharing/partnerships/team membership;
- language and communication e.g. following/giving instructions;
- thought and behaviour e.g. problem/solving, predicting/anticipating the problem/solution;
- fine and gross motor control e.g. spatial awareness, planning and sequencing movements.

(DfES, 2003)

Clearly pupils with ASD have specific barriers to their learning that the PE teacher must try to overcome and go beyond the previous examples of differentiation included in this chapter. However, although the methods and strategies may be different, the principles remain the same. For example, suggested strategies provided for helping pupils with ASD to develop skills in physical activity are shown in Table 5.3.

Table 5.3 Strategies for helping pupils with ASD develop skills in PE

Strategy
• Analysing the essential elements of the task and set parameters of level of difficulty and
• Duration (*differentiation by task*)
• Praise the performance at the pupil's individual level (*differentiation in setting goals*)
• Giving clear physical and visual prompts. However, beware of pupils who get upset at being
• Touched at all (*teaching and learning styles*)
• Limiting the space being used (*differentiation by task*)
• In a one-to-one situation explore space alone with pupils when hall is empty (*differentiation by support*)
Source: adapted from DfES (2003: 21).

Once again the clear message is that to successfully include all learners, it is vital to start with the learner and their needs in mind and then to select the appropriate differentiation methods of organisation, presentation and content. Inspiring your pupils to perform at a level they find challenging and yet achievable requires imagination, flexibility and planning.

Reflect

What do you think are the differences between the terms 'integrating' and 'inclusive'?

Reflect

Read Chapter 2 on assessment in this book; would a department/school's assessment strategies need to be adapted to include pupils with SEN?

Summary

The provision of an inclusive curriculum is recognized as a fundamental human right and as such the statutory inclusion statement sets out the principles for developing one. The non-statutory guidance is crucial in supporting this principle and providing pupils with relevant and challenging learning. The trainee PE teacher will particularly contribute to this through the lessons they teach (in addition to other ways, such as out-of-school hours' clubs).

Successful differentiation requires planning and thought given to the organization, presentation and content of the lessons you teach. Although there are many ways in which a teacher can successfully differentiate, it is important that the strategies chosen are based on the learning needs of the pupils. When you teach pupils with SEN, it is important that a knowledge and understanding of the learner's specific needs enable you to effectively support that pupil and enhance their learning experiences. Your school and department will continually be working towards a curriculum that is personalized and inclusive; your aim at this moment in your career is to try and achieve this in the lessons you teach.

A trainee teacher's lesson observation notes

Most of the students were placed in the correct area of the pool in relation to their ability and the tasks set for them were differentiated and correctly levelled. This was achieved through the use of prepared laminated task cards showing a good use of ICT. Could you differentiate these further through the use of diagrams for the less able and maybe technical information and challenges for the more able?

Sample interview questions and developing a personal philosophy for teaching

Interview questions

- How would you address the problem of an able pupil suddenly becoming uninterested?
- What do you understand by inclusion and how might it impact on your lessons?
- How do your ensure that pupils with SEN receive the best possible education in your lessons?
- What are your views of teaching mixed-gender and mixed-ability groups in PE?

Is this you? Do you agree?

Could you describe what you think makes a good PE teacher?

Someone who can motivate, encourage and make a child feel good about themselves.

Paul Evans, Athletics, Marathon

www.sportingchampions.org.uk

Further reading

Bailey, R. (2001) *Teaching Physical Education: A Handbook for Primary and Secondary Teachers*. London: Kogan Page.

Bailey, R. and Morley, D. (2008) *Physical Education Quality Standards for Talent Development*. Youth Sport Trust (accessed 26 July 2008 from Youth Sport Trust: www.youthsporttrust.org/downloads/cms/Xchange/TALENT_DEVELOPMENTFINAL.pdf.

Capel, S. (1997) *Learning to Teach Physical Education in the Secondary School: A Companion to School Experience*. London: Routledge.

Capel, S., Breckon, P. and O'Neill, J. (2006) *A Practical Guide to Teaching Physical Education in the Secondary School*. London: Routledge.

DfES (2003) *Children with Autism: Strategies for Accessing the Curriculum, Physical Education*. London: Department for Employment and Skills.

Dymoke, S. (2008) Learning and teaching contexts, in S. Dymoke and J. Harrison (eds) *Reflective Teaching and Learning*. Los Angeles, CA: Sage Publications.

Gardner, H. (1999) *Intelligence Reframed: Multiple Intelligences for the 21st Century*. New York: Basic Books.

Kolb, D.A. (1984) *Experiential Learning: Experience as the Source of Learning and Development*. Englewood Cliffs, NJ: Prentice-Hall.

McCormick J. and Leask M. (2005) Teaching styles, in S. Capel, M. Leask and T. Turner (eds) *Learning to Teach in the Secondary School*, pp. 276–91. London: Routledge.

McNamara, S. (1999) *Differentiation: An Approach to Teaching and Learning*. Cambridge: Pearson.

Mosston, M. and Ashworth, S. (2002) *Teaching Physical Education*, (5th edn) San Francisco, CA: Benjamin Cummings.

O'Brien, T. and Guiney, D. (2001) *Differentiation in Teaching and Learning Principles and Practice*. London: Continuum.

Pickup, I., Price, L., Shaughnessy, J., Spence, J. and Trace, M. (2008) *Learning to Teach Primary PE*. Exeter: Learning Matters.

QCA (2008a) National Curriculum (accessed 18 May 2008 from Qualifications and Curriculum Authority: http://curriculum.qca.org.uk.

Subject: PE

Subject: Year 7 Health-related exercise
(Exercising safely and effectively)

Trainee target(s)	Standards	Pupil preparation for next lesson (homework)
Know how to make effective personalized provision for those they teach, including those for whom English is an additional language or who have special educational needs or disabilities, and how to take practical account of diversity and promote equality and inclusion in their learning.	Q19	Plot your heart rates from this lesson as a graph.
Know and understand the roles of colleagues with specific responsibilities, including those with responsibility for learners with special educational needs and disabilities and other individual learning needs.	Q20	

Date & time	Class	Lesson sequence	Curriculum references: (KS3/KS4/KS5)
	Year 7 30 mixed ability pupils	3 of 8	Key concepts: 1.1c; 1.4a; 1.4b Key processes: 2.3a; 2.3b; 2.5c Range and content: 3f Curriculum opportunities: 4a.

How does this lesson address gaps in pupils' learning from the previous lesson?
Pupils have completed a range of fitness testing and understand what areas of their fitness they need to improve. They designed varieties of circuit training the previous week, looking at the type of exercises and how they relate to the fitness tests. This lesson challenges the pupils to recognize the effects that different types of exercise have on their heart rate.

Learning objectives (*This is what the pupils are going to learn by the end of the lesson – what the pupils should know, understand and do. It should be presented to pupils as 'We are learning to:' WALT*)

By the end of the lesson pupils will know how to record their own pulse rate and understand why it fluctuates.
They will understand the different muscle groups of the body and be able to do different exercises to improve specific muscle groups.

The big picture – unit outcomes – linked to key processes relating to them being able to:

• recognize how to improve their muscle strength, stamina and speed;

• recognize how to improve flexibility and move their joints through their full range.

• improve their confidence and determination to have a go at challenges they are set.

Learning outcomes *(This is what the results of the teaching will look like – the success criteria. It should be presented to pupils as 'What I'm looking for: WILF)*

All pupils will:
- work on exercises that work different parts of the body;
- identify how to perform different exercises safely;
- be able to identify how to take their heart rate.

Most pupils will:
- work on exercises at a suitable intensity to their learning needs;
- identify how to perform the exercise safely and what they can do to ensure no injuries occur;
- identify how to take their heart rate and record their own heart rate.

Some pupils will:
- be able to explain which exercises are relevant for their favourite sport;
- know which exercises made their heart rate increase and explain why.

Addressing the needs of individuals: strategies you will use to ensure inclusion.

> Opportunities exist for pupils to personalize the lesson.

Setting suitable learning challenges; pupils will be able to choose whether they exercise at a green, yellow or red level as well as choose the exercise they wish to do.

Responding to pupils' diverse needs; each station will have a pupil who will demonstrate the exercises, as well as an individual card with the exercises shown visually and verbally. Pupils decide what order they complete the exercises in.

Overcoming potential barriers in learning and assessment for individuals and groups of pupils: the gifted and talented pupils are encouraged and supported to make the exercises specific to their sport (creative ability). A pupil with EAL will move around the circuit with their 'buddy'.

How I will assess the learning objective/s (*HIWALO*):
- Pupils will record their pulse after each activity on a 'recording card'.
- They will also complete the sheet and hand it in following the lesson.
- Pupils will answer questions in the plenary and discuss their answers with their partners.

> Assessment takes into account both performance and understanding.

> Planned strategies for inclusion include differentiation to consider organization, presentation and content.

Cross-curricular links (with specific curriculum references)		
PLTs	Functional skills and key skills	Other links
Team workers	Read and understand texts and take appropriate action.	ECM – develop a positive sense of their own identity and self-esteem.
Effective participants	Recognize that a situation has aspects that can be represented using mathematics.	ECM – develop the confidence to take on new experiences and ideas safely.

Resources (including ICT)
Task cards for each station
Stop watch, whistle, skipping ropes, weight bands, speed ladders, benches, variety of balls, wobble boards, gym mats, cones, poles, music

TIME	ACTIVITY	ORGANIZATION & EQUIPMENT	TEACHING POINTS	DIFFERENTIATION
	Set up equipment prior to the lesson	The 'Super 12 Fitness Circuit' is organized as follows: 12 exercise stations are located around the sports hall based on muscle groups and components of fitness. 1. Biceps 2. Quadriceps 3. Coordination 4. Triceps 5. Reaction time 6. Hamstrings 7. Speed 8. Pectorals 9. Agility 10. Gluteals 11. Balance 12. Hip flexors		
		Pupil will have 'recording card' to complete throughout the lesson (exercise completed, intensity competed, recording resting heart rate, heart rates during exercise and recovery heart rate).		Extra support provided if required by the pupil.
		Three exercise cards are placed at each station (on a wall/bench) that provides a visual illustration and verbal explanation of the exercise. Also attached to each station are three levels of intensity (e.g. red = 30, yellow = 20, green = 10). Sometimes these are time based		On the back of the card there is a picture and description of locating your pulse at the carotid and radial artery for those pupils who require it. Pupils will choose an exercise and decide the intensity that they work at.

Differentiation by task, decided by the pupil.

Phase	Activity	Teaching points / Questions	Differentiation
Introduction of learning objectives	Pupils are informed that they will be completing a 15 minute circuit that they think best matches their individual fitness needs.	Questions are used to recap previous ideas, concepts and Knowledge.	
Finding your pulse, measuring and recording resting heart rate.	Pupils find their pulse either from their wrist (radial artery), or neck (carotid artery).	Pupils are shown how to find, measure and work out their resting heart rate and record this on their 'recording card'. Levelled Q and A on why there might be differences among the class.	Within the questions the teacher can vary the terminology used (e.g. wrist/radial artery). A variety of mathematical ways of calculating the resting heart rate are provided.
Warm-up	Pupils jog around the centre circle using different movement patterns. When the teacher calls out a number 1–12 they move to that station to find out what takes place there. After the demo the pupils move back to jogging in the circle.	Each of the 3 exercises are demonstrated and the location of the cards shown. Pupils stretch while listening to the demonstration.	Sometimes pupils are selected to demonstrate alongside the teacher.
Planning their individual circuit	On their card the pupils write down the order that they wish to do the circuit (just by putting in the order of the numbers). They will decide which exercises and the level of intensity when they get there.	Q and A to revolve around what the individual pupils wants to improve upon. They are also told that at any time they need to rest they can be a 'fitness coach' at one of the stations.	Teacher can work with pupils who struggle at planning realistically for their own ability levels
Play the music!	For the next 15 minutes the pupils will work on their own circuit. Going to the stations in the order they planned. They choose the exercise and level that they work at, and then record that information plus their heart rate, before	The teacher oversees the exercises being performed and listens to the advice being given by the fitness coaches. Halfway through the time the	The teacher can work with the G and T pupil on making the exercises more specific to their sport.

Callout boxes:

- The teacher varies the terminology, task and questions to suit individuals.
- Pupils who struggle to follow verbal instructions are used to demonstrate.
- Differentiated by task and support.
- The task will be graded and differentiated by the pupil.

Play the music!	moving on (or staying as a 'fitness coach' if they need to rest).	teacher can stop the class and allow them some time to re-evaluate and change their plan.	Again the teacher can work with specific pupils on this.
Cooldown	As above. In whatever station they finished on the pupils conduct a cool down among themselves.	Every two minutes the pupils record their heart rate.	Some pupils are selected to lead the group's cool down and encouraged to describe (as well as show) the stretches they are doing.
Plenary	In pairs pupils show a partner their 'recording card' and discuss a) what they did and b) the similarities and differences in their heart rates before the class discuss it together.	Principles of training including specificity and intensity. The effects of exercise on heart rate.	Initially closed questions such as: • What happened to your heart rate? Become more open • Why do you think some exercises raised your heart rate more than others? • If you repeated the same circuit for the next 8 weeks what do you think would happen to your heart rate?
Homework	The pupils collect some graph paper on their way out and will plot their results and bring it in for the PE 'cross-curriculum' notice board		

Questions progress with regard to the detail of answer required. Pupils have had time to think and discuss answers with a partner.

6 Teaching cross-curriculum aspects within physical education

Harvey Grout and Gareth Long

A teacher's story

I guess that my understanding of 'cross-curriculum' aspects has changed significantly over my career. Initially, I viewed my role as a PE teacher as being purely to teach PE. If I'm being honest I previously felt that cross-curriculum aspects such as literacy and numeracy rather 'got in the way' of my teaching and were perhaps 'irrelevant' to my subject. In a way I felt that these could be taught better by my colleagues who were trained to teach English and Maths.

Gradually, I began to see my role differently and I recognized that all teachers had a responsibility to develop all aspects of learning and that my subject was actually a great vehicle to contribute to this. As a result, I like to think that I seized upon opportunities to develop areas such as literacy and numeracy within my lessons, but, once again if I am being totally honest, this was usually '*ad hoc*' and rarely did cross-curriculum themes inform or impact upon my lesson planning. I suppose that in reality any cross-curriculum content in my lessons was usually reactive rather than part of any pre-planning.

I am much more comfortable with the way the National Curriculum now outlines and explains cross-curriculum aspects. For example, the emphasis upon pupils' personal learning and thinking skills (PLTS) has made me realize that in actual fact I had always tried to develop these skills in my lessons, but now I had a framework and structure that would enable me to make the essential skills required for personal development more transparent and relevant to my pupils.

As a school and department, we have tried to identify what the strengths and weaknesses of our pupils are with regard to their learning. This has enabled us to embed the relevant functional skills and PLTS into the PE curriculum and as a result they now impact on my lesson objectives. Hopefully, this will go some way to ensuring that my pupils meet the aims of the curriculum and also the outcomes of *Every Child Matters*.

Katherine, PE Teacher, age 29

> **The learning outcomes of the chapter are:**
>
> ☑ To understand the potential that PE has in assisting pupils in their personal development and their attainment of cross-curriculum skills
> ☑ To understand that cross-curriculum aspects can impact on the lesson objectives in PE
> ☑ To show how the cross-curriculum aspects compliment much of the content of the PE programme of study

The professional standards for qualified teacher status (QTS) addressed in this chapter

> **Q15:** Know and understand the relevant statutory and non-statutory curricula and frameworks, including those provided through the National Strategies, for their subjects/curriculum areas, and other relevant initiatives applicable to the age and ability range for which they are trained.

The school curriculum

Designing a school's curriculum includes more than just the lessons taught by teachers. Other aspects include the locations and environments in which learning takes place, school events and the learning that takes place in extended hours and out of school. In addition, the school's routines (e.g. assemblies) also require consideration if agendas, policies and initiatives are to be successfully embedded in a curriculum.

The new National Curriculum (QCA, 2007a) allows for schools to organize learning through a variety of curriculum opportunities. This chapter acknowledges that some schools may choose to develop cross-curriculum skills and values through a variety of different ways (e.g. themed days, activity weeks, educational visits and the use of outside experts).

Therefore, although this chapter recognizes that curriculum pathways include opportunities within and beyond school hours, and that opportunities are best planned via a coherent whole curriculum experience, this chapter particularly focuses on how cross-curriculum experiences may be developed through the PE lesson.

However, at the core of this chapter are the following arguments:

- An integrated and coordinated approach whereby cross-curricular skills, such as functional skills and PLTS, are embedded into the curriculum, which will encourage pupils to better transfer and apply their skills.

- The key concepts and key processes for PE have a clear potential for developing functional skills and PLTS.
- The subject should and can contribute successfully to pupils' personal development and the skills required for learning, life and employment.
- The planning of these skills and qualities should be based on the needs of the school's learners rather than the activities themselves. For example, the PLTS of 'team workers' should not just be included because outwitting opponents through games is being taught, but instead because perhaps your pupils argue when working in groups and are not confident at expressing their ideas to others.

This chapter provides a brief overview of how the *Every Child Matters* (ECM) agenda and the National Curriculum's cross-curriculum dimensions relate to PE as a subject. It then uses examples of functional English and Maths skills (Information and Communications Technology (ICT) is discussed in further detail in Chapter 7) and personal, thinking and learning skills to highlight how cross-curriculum aspects can be developed through the PE lesson.

Personal development and ECM: a brief overview

ECM was introduced by the Children Act in 2004 and states that every child, whatever their background or circumstances, should have the support they need to:

- be healthy;
- stay safe;
- enjoy and achieve;
- make a positive contribution;
- achieve economic well-being.

(QCA, 2008c: 1)

The personal development of pupils encompasses their spiritual, moral, physical, emotional, cultural and intellectual development. The school's curriculum is central in demonstrating how the school is contributing to the ECM outcomes in order to promote individuals' well-being and developing opportunities for pupils to become healthy, enterprising and responsible citizens.

Reflect

Consider how the five social and emotional aspects of learning (SEAL) programme (self-awareness, managing feelings, motivation, empathy and social skills) can contribute to the ECM outcomes.

PE can make a hugely valuable contribution to help a school support pupils to achieve the ECM outcomes. The following provides very simplistic examples of how this could be achieved (this is certainly not meant to serve as an exhaustive list!):

- *Learning to be healthy:* developing a personal fitness programme.
- *Learning to stay safe:* learning the importance of warming up correctly and following rules appropriately.
- *Learning to enjoy and achieve:* taking part and achieving in a range of activities and roles and making links between them.
- *Learning to make a positive contribution:* understanding the importance of adopting sportsmanship, responsibility and etiquette within activities.
- *Learning to achieve economic well-being:* understanding how the skills required for solving problems in PE can translate to the world of work.

Reflect

What other ways can PE help achieve the ECM outcomes?

Reflect

Some Year 9 pupils at Cramlington Community High School in Northumberland were set the challenge of researching and producing a fitness video with advice on exercise and nutrition. What other 'PE ideas' could facilitate an integrated approach to all five outcomes of ECM?

Reflect

How has your department/school responded to the ECM agenda?

The cross-curriculum dimensions: a brief overview

Cross-curriculum dimensions aim to provide pupils with an understanding of themselves and the world around them and in particular they serve to give the curriculum relevance and authenticity (QCA, 2008c). The cross-curriculum dimensions include:

- identity and cultural diversity;
- healthy lifestyles;
- community participation;

- enterprise;
- global dimension and sustainable development;
- technology and the media;
- creativity and critical thinking.

As with other cross-curricular aspects, these dimensions provide opportunities for work within PE and between PE and other subjects. Although some of the dimensions clearly possess a stronger relevance to PE than others, all the dimensions should be explored in and through the subject. Once again these dimensions should not be seen as isolated 'subjects' as they interlink and provide a framework to help pupils achieve the aims of the curriculum.

Reflect

Visit the QCA website www.curriculum.qca.org.uk to look in further detail at the cross-curriculum dimensions. Identify where in the programmes of study for PE these dimensions fit best.

Reflect

Droitwich Spa High School (National Curriculum, 2008) led a cross-curriculum topic linked to the cross-curriculum dimension of healthy lifestyles, creativity and critical thinking and technology and the media based around the energy cycle (respiration equation). This work involved the physical education, science and maths departments working together on the day. What other 'cross-curriculum' days do you think the PE department could be involved with?

Personal, learning and thinking skills: a brief overview

To become successful learners, confident individuals and responsible citizens, pupils need to develop personal, learning and thinking skills (QCA, 2008). The PLTS framework is made up of six groups of skills:

1 independent enquirers;
2 creative thinkers;
3 reflective learners;
4 team workers;
5 self-managers;
6 effective participants.

Reflect

- What links do you immediately see with the groups of skills listed and the key concepts and key processes related to physical education?
- How could these skills help a pupil improve in PE?
- How could PE help a pupil improve in these skills?

Immediately it has probably become apparent that there are strong links between the essential concepts, skills and processes that pupils need to learn and understand in PE and the PLTS required for achieving success in learning and in life.

Functional skills: a brief overview

Functional skills are the core elements of English, maths and ICT that enable pupils to progress through education and through to employment. Although these skills are embedded in the programmes of study for English, Maths and ICT, they are not limited to these subjects. The programmes of study for physical education can provide an opportunity for functional skills to be applied in real-life contexts. As with all the cross-curriculum aspects, the functional skills should not be viewed in isolation and pupils should be encouraged to use the skills in an integrated way.

How it all fits together: a coherent and planned approach

You may well be forgiven for being slightly overwhelmed by all this! How do you try and ensure that your lessons:

- contribute to the aims of the National Curriculum;
- achieve the outcomes of ECM;
- develop pupils' PLTS;
- make links with other subjects?

Well, first of all, let us remind ourselves that all the above is not expected in one lesson! However, it is perhaps pertinent to remind ourselves that the above four aspects should not be seen as separate entities but rather as connected.

For example, by providing opportunities for pupils to:

- identify the type of role (e.g. a sports coach) they would like to take on (key process: making informed choices about healthy, active lifestyles);

pupils may begin to:

- identify improvements that would benefit others as well as themselves (PLTS: effective participators).

To do this, pupils will need to be able to:

- be flexible in discussion, making different kinds of contribution (functional English skill).

If successful over time this will help the pupils to:

- develop the skills and strategies to form effective relationships in a variety of roles (ECM: make a positive contribution – form relationships and participate in society).

This ultimately may enable pupils to:

- work cooperatively with others (aims of the curriculum: responsible citizens).

The purpose of the above example is by no means intended to simplify the complexities of the teaching and learning that would be vital over an extended period of time, but rather to illustrate how the PE programmes of study are linked to a pupil's essential skills, qualities and personal development needed to meet the aims of the national curriculum.

Planning to ensure that PLTS form an integral part of teaching and learning within the PE lesson

It is important to recognize that although each group of PLTS are distinct, one particular learning experience may well develop more than one of the skills. With this in mind the following examples aim to highlight how learning experiences within PE lessons can contribute significantly to developing pupils' PLTS. As examples they do not show the context of the lesson with regard to the needs of the learners, but rather they aim to highlight how PE may contribute to developing PLTS.

Example 1

Year 11

> **Sample key process:** making and applying decisions; refine and adapt ideas in response to changing circumstances.
> **PLTS:** developing independent enquirers, creative thinkers and reflective learners.
> **Range and content:** performing at maximum levels.

This part of a lesson is based around an athletics team challenge. The groups (e.g. four pupils in each group) are told that the team will have to complete 10 laps of the 150m track (marked out with cones). These are the rules of the race:

- Only one team member can run at a time.
- Each team member must complete at least one lap (this does not have to be in one go).
- The team can change the baton at any place on the track.
- The first team to complete 10 laps wins (they have to shout out the number of laps run each time they cross the line).
- Pre-planned tactics are allowed to change at any time.

The teacher allows a set period of time for tactics to be discussed. Pupils are encouraged to relate this challenge to their previous work (on pacing and race tactics) to devise a race strategy. The teacher then poses some 'problems' while the teams are planning their strategy: 'What would you do if one of your team is slowing down and struggling to complete their designated stage of the race?'; 'What would you do if you are running and feeling really strong and feel that you can carry on for longer than planned?'; and 'How will your tactics ensure that your team runs the second half of the race quicker than the first?'

It is emphasized that a pre-planned strategy may not always go to plan and that team members will need to assess their tactics and possibly change them while the race is taking place. At the end of the race pupils are not only encouraged to evaluate and analyse the team's strategy but also to identify the successes and problems they encountered (e.g. having the confidence to change something that wasn't working or taking responsibility for making the changes).

Within the plenary the 'lessons learned' are applied to the revision that the pupils are currently engaged in for preparation for their forthcoming exams. Links are made between how an athlete/team has a plan for competition success, yet how they also need to be flexible and critical enough to adapt and refine this plan.

Within this lesson the pupils will have experienced the following opportunities (among others) to develop their PLTS:

1 They had to plan what they and their team were going to do. These decisions were based on their previous knowledge of pacing and race tactics (independent enquirers).
2 The plan required the pupils to respond to what was happening and required a degree of creative improvisation (creative thinkers).
3 After the race had been run, pupils were required to reflect upon their plan and subsequent performance and to refine what they would do in future (reflective learners).
4 This was then applied to an aspect of their education, which in this case was the need for a revision plan/strategy in preparation for examinations.

Once again, it is important to reiterate that it is not expected that because of this lesson pupils have suddenly become independent enquirers, creative thinkers and reflective learners, but rather that in order to do so these skills will need to be developed over a period of time and within a number of different contexts.

Reflect

What would you need to consider about your role as a teacher and your own pedagogy if you were trying to develop independent enquirers, creative thinkers and reflective learners within your lessons?

Example 2

Year 9

Sample key process: making informed choices about healthy, active lifestyles; identifying the types of activity they are best suited to.

PLTS: developing team workers, self-managers and effective participators.

Range and content: accurate replication of actions, phrases and sequences.

In this example pupils are beginning a sport education module (Siedentop, 1994) using TeamGym as the focus. The pupils are given the 'big picture' that at the end of the 'season' their 'teams' will perform a group display in a class gymnastics festival. Along the series of lessons they will experience a range of 'mini competitions' in which their group will be scored by other members of the class. The teacher has already allocated which pupils will belong to each team.

The pupils are told that within the next couple of lessons, they will need to designate roles for each member of the team (e.g. floor routine choreographer, display choreographer, tumbling choreographer, warm-up coach, judge, music coordinator, equipment manager, video analyst) and produce a team identity (e.g. team name and logo). After a warm-up, the class are shown a video of a TeamGym display and the discussion revolves around the strengths of individuals witnessed in the video as well as the strengths of the team.

As the first 'mini competition' will be a '3 run springboard display', the rest of the lesson focuses on timing, quality of the move, height, flight and landing. The pupils experience different ideas that could be included in a '3 run springboard display'; they are then encouraged to consider what the technical strengths of each pupil are and what the characteristics of an effective display team would be. The rules of the competition state that in the first run each member of the team must perform the same move, while in the other two runs the moves can differ. The judging criteria are used in the plenary to introduce what will be learned in the next lesson (e.g. 'close and safe streaming' will be judged better than a run that exhibits longer time delays between performers' moves).

Within this lesson the pupils have begun to experience and consider the following:

1   How they will take into account each other's strengths and weaknesses and decide on a way forward for their team (team workers).
2   As a result the pupils will have a choice about the activity and role that they will get involved in (effective participators).
3   The pupils recognize that they will need to take initiative to manage and organize aspects of the activity (self-managers).

This example once again shows clearly how the key processes linked to physical education can successfully complement some of the personal, learning and thinking skills to help achieve the aims of the curriculum.

Reflect

What would you need to consider about your role as a teacher and your own pedagogy if you were trying to develop team workers, self-managers and effective participators? How does your answer compare to the previous reflection task?

Planning to ensure that development of English and maths functional skills are integrated into the PE lesson

What follows here are two examples that serve to demonstrate how the functional skills of maths and English may be developed through the physical education lesson. Once again, remember that decisions on which particular functional skills are to be developed through PE will probably have occurred at a whole-school level and arisen from an identification of those skills that your pupils require more support in. Although in the following examples specific functional skill standards have been used (for clarity), it should be remembered that these should not be considered in isolation as they are often inextricably related to other cross-curricular aspects.

Example 1

Year 2

Sample key process: evaluating and improving – make informed decisions about how to improve the quality and effectiveness of others' performances.
    Sample level 2 functional skill standard (**maths**): interpreting – interpreting and communicating the results of the analysis. Interpret results and solutions.
    Range and content: outwitting opponents.

The pupils are organized into groups of four and paired up as a coach and player partnership. The two coaches receive a tennis match statistics sheet (such as the one shown in Table 6.1) and are informed that they will need to record the match statistics of their player. Both coaches and players agree altogether what categories will be recorded by the two coaches when the game begins and therefore prepare a simple tally sheet to use to record their match statistics. At the end of a set period of play the coaches compare information and use this information to try and improve their player (e.g. if a player is losing a high percentage of net shots, the coach may offer advice on how to perform this shot better, or change the player's match strategy). After the game is completed, the coach and player swap roles, but before the next game begins all four members of the group adapt the categories on the analysis sheet based on the usefulness of the initial attempt.

Table. 6.1 Match statistics for 2008 Men's Wimbledon Final

Roger Federer SUI (1)	4	4	7^7	7^{10}	7
Rafael Nadal ESP (2)	6	6	6^5	6^8	9

Match Summary

	Federer (SUI)	Nadal (ESP)
1st Serve %	128 of 195 = 66 %	159 of 218 = 73 %
Aces	25	6
Double Faults	2	3
Unforced Errors	52	27
Winning % on 1st Serve	93 of 128 = 73 %	110 of 159 = 69 %
Winning % on 2nd Serve	38 of 67 = 57 %	35 of 59 = 59 %
Receiving Points Won	73 of 218 = 33 %	64 of 195 = 33 %
Break Point Conversions	1 of 13 = 8 %	4 of 13 = 31 %
Net Approaches	42 of 75 = 56 %	22 of 31 = 71 %
Total Points Won	204	209
Fastest Serve	129 MPH	120 MPH
Average 1st Serve Speed	117 MPH	112 MPH
Average 2nd Serve Speed	100 MPH	93 MPH

Note: match statistics accessed from www.2008.wimbledon.org.

Although not made explicit in this example, it is probably clear that this lesson would also contribute towards the enhancement of the pupils' PLTS.

Reflect

Familiarize yourself with the functional skill standards (maths). Which ones do you think could be developed through your teaching of PE?

Example 2

Year 9

> **Key process**: making informed choices about healthy, active lifestyles – identify the types of role they would like to take on.
>
> **Level 1 functional skill standard (English)**: present information/ points of view clearly and in appropriate language in formal and informal exchanges and discussions.
>
> **Range and content:** outwitting opponents.

In this handball lesson the emphasis is placed on the role of the two referees. Before the start of the game each referee of a small-sided game is given a 'poor referee card' in which they are required to 'role play' refereeing in a certain way (e.g. don't explain your decisions, be overly aggressive in your explanations to players, or explain every decision in a long and complicated manner). The other pupils (as well as playing) have to try and guess what was written on the card by the end of the three-minute game. Before handing out new cards to different referees discussions take place on the importance of effective communication for a referee and how this may change depending on different contexts (e.g. a game for 8-year olds, or when a deliberate foul has taken place). As the lesson develops the emphasis evolves from a focus on the referees' communication skills to the players' listening skills and how these are affected by the style of the referees' communication. At the end of the lessons some of the handball referee hand signals are shown to introduce how effective communication in this situation can be helped by the use of non-verbal communication.

Reflect

Familiarize yourself with the functional skill standards (English). Which ones do you think could be developed through your teaching of PE?

Summary

This chapter has argued that there are inextricable links between the PE programme of study and ECM, cross-curriculum dimensions, PLTS and functional skills. With this in mind, it is important that as a trainee teacher you observe, and begin to consider, how the PE lesson can support pupils in developing these skills and help pupils to meet the outcomes of ECM. This planning of cross-curriculum (as with other aspects) should be process driven ("what do my pupils need?") as opposed to activity driven ("what can I teach through team games?"). Although this chapter has focused on the *content* of lessons designed to support the teaching of cross-curriculum aspects, it is also important that you reflect on your own values as a teacher. For example, the positive demonstration of your values and attributes will arguably have more impact on a pupil 'enjoying and achieving' (ECM outcome) than the 'content' of a lesson.

A trainee teacher's lesson observation notes

More consideration for the cross-curricular aspects are required here to show that you understand the responsibility you have as a teacher rather than just a subject teacher. Personal, leaning and thinking skills can be key to the success across all subjects, so try to offer an indication of where you may be able to include them within your teaching.

Sample interview questions and developing a personal philosophy for teaching

Interview questions

- How do you feel that PE may help raise a pupil's self-esteem?
- What do you feel about the statement that 'all teachers are teachers of English'?
- How do you try and develop pupils' creativity in your lessons?

Is this you? Do you agree?

Could you describe what you think makes a good PE teacher?

They should be enthusiastic about sport and working with young people. They should treat pupils as individuals but with regard to discipline treat all the same.

Craig Heap, Gymnastics – Men's Artistic

www.sportingchampions.org.uk

Further reading

DCSF (2008) *Social and Emotional Aspects of Learning (SEAL) Curriculum Resource Introductory Booklet.* London: Department for Children, Schools and Families.

QCA (2008a) *Physical Education Programme of Study.* (accessed August 2 2008, from Qualifications and Curriculum Authority: www.curriculum.qca.org.

QCA (2008b) *Every Child Matters: At the Heart of the Curriculum.* London: Qualifications and Curriculum Authority.

Siedentop, D. (ed.) (1994) *Sport Education: Quality PE Through Positive Sport Experiences.* Champaign, IL: Human Kinetics.

SECONDARY ITT LESSON PLAN PROFORMA	Subject:	PE (exploring and communicating ideas, concepts and emotions, as in dance activities)

Target(s) from:	Standards	Pupil preparation for next lesson (homework)
Know and understand the relevant statutory and non-statutory curricula, frameworks, including those provided through the National Strategies, for their subject/curriculum areas, and other relevant initiatives applicable to the age and ability range for which they are trained.	Q15	

Date & Time	Class	Lesson sequence	Curriculum references:	Attainment range
	Year 8	5 of 8	Key Concepts: 1.1b, 1.1c,1,3a, 1.3b Key Processes: 2.2a, 2.2b Range and Content: 3c Curriculum opportunities: 4g	Level 4–6

How does this lesson address gaps in pupils' learning from the previous lesson?
Pupils have been introduced to 'rhythm and timing' and can create short compositions in a duo. Many pupils need to understand how to express and communicate an idea through movement.

Learning objectives *(We are learning to: WALT)*	The big picture
• Communicate an idea or theme through movement. • Have knowledge and understanding of a variety of choreographic devices. • Create, refine and perform a group composition.	Pupils are working towards creating a dance piece that communicates an idea or theme and can be used as an assessment piece at the end of the unit to achieve a good NC level.

Learning outcomes *(What I'm looking for: WILF)*	How I will assess the learning objective/s: *(HIWALO)*
All pupils will:	Observe each group during the choreography process. Assess/ evaluate each performance. Q and A after each performance and the plenary.
• understand how to communicate through movement, without using verbal communication.	
Most pupils will: • select four ideas and create freeze frames that will communicate the ideas; • create transitions or travelling movement to link each freeze frame to create a sequence; • select and apply a variety of choreographic devices; • perform in a small group.	
Some pupils will: • work effectively in a small group; • lead in student discussions and ideas; • recognize the strengths and weaknesses of others; • be able to verbally appreciate the work of others.	

Addressing the needs of individuals – strategies you will use to ensure inclusion:
• grouping
• differentiation by task and outcome;
• leading questions used in Q and A.

PLTs	Functional skills and key Skills	Other links
Creative thinkers – use imagination and own ideas for creative improvisation.	Make relevant contributions to discussions, responding appropriately to others.	Creativity and critical thinking (cross-curriculum dimensions).
Effective participators – active participation and engagement of pupils.	Recognize that a situation has aspects that can be represented using mathematics.	

	Resources (including ICT)
	Music system
	CD (Chemical Brothers – Block Rockin Beat)
	Whiteboard and whiteboard markers

ACTIVITY	ORGANIZATION & EQUIPMENT *Please use diagrams to illustrate*	TEACHING POINTS	DIFFERENTIATION
Introduction How can we communicate with each other without speaking? Through movement we can communicate ideas and feelings e.g. happy/sad.	Pupils sit facing the teacher. Give the pupils 30 seconds to discuss the question with someone close to them. The use of clear pupil responses are required and key words highlighted.	Demonstrate to the pupils a happy walk and a sad walk. Ask them to explain the difference.	If a student within the class has social difficulties then select who they are going to discuss questions with.
Discovery travel (cardiovascular)	Pupils use all the space.	Travel on: • two feet; • one foot, two hands; • no hands or feet.	
Traffic lights (dynamic and static stretching) Simple maths skills are incorporated into the warm-up. The number they make can also be arrived at through a maths equation. At times the teacher says a word and the pupils have to create the number of letters in that word.	When pupils are requested to get into groups they do so as quickly as possible and create the word or number selected by the teacher. When the pupils have created the word or number, ask them to make it 30% bigger and hold for 8 counts. This is a good alternative stretching exercise.	Green = jogging around the room in any direction Amber = walking in time with the music Red = stop The teacher can then set a challenge. Get pupils into small groups and ask them to spell words using their bodies (i.e.) in groups of 4 spell 'BOLD'	Due to time constraints, pupils will not isolate any individuals. They will not have time to 'pick and choose' their groups Groups are also asked for their words to reflect their meaning (e.g. through the use of gesture)
Discuss Why we warm up and why the	When pupils are sat down, ensure that they are sat upright and not	Do not discuss for long, keep it brief and to the point.	Identify pupils to answer questions. This will keep

'traffic lights' warm-up was relevant to communication.	leaning against anything. This is to increase their strength and posture.	The 'traffic lights' warm-up creates shapes with the body to communicate a letter/word. It also stretches the muscles in an unconventional way.	them focused. Use more open and leading questions for some pupils.

> Rules of the activity are reminded throughout; also to prepare for the etiquette of watching performances.

> Again the concept that communication is more than just words. The example is given of a teacher who might give praise without sounding like they *mean* it, or without smiling.

Extreme sports Freeze frames List any extreme sports on the white board In pairs choose two extreme sports and make a freeze frame of them.	If you have enough board markers let the pupils come up and write ideas on the board themselves. The teacher should try to guess what sport the pupils are trying to communicate.	Sky Diving, Bungee Jumping, Snow Boarding, White Water Rafting, Surfing etc. Pupils should exaggerate movements	
Join two pairs together to make a group of four. Ask each pair to demonstrate their freeze frames to the other. Each group of four should create four freeze frames.			
Using music, ask pupils to perform freeze frame 1,2,3 and 4 one after the other without talking.	Insist that it is a performance and there is to be no talking.		
Transitions or linking movements Discuss what would make the performance better.	All pupils will be walking or shuffling into their next freeze frame. It will look messy and un choreographed.		
Introduce the word 'transition' or 'link'. Tell the	Twisting Turning		

> Previous work has focused on working with a variety of different groups and individuals.

> The responsibilities of performers and observers are explained.

pupils to use a variety of travelling movements (some from the discovery warm).	Jumping Rolling		
Choreographic devices Introduce and explain four basic 'choreographic devices: • Unison • Canon • Levels • Direction Ask the pupils to incorporate at least two of the above choreographic devices into their choreography.	Give demonstrations of each. New specific terminology is introduced to the pupils	Unison – when all pupils dance the same move at the same time. Canon – when pupils dance the same movement at different times (like dominoes falling) Levels – change levels and heights direction – Vary direction of dancers	Challenge the more able by asking them to incorporate all four choreographic devices.
Performance and appreciation The audience should guess what extreme sports the performing group have used and explain how these know this.	Split the class into 2 groups. One group performs, the other observes. Then change over.	Performance rules • No talking or giggling • Hold the finish position until everyone has finished • Positive feedback and constructive criticism can be used	Pupils are helped to structure their feedback.
Plenary	Sit the pupils in their performance groups.	Ask each group to discuss what section another group's dance they thought was most effective at communicating the extreme sports Idea and why? How did the choreographic devices help?	EXTENSION – question the pupils why?/ promote key words.

7 Information and Communications Technology in physical education

Stuart Taylor

A teacher's story

During a full OfSTED inspection, I was observed teaching a GCSE theory lesson. As it might have been likely that an inspector would watch the lesson, I planned to pull out all the stops by using as many forms of multi-media as I could to impress him. Although I had used video, DVD and PowerPoint before in lessons, it was only the second week of us being able to use our newly converted PE theory classroom and I was still getting used to using all the equipment in the room. Sure enough the inspector arrived and sat at the back of the class looking around as if they were impressed with our newly acquired PE room. The lesson started well but soon the worst happened. While switching between the computer and the video player for the first of my multi-media learning experiences, I lost how to switch between the two items of ICT and as time ticked on I could feel the anxiety rising within me (in my defence it was an awkward 'switching' process!). Thinking on my feet, I quickly asked one of the students near the front to get another member of staff to assist so that I could proceed with the lesson in a seamless fashion. Needless to say the member of staff came and with a few pressing of buttons got the video working straight away (to my disgust – and secret relief!). Luckily, the lesson went extremely well from that point in and the inspection team commended the lesson at the highest level, but I will never forget that sinking feeling …

Graham, PE Teacher, age 34

Reflect

Put yourself in Graham's shoes. Would you have pulled out all the gadgets and multimedia experiences to impress an onlooker or even an inspector or would you play safe? Come up with strategies that will help you if such a scenario occurs in a lesson, practical or theory, in which you decide to integrate ICT into the activities. What's your 'Plan B?'

The learning outcomes of the chapter are

☑ To understand the rationale for Information and Communications Technology's (ICT's) inclusion across the curriculum subjects and how this can be achieved

☑ To know what opportunities you are expected to plan for with regard to ICT's inclusion within your subject area

☑ To become aware of what ICT resources are available to enhance learning opportunities within your lessons through an appreciation of learning theory

☑ To become familiar with the resources that are currently and will soon be available to you as a practitioner

☑ To understand how you, as a trainee, are required to show your own skills and offer your pupils opportunities to develop their ICT skills within lesson activities

☑ To be aware of possible cross-curricular collaborations that could assist you to fully 'embed' ICT skills within your pedagogy

The professional standards for qualified teacher status (QTS) addressed in this chapter

Q16: Have passed the professional skills tests in numeracy, literacy and information and communications technology (ICT).

Q17: Know how to use skills in literacy, numeracy and ICT to support their teaching and wider professional activities.

Q23: Design opportunities for learners to develop their literacy, numeracy and ICT skills.

Introduction

The integration of ICT into the curriculum subject of physical education (PE) has previously been seen as a distraction from the practical active focus by teaching staff (OfSTED, 2002). With the introduction of skills tests for initial teacher trainees (ITTs) and a sharp focus on the ICT 'literate' trainee being emphasized by the Teacher Development Agency (TDA), teachers today are expected to embrace and integrate themselves and their subjects into the digital age (TDA, date unknown).

Reflect

Think about your experiences of using ICT at school. Was it a positive experience? If so, what could you take from the experience into your own teaching and if not what would you like to change so that it informs your teaching, specifically in the specialist area of PE?

This chapter intends to highlight the issues that can be faced from a PE practitioner's standpoint with regard to ICT integration into its subject. Through examples of a Year 7 shot-put lesson, it will show how ICT can be structured into lesson planning, teaching and reflective evaluation, to maximize learning opportunities and create an engaging climate within a PE lesson. The chapter is taken from a pedagogical perspective rather than a review of how and when ICT has been formulated into its current curriculum structure. For such a review look towards details published by the British Educational Communications and Technology Agency (Becta), the government's ICT sidearm organization, who deal with educational policy (www.becta.org.uk). To be ultimately successful in your pedagogical strategies with regard to ICT in PE, it is suggested you approach this area with an open mind, and a flexible outlook as often steps forward are accompanied by failings and/or backward steps similar to many facets of your training.

ICT has been introduced into the curriculum in many formats over the past 20 years. In its own right, ICT claimed a stake of the curriculum timetable allocation in the early 1980s with affordable personal computers becoming available. Just after the turn of the millennium Becta (2003) outlined their stance on ICT in education:

> To prepare pupils for a future in an increasingly technological reliant world, ICT should not only be a core subject in its own right, but also an integrated element in the teaching of every subject to all age groups.

Since then ICT's integration across all curriculum subjects has been evident with a strong undercurrent of basic 'functional' skills development for all pupils. Furthermore, the revised National Curriculum places an even greater focus on the integration of these 'functional' skills due to them being at the heart of the independent learner (QCA, 2007c: 6).

Reflect

Look at the exemplar 'functional skills' in the Key Stage 3 Programme of Study for Physical Education. Consider how you may include these within your lesson plans.

Suggestions have been made with regard to the limited impact of ICT provision in classroom practice (Underwood, 2004: 137). Thus, with such a practical slant, this research could further support the fact that many see ICT; induction into practical PE lessons as being inconsistent (OfSTED, 2004: 10). However, it should be noted that trainee teachers and present practitioners, with good skills in ICT and sufficient resources available to them in schools, can provide fantastic opportunities for their pupils to learn through the medium of ICT that may otherwise have not been realized.

Questions remain regarding why to include ICT into such a physically active curriculum area and just how much benefit can be gained by doing so? Contrary to many beliefs, such as the typical response that 'PE should be about doing – not sitting in front of a computers', this chapter highlights that ICT does have a significant place within such a practical subject (Becta, 2005a: 3). Some practitioners suggest that PE could benefit from the impact of ICT to a greater extent than many other curriculum subjects (Tearle and Golder, 2008).

Reflect

Consider why PE can potentially gain greater benefits from the introduction of ICT compared to that of other subject areas. Does the performance element of PE create learning implications that other subject areas do not?

Gadgets, gadgets, gadgets!

Due to its nature, ICT implementation means the use of equipment and resources that have some form of digital or electronic function within a lesson context. This leads us to our first major issue that strikes fear, and at times, resentment into the hearts of many PE practitioners. ICT equipment, as with many types of machinery, has, at times, a tendency to break or go wrong; unfortunately, that is a fact of life. If you could liken PE teaching with ICT to any other profession, it would be to the TV presenter working with children and animals – when you do it something strange always happens. PE departments also spend particularly large amounts of money (known as capitation) on basic supplies, such as balls, implements and specialist equipment. To spend even more on a single item of ICT, such as a digital camera for example, and then find it does not work, or worse, to break it tends to cause a reluctance to integrate ICT into PE from the outset.

> If it is a choice between spending £100 on software or on footballs, footballs win.
>
> (Becta, 2005a: 3)

However, with the cost of electrical items reducing (both in cost and size) and with their increasing reliability, robustness and mobile ability, PE can start to find resources that can be used in the practical setting. With such developments in the digital world gaining momentum, technophobes face being flattened by the ICT steamroller.

Previously, educational initiatives have seen schools and teachers benefit with a range of hardware and software purchasing schemes including the New Opportunities Fund (NOF), e-Learning Credits and the Laptops for Teachers' Scheme. Such initiatives have benefited the resourcing of PE departments with a number of 'gadgets'. To list the available electronic resources here would be futile as the development of technology is evolving so quickly; however Figure. 7.1 shows opposite ends of the spectrum with a few of the 'essentials' and a few of the 'if you're lucky' items listed.

Figure 7.1 The spectrum of ICT resources

It may be useful to categorize the type of technology by 'type' prior to considering its need and potential use in your lesson plans. The application of different sorts of technology can vary depending on your facility and the environment in which you are teaching. It goes without saying that poor weather conditions are particularly difficult to work in but try to consider other issues such as sunlight on LCD screens and power issues. You may like to consider whether the resource is web-based, that is, it needs an internet connection to work (e.g. YouTube), is standalone and static (e.g. a desktop personal computer or a treadmill), or is mobile (e.g. a calculator, stopwatch, laptop, GPS navigator). It is essential to take into account such logistical and pragmatic issues when you plan your lessons.

Reflect

Create a *'wish list'* of what ICT resources you could see yourself using in the scenarios below:

- A Year 7 gymnastics lesson in a traditional gymnasium.
- A Year 10 GCSE athletics lesson on the field in the sunshine.
- A Year 9 cricket lesson on the field in the rain.
- A Year 8 swimming lesson in the pool.
- A Year 11 health and fitness lesson in the multi-gym.

(Note: activity-specific examples are used here to focus your reflection.)

Before we explore specific ICT items and discuss the pedagogical approaches to their implementation, we must finally agree on a fundamental context in which we offer ICT experiences. Previously, ICT has been seen as an element that had to be 'added to' existing practice and structure within the lesson (Tearle and Golder, 2008). This is where the problem lies. ICT must only be used in a lesson if it benefits the teacher, pupil or A.N. Other (e.g. teacher assistants, adults other than teachers (AOTTs), administrators) in some shape or form. As the next generation of teachers, you must now strive to eradicate the situations that have previously occurred where you hear of stories from ICT-'rich' PE departments that they only wheel their kit out when journalists or inspectors visit (Becta, 2005a: 4). Although it is a challenge, ICT should offer newer, better and more sustainable learning opportunities for your pupils engaging them in the subject. Furthermore, it should not be seen that only specific items of ICT equipment are viable for PE pedagogy.

> In addition to the benefits of assistive technologies for pupils with particular needs, ICT can allow the personalisation of the curriculum for most, if not all, pupils and help them to overcome barriers, raising self-esteem as well as achievement.
>
> (Condie and Munro, 2005)

Many departments have decided to purchase and run expensive digital video equipment and analysis software that offers PE the chance to show its links to the world of ICT. Although this can be one method of practice, it is far from the only way you can offer a range of beneficial learning opportunities that build on pupil experiences. The following sections look to offer an insight into these technologies and also offer a number of alternatives to such expensive systems by considering ways of integrating more common items of ICT.

Reflect

Now reconsider the *'wish list'* that you previously created and consider alternative resources that you will probably find available to you in schools or at home. Could these be used to get the same or similar results?

Teaching and learning

The QCA (2007: 4) outline that 'the new National Curriculum is much more than a set of content to cover: it is the entire planned learning experience, including lessons, events, the routines of school, the extended school day and activities that take place out of school'. This more cohesive and common framework should offer pupils the opportunity of understanding the links between subjects rather than a fragmented approach as is sometimes seen where discrete elements are offered. This holistic view of pupil development is crucial when looking to structure teaching and learning opportunities from which pupils can achieve. Herein lies the first of many issues that inform our rationale for ICT involvement within PE. Therefore educating pupils through the development of 'skills' that are used later in life is essential. Many forms of technology are seen as commonplace in the world of professional sport with Hawk Eye, 'player cams' and the video referee to name but a few. With this in mind, it is essential that you offer pupils similar approaches and experiences to those they could be faced with outside of the school environment. More obvious applications to such a rationale could be that by offering functional ICT skills (embedded in such an engaging medium as PE), pupils become more motivated to try and develop these skills further.

Reflect

Consider how ICT and technology in general has influenced the sporting arena. Can these examples be used to motivate and engage students within your lessons to appreciate real-life scenarios?

This brings us on to our second issue informing our rationale that targets the fact that ICT can offer your pupils a wider range of learning experiences and opportunities. In order to be a successful teaching practitioner, it is vital that you understand your pupils, and are able to realise this through the application of learning theories. The topic area of learning theories is far too wide for this chapter alone; however, it is vital that we outline some of the crucial links between those theories and ICT integration into physical experiences you provide.

> The success of ICT use depends on our familiarity with good practice firmly rooted in an understanding of how pupils learn
>
> (Pachler, [1999]2005: 6)

With the introduction of ICT and new technologies into our lessons, the role we adopt as a practitioner is changing; however, you should never accept that the use of ICT replaces you as the teacher. It is *your* input and facilitation with regard to how the ICT equipment is used within the lesson that will ultimately decide if your pupils are successful. These views can be further explored in Norbert Pachler's chapter 'Theories of Learning and ICT in Learning to Teach Using ICT in the Secondary School' ([1999] 2005). Ultimately, the introduction of ICT-based learning applications can cause a shift away from the 'formal' setting or transmission of knowledge (behaviourist theory) to that of the 'informal' setting where the learner discovers (cognitive theory) in an active style (MacGilchrist et al., 1997: 20). However, this is totally dependent on how you choose to implement the ICT resource in question. For example, in our lesson if we choose to use a 'best practice' clip of a shot-putter in action, we would follow a behaviourist approach if the teacher highlighted the exact responses required from the pupils based on the observed performance (e.g. T shape between upper arm and chest). Because the response that follows the use of such a technique is a positive one, the pupils will strive to achieve this. However, the same clip viewed without teacher reinforcement of the correct technical points and used in a guided discovery trial-and-error format would utilize a cognitive approach. This highlights how flexible ICT provision can be and also how important it is for the teacher to take on a pivotal role in the pupils' learning experiences.

The use of ICT within the lesson provides opportunities for pupils to observe, reflect and analyse performance (which can obviously be their own, their peers or role models). This is probably the most widely used and integrated responses to ICT within PE.

Reflect

Consider your existing knowledge on learning styles. Using the lesson plans outlined in each chapter plan, how would you offer learning opportunities through ICT for pupils with different learning styles?

By considering your pupils' learning styles and having an understanding of the learning theories that underpin them, your lesson planning should become more effective with regard to meeting the pupils' needs. Due to this effective planning, it is possible that the lesson will offer more opportunities than just developing the ICT skills used within that lesson. These experiences can reinforce skills learned while using ICT in other subjects, and further literacy and numeracy development through various follow-on tasks (Poole, 1998). Indeed, there are many occasions where a certain level of ability in literacy and numeracy will be required, prior to, and in order to use ICT effectively, and on other occasions where a certain level of ICT ability is needed to demonstrate adequate literacy or numeracy (Kennewell, 2004). Such links are vital to develop skills for later life providing a rationale for ICTs to be embedded across all curriculum subjects.

> Trainee teachers therefore need to understand what learning means and what approaches are conducive to support and enhance learning in PE using ICT.
>
> (Tearle and Golder, 2008: 55)

Providing your pupils with a range of engaging, stimulating and achievable tasks is vital to create a successful and positive climate in any classroom – regardless of whether it is indoors or out. Initial planning is vital for the success of any lesson, especially if additional resources are to be incorporated into the lesson. Familiarizing yourself with the technology initially is a crucial aspect of preplanning the lesson and how you intend to use the resource within your teaching setting. The essential 'getting to know how it works' stage is often something that teachers leave out, and consequently when things go wrong in the pressure situation of a lesson, this can lead to panic setting in. As well as getting to know the equipment it also gives you a chance to understand the capabilities of the resource, allowing you to plan the introduction of the equipment more effectively and efficiently.

Reflect

While on school-based training, identify an area of technology that you have not had much or any previous experience of use with regard to lesson delivery. Consider how you could get further experience of this identified area, what and who you need to assist you in developing this area?

'Playing' and becoming familiar with the equipment is not the only part that makes the introduction of ICT into your lesson successful, it is vital that you consider the learners' needs and what benefits the use of such equipment will have to them. The use of ICT could primarily be there to support lower-ability pupils, allowing them a form of prompts to achieve successful results. Slow-motion video or DVD imagery, key word or phrases and voice recordings can all be used to allow pupils to revisit the teacher's original teaching points and/or instructions. More complexly, ICT could vary in terms of usage with some learners becoming more involved with the resources. Due to the flexibility in the curriculum and with an emphasis on personalized learning, ICT could be used to lead some pupils learning while it extends or reinforces others. This diversity and range of opportunities is particularly worthy of note in PE.

So what key factors must we look for prior to introducing ICT? Well, in the teaching and learning environment, we must justify and establish the reasons for introducing the equipment. There can be several reasons for this:

- Does it increase the ease in which a pupil grabs a concept, idea or skill?
- Does it create less off-activity time with regard to the whole group?
- Does it motivate pupils?
- Does it help the more able pupils to extend their knowledge, understanding or application of the tasks and concepts?
- And, finally, does it allow pupils to gain or reinforce their ICT skills by you providing such opportunities in your lesson?

Not only is it important for you to consider such areas, it is important for you to signpost or highlight your choices to the pupils to integrate their understanding of ICT use within the lesson, thus giving them an insight into your reasoning.

Once you have decided on the learning outcomes you wish to address, make sure that your lesson outcomes can then utilize the ICT resource fully. Let us take the idea of motivating the pupils. Teachers often used ICT resources to enhance the process of learning through motivation. Due to a wide range of ICT resources used by pupils at home, they are familiar with the digital age and are happy to use such resources. Pupils will often grasp the concepts of how and when to use the technology before many adults. Therefore, some pupils are happier with the challenge of using technology in the unknown environments and engage in the tasks more openly and successfully. To motivate the pupils, it could be as easy as using a digital camera, or to integrate video through a DVD player showing successful practice that they aspire to perform. This not only allows the pupils a motivating and engaging platform from which to learn, it also offers a variety of learning dimensions from which pupils can select and apply, providing them with a more personalized learning approach.

Assessment

Although assessment has already been discussed in Chapter 2, it is vital to briefly highlight key areas in which ICT has and can benefit you with regard to this area of teaching. Formative assessment that informs planning so that you can track, monitor and affect changes in your lesson for the good of pupil development is vital. ICT has revolutionized the way in which schools and teachers log, chart, store and present assessment details for every pupil. In our sample Year 7 lesson (at the end of this chapter), you can see the use of a mobile personal data assistant (PDA) or handheld PC, which has a class spreadsheet loaded onto it to record the pupils' attainment details or comments provide us with key information for you to plan and deliver the lesson's content. Furthermore, you could send this detail wirelessly back to a central database in the PE office if the school has wireless capability. This can also be replicated with specific performance details in a shot lesson by noting the distances achieved for each pupil. Other approaches, such as videoing the pupils' performances, allows department standardization of attainment judgements and offers the chance to disseminate good practice opportunities throughout the school.

Reflect

Consider what method your school placement administration use to collate and track your pupils' assessment. If possible try and get experience of the system with the assistance of your subject mentor or try and use your IT skills to design and complete a database system.

Other ongoing practical assessment opportunities, such as assessment for learning (AFL), self- and peer assessment, can be embraced through pupils using digital video media. Small rechargeable DVD players (such as those found in cars), PDAs, laptops or personal computer's holding analysis software can all be used by the pupils to observe, analyse and compare their own or their peers' performances. Furthermore, simple and inexpensive video cameras that allow pupils to record their own and others' performances can replicate this process informing pupils of their level of success at any given time.

The use and storage of such digital content has become more prevalent at examination level where exam boards offer the opportunity to submit such details electronically. More recently exam boards have also piloted and moved towards e-portfolios and online testing for examination purposes.

Reflect

Visit the website from the exam board that your current school experience uses and search for online versions of exams and/or test material. Go to www.testbase.co.uk/sec/index.asp for further details.

We now take a look at particular areas in which ICT can be involved, highlighting good practice and explaining some of the 'pitfalls' to avoid in your quest to successfully introduce ICT into your lessons.

Examples and uses: equipment

The next section offers you a summary of the equipment that is available to you in most schools or could be made available if funds allow. Think about how the inclusion of such a piece of ICT equipment can enhance your lesson. On that note, it may enhance the lesson for all learners or it could be specifically for individuals. Furthermore, the introduction of ICT equipment can motivate and stimulate learners. This could be its prime purpose?

This broad topic is divided into two sub-sections: fixed and mobile equipment. It is appreciated that although some items fit in both categories here, it is placed under one heading only.

FIXED technology

Whole-school provision: intranets, learning platforms and virtual learning environments (*VLEs*)

As technology develops, education has managed to realize the potential of some key facilities that assist the day-to-day running of the school. Accessibility has been a driving factor into the development of school intranets, learning platforms and VLEs. Key government documentation and policy with the extended schools programme, together with the fact that the majority of homes have some sort of internet access, have seen a particular rise in these digital environments being developed by schools. Individual schools offer these resources at varying levels of complexity, going from a basic school website containing vital information to that of the school that has a fully interactive site offering an interactive interface between school, parent and pupil. The latter is becoming more widely available offering the ability to track timetabled lessons, register absence and gain assessment data.

Using the well-developed and resourced ICT school as an example, consider how you could link, support and extend your pupils through this medium. This environment allows teachers to introduce key lesson content prior to the actual lesson being delivered. Many VLEs provide the opportunity for pupils to interact with their timetabled lessons where teachers can post details (such as the lesson plan, introductory and prep work) so that pupils can engage in the lesson before they actually turn up!

Assuming that your shot-put lesson is the first real shot-put experience the pupils have been exposed to (and dependent on your selected learning objectives for the lesson), offering a simple video clip or photo storyboard could decrease the amount of time needed to unpack the initial activity. It could be that you asked the pupils, as homework from the previous lesson, to visit this area where you have posted a question sheet that asks the pupils to offer health and safety rules for the lesson or to find key teaching points that will be used within the lesson. Remember, one of the benefits of electronic media is its 'reusability'. These are often known as reusable learning objects (RLOs) that could be assigned to groups or specific individuals year after year. Your initial outlay of work is then dispersed over time, other than you revisiting each resource if needed to amend or update. Another benefit of such a virtual environment is that it is possible to 'track' the number of times it is accessed and by whom. If such tasks are used for homework, this offers you the capability to see who has completed their homework or not. If you can create a positive culture forming an expectation of the pupils to do this, then this can have a positive impact on the teaching and learning in your lessons.

Reflect

Find an appropriate short video clip of a successful shot-put performance and create a simple Word document that asks the pupils to submit their ideas for safety and teaching guidelines. Now consider post-lesson activities. What tasks and/or, activities might you post up on the VLE to consolidate or extend the pupils' learning in the area of athletic throws?

Class ICT suites: 'the computer room'

Although it is important not to lose physical opportunities in your PE lessons, the use of 'the computer room' has potential benefits to enhance teaching and learning. Classroom ICT suites of personal computers (PCs) are often seen as 'whole-school' resources but are rarely used by the PE practitioner. Class suites offer the ability to engage pupils in a one-on-one interaction with the lesson's content. This enables pupils to work at their own pace and for particular pupils to show that they possess particular skills not always seen in such a practical subject. A 10-minute slot either as a starter or a plenary could be enough time to create a purposeful engaging climate within your group and support learning. Offering tasks such as navigating to internet pages of a shot-put performance offers an alternative method of engaging the pupils with the topic material. Other tasks could incorporate simple word processing or drawing packages such as Word or Paint to complete worksheets or annotations on a image to gain an understanding of the main technical points of a successful shot-put performance. Many ICT suites have the capability to show a specific computer on the main screen at the front of the class allowing you to highlight particularly good examples found by the pupils. Recent research has shown that PE teachers find the booking of ICT suites within their schools difficult (Tearle and Golder, 2008); maybe this is your chance to change this culture?

Reflect

While on school-based training, find out how the school ICT suites are timetabled and see if it is possible to timetable one of your lessons there. Consider whether you will need the whole or only part of the lesson to achieve your learning outcomes using the ICT available.

TOP TIP: remember, it may be helpful to observe or discuss with another member of staff who is experienced in teaching in such a room, prior to your usage.

Research suggests that classroom ICT provision for physical education rarely features prior to some Key Stage 4 involvement (Cox et al., 2003). It goes without saying that examination or theory lessons lend themselves to using whole-school computer suites compared to that of practical sessions mainly due to logistics alone. Many tasks that the examination class teacher would wish to complete can be done efficiently and thoroughly using the PC as a simple ICT resource. Alongside the independent study activities, such as research and investigation on a particular topic (e.g. sports injuries or the organization of sport in the UK), a computer's use is limited only by the software that is loaded onto that system.

Word processing, spreadsheet and presentation packages, such as the ones you as a trainee will have to show competence in using for qualified teacher status (QTS), can be enough. Group presentation tasks on an area of the specification in a BTEC core unit or a written summary of a video interview that looks at sport in the media could be your major focus. Remember that lesson time is valuable and you need to balance the need for the pupils to engage in this form of ICT with the benefit to the learner. Is it possible to set work that pupils can complete at home? A more productive way of using school resources could be seen in light of this dilemma. What experiences can't your pupils access at home that could be beneficial to their learning? Schools may have invested in communications software that allows you to weblink via web cams to other partner schools both in the locale and further afield; how can this enhance your pupils' understanding of particular topics? Moreover, the specifications ask the pupils to gain an appreciation of sport globally. What better way than to offer links to schools in the studied countries such as the United States of America or Australia. This will benefit your pupils' examination understanding and also provide many opportunities to access cross-curricular themes and principles with regard to citizenship and socio-cultural factors. In response to international dimensions within the world of education, the government has set up the organization Global Gateway (www.globalgateway.org.uk). They have lists of schools from other countries that wish to be involved in such projects, which can certainly short-cut the initial issues of finding appropriate partners.

Software

It would be unwise to offer a range of software titles here as technology progresses at such fast rates that specific software will become superseded and updated. However, it is possible to consider generic areas of software availability based on areas of involvement within our example lesson. For this section, rather than following our normal format of practical and theoretical applications, we take each area of software and then express integration options based on practical and theory application. Remember, this is not an in-depth review of specific software; however, some may be named specifically to assist in giving examples.

Desktop applications – Microsoft Office's packages (and alike)

These basic packages are typical of the everyday software you will find on your home computers as standard. As a trainee you must complete and pass your 'skills tests' in order to progress through Transition point 1 gaining QTS. The skills test in ICT covers basic entry-level applications in word processing, spreadsheets, databases, presentations, e-mail and browser applications. It is worth taking the time to practise/view the skills test at the TDA website prior to your test date that either you or your training provider (university) will book for you.

Reflect

Go to www.tda.gov.uk/skillstests/ict/practicematerials.aspx and complete the practice ICT skills test. You may wish to complete this skills test for real as early as possible in your training period so that it isn't a 'must have' award at the end of your training period.

Let us take the widely used Microsoft Office package and see how each common element could be applied to both our shot-put lesson and your own CPD. Remember, this chapter is not a review of each package as this would be far too great to achieve here. For such details, look at www.bbc.co.uk/learning or gain information from the series of 'Dummies guides' available on the market. First, let us look at the Microsoft Word package. More recent versions of Word are more capable than previous and offer a large range of drawing and chart wizards that are great for task cards and worksheets. The use of task cards prompts pupils to reflect upon their own and their peers' performances allowing reciprocal approaches and tasks that have been highlighted as good practice and creating high-quality PE lessons (DfES, 2004e) (see Year 7 lesson plan at the end of this chapter for more details). By using your internet browser, you can navigate to various sites to gain the information needed to integrate into your task card. Remember, you may need to laminate these if you are taking them outside and also consider the logistics with regard to what happens if it is windy!

Excel is a well-known spreadsheet package that is widely used in schools. Tables of data can be collated, manipulated and expressed. With regard to our Year 7 shot lesson, consider the use of tables to collect individual performance scores so that you have a measure of success. This could be as a raw distance score or through an agreed 'level' or 'medal' system that is standard within the department. It may be possible (weather- and logistics-dependent) to take a piece of mobile equipment, such as a laptop or palm top, with you to add the data as the event is completed; better still, could the pupils compile the results as they compete? Once the data are saved, they can be manipulated depending on how you intend to use them. As a teacher you could use the information to guide your planning (formative assessment) for future lessons, publish it either individually or publicly, the department may use it for selection purposes for athletic events/sports days but ultimately measures give the pupil a means of assessing their own performance that is crucial for continued participation.

Reflect

Using the lesson plans in each chapter, adapt the plans to integrate the outlined forms of software available.

Video editing/analysis software (e.g. Movie Maker/Nero/Roxio and DartFish, Silicon Coach, Kandle, Sportscode)

Probably the biggest area of development and integration with regard to ICT's integration into the PE subject area is that of digital images, either through video or stills (Stratton and Finch, 2001; Green, 2002; Morgan and Kinchen, 2003; Kibble, 2005). Although the use of digital images is discussed later in the chapter, it is vital to understand that the use of clips and footage can be of greater use than just being held on camera for review at a later date. Basic software such as Microsoft's 'Movie Maker,' found on most new PCs or laptops, can change basic video into useful resources. Movie Maker and many other video-editing suites can cut, split, slow down and speed up footage allowing you to create effective analysis to be used in future lessons for either review with the same group or to engage and enhance the learning process with different groups. Titles, annotations and diagrams can easily be added to video, creating sequences of action and or instructional video that can be used to highlight key elements in our lesson. It is worthy of note that in order to 'author' a DVD, you will need to send the finished clip to another piece of software. Authoring allows a DVD to be made that will run on any DVD player rather than an unauthored disk that only allows playback to occur on a computer. Purchasable software such as Nero, Roxio and Adobe Premiere will author all to disk and allow you to capture and edit your video prior to this phase, giving you the whole package in one software bundle.

> **Reflect**
>
> Using the footage gained from your Year 7 shot-put lesson, plug the camera into your computer and capture the footage. Using the software, create a 'good technique guide' for the shot-put focusing on the specific areas of the technique at particular phases, for example, preparation, execution and follow-through. Also create a 'common mistakes' video to highlight errors and how to fix them.

In recent years schools have integrated more specific sports performance software with a view to creating a workable link between ICT and PE. Software providers such as DartFish, Kandle, SiliconCoach, Focus and SportsCode have all targeted the educational market looking to capitalize on this integrated approach between technology and curriculum subject. This area of technology links the opportunities created by digital video that can now be seen as one of the most readily used forms of ICT media in today's PE lessons. These software packages allow for capture, manipulation and storage of footage taken in lessons concentrating particularly on observational and analysis skills.

As with all the areas covered so far, the use of digital analysis software could fulfil a chapter in its own right, so it is vital that you look to the department that you work or train within and discover the issues relating to such ICT applications. In many school environments, such technology has presented barriers to 'normal' teaching due to its complexity with regard to use and or set-up; however, it is vital that you look forward with an open mind and attempt to 'iron out the bumps' with regard to its use. You may find that some schools purchase this type of analysis software only to never use it or even get it out of the box! Much of the criticism that comes with these applications is justified; however, much of it is not insurmountable. The following short paragraphs look to highlight common issues and attempts to provide short examples of use and ways in which such issues can be addressed.

COST

This is probably the first and foremost issue when departments discuss computerized analysis software. Initially, companies that produced analysis software for professional sports applications, such as golf swing analysis and professional football analysis, sold similar items to education that often provided a poor fit with regard to cost and usability as the education market had differing needs to those of professional environments. However, in recent years software has adapted to the needs of the education market and has reduced in cost. It is not vital that for effective use you need the all-singing, all-dancing versions of the software available; in fact, most of the time basic packages will be more than effective. Consider what you want from your software. Look at packages that offer upgrades so that if you find that you need additional features, you can gain credit for being an existing customer. Many software providers have developed web-accessed packages that allow a single licensed application to be used on any suitable computer throughout the school rather than assigning it to one computer or laptop, which is vital for the 'mobile' user such as a PE practitioner. Finally, remember to factor in the need for a video camera and a computer in the financial equation.

TOP TIP: Consider whether you actually require software – can you do what you want with simple 'handheld' or 'mobile' resources alone? See the 'mobile' sub-section below for further details.

TRAINING/COMPLEXITY

Anecdotal evidence suggests that a major factor raised by teachers and trainees alike was the lack of training with regard to using such ICT resources. Some companies offer training; however, the cost is usually high. Prior to enrolling on a training course, check within your school partnership if some teachers have particular skills within this area of pedagogy and can share some good practice. Ultimately, the need to 'have a go' with these items is vital. Think about how early attempts can be made without impacting negatively on the pupils by experimenting within extra-curricular or observational lessons prior to introducing items fully into your taught lessons.

SET-UP

This is seen as another major bone of contention with regard to such systems due to the nature of needing some sort of method of acquisition, usually a video camera, some means of processing the images and hosting the software, usually a PC or laptop, and finally, some way of presenting the image to pupils, a projector or screen of some description. The latter piece of hardware need not be used if small numbers of viewers or users are involved as the PC/Laptop involved can be sufficient to display the images. Obviously, there is a clear issue with regard to whether the activity is based indoors or outdoors. Consider the shot-put lesson where you would need to take out a camera, tripod and laptop. If it was raining, this may be entirely inappropriate. It may also be inappropriate on a bright day due to the screen's effectiveness in sunlight. Another factor is be power as batteries are renowned for their short life span. How can you make it possible to use such software? The simple answer is you need to be flexible in your approach and realize the constraints that are imposed upon you. Furthermore, look towards using simple set-ups that the pupils themselves can be trained to establish just as they do with regard to other forms of equipment (balls, goals, etc.). Finally, always consider health and safety as the last thing you want is to have cables trailing across the practical space from camera to computer or computer to plug sockets.

USAGE

Depending on your learning outcomes for the lesson, the amount of involvement in the software application will differ. On a more basic level, you may have the software running on a delay function that stores the image and presents it on the computer screen at a later time allowing pupils to complete an activity and then view their own performance. Or on a more complex level, you may have reference clips stored in the software and acquire images from the pupils live in the lesson followed by a whole-class discussion about the comparisons between the two performances. The latter will take more time away from the practical involvement and should only be considered where appropriate. You will notice that in our sample shot-put lesson, we have included the former example of usage with the proviso that if not appropriate other methods of self-evaluation can be used due to environmental or practicality factors. Such flexible approaches are paramount to the successful inclusion of ICT in PE.

As discussed previously, the use of computerized analysis software in the PE arena is seen as somewhat contentious and can raise many issues, some of which have been dealt with above. However, it is vital that you realize the potential of such resources and attempt to use them within your practice when appropriate.

Presentation hardware: interactive whiteboards (IWBs)/fixed projectors/TVs

Due to the nature of the equipment in this area, it is obvious to realize that such items can only be used in a number of indoor environments. The use of images and or video has developed in PE over recent years and can be seen to reflect professional sports integration of technology. However, many schools are resourced to the tune of having an old TV on a stand that the pupils congregate around. But times are changing and with technology becoming ever cheaper, it is not uncommon to see schools invest in a number of flat-screen TVs and/or have projectors fixed in each teaching venue. Arguably, projectors were originally thought to have been seen as a better way of creating large-scale images in large environments, such as sport halls or gymnasiums. However, the practicalities with expensive replacement bulbs, specialist lenses and probably PE's biggest venue issue, that of the inability of being able to control the amount of light present, have major effects. Regardless of what media you have in your venue, try and think of ways that can benefit the pupils' learning opportunities within your lessons rather than something that distracts them from the actual lesson content. Support material for lower achievers or extension activities for gifted and talented pupils could be displayed on the screen via a simple PowerPoint. A 'good practice' set of video clips could be viewed reinforcing the key teaching points you as a teacher have outlined in an earlier demo through a DVD or video. Let us go back to our shot-put lesson. Although we would have to use alternative equipment such as Futball de Salo's or actual indoor shot-puts in the sports hall, a looped high-quality action/performance as a reference clip could be an effective strategy while the pupils practised. This could also allow the pupils to interact with the media and each other by providing structured opportunities for both self- and peer-assessment based on the video content. This has proved positive with regards to both pupil motivation and attainment within PE (Hay McBer, 2000).

TOP TIP: Look out for televised coverage of the major competitions (Olympics and World Cup events) in athletics as they often have well-structured 'guides to' the events before the competitions get under way. These can act as excellent teaching resources.

IWBs or 'smart' boards are featured here as ultimately they are forms of controlling computer-projected images. IWBs have become more prevalent in classrooms across the country; however, PE practitioners are yet to have full access to them (Becta, 2005a). If a PE department is lucky enough to have a projector in a PE teaching environments few have whiteboards linked to this piece of hardware. To the basic user, an IWB pen can be a useful tool acting as a remote mouse allowing you to control the computer from the display area. However, with regular use you can become a whiz-kid with regard to what is on offer. IWBs can offer a number of effective tools dependent on the software packages linked into the computer. One of the most useful tools in an everyday lesson situation could be the drawing and annotation tools. These basic text and drawing options allow the teacher or pupil to highlight key aspects on a image or video being projected on the screen. Basic Whiteboard software allows an overlay-style effect where all the annotations and drawings are separate to that of the actual image being produced. Considering our example lesson, it would be possible to use the overlay while asking the pupils to verbalize the key positions. It could also be possible for pupils to develop their observation and analysis skills through evaluating a performance and suggesting key points for improvement. Being able to provide pupils with opportunities to view and evaluate performances and offer ways in which it can be improved are crucial to high-quality PE. A downside to an expensive piece of equipment such as a whiteboard is that it can be damaged especially if in a sports hall with moving objects, for example, a cricket ball.

> Evidence of the impact on learning and teaching indicates that, where the use of ICT is most effective in enhancing the learning experience, teachers have been able to integrate a number of technologies such as laptops, interactive whiteboards and the Internet. Such combinations of hardware, software and connectivity allow them to develop innovative approaches to learning and teaching.
>
> (Condie and Munro, 2005)

Reflect

While on school-based training or placement, set aside some time to use a classroom with a member of staff that uses an IWB in their daily teaching; this may be from another subject area (perhaps outside of school hours). Practise using its basic tools over some shot-put video using the whiteboard to control the video player. Try to pause the video at specific points where you can then annotate on the screen using the drawing and the text tools. Remember, if you don't have any shot-put video to hand at this stage, navigate to youtube (if possible) or other athletic video sites (www.mysport.net) and maximize the video window.

Theory

As previously mentioned, these items, due to their nature, are more readily found in the indoor or classroom environment. If you are lucky enough to have your own PE classroom to teach theory you may be well resourced. Many PE classroom teachers are still nomadic, having to adapt to whichever room they may find themselves in; ironically, you are probably more likely to find an IWB in these rooms. As well as providing a variety of methods of delivery, viewed media can offer a range of possibilities for individual and group work. Pupils with particular difficulties in literacy (written and spoken) and numeracy can benefit from a range of software that allow pupils to access the content at various levels. Read the examination PE in Chapter 8 for a more comprehensive overview of teaching theory PE.

HRE equipment

Due to the boom in the health and fitness market, it is now commonplace for health and fitness equipment to be loaded with interactive technology offering users feedback on their performance. As PE professionals, we should take advantage of this development allowing us to monitor and track performance of the pupils as they use the equipment. Basic measures of heart rate, energy expenditure, distance, speed and resistance are normal even on the lowest of base models. Depending on the equipment itself, some items allow the user to 'download' the information into a program (e.g. Polar heart rate monitors) allowing the pupil to track progress similar to simple data loggers used in science and other curriculum areas. Other more recent developments allow more than one piece of equipment to be linked together. This is similar to online gaming where you can challenge opponents from a distance via your internet connection. A successful application of this technology in schools is in the form of the Concept II rowers which, with some simple downloadable software, can offer competitive races both on a single and multiple enviroment.

It is worth noting that such equipment would not necessarily fit into our example throwing lesson (apart from maybe a Key Stage 4 application through a training programme). However, with current developments in gaming technology, such as the Nintendo Wii, we may see a 'virtual' Olympic environment where specifically designed equipment can track the flight and trajectory of a specialist shot giving us the ability to compete against others in an online environment. These virtual environments could also be furthered to actually allow us to replicate desired movements without completing the shot itself as in the production of animation-style movies where computer simulation creates the final image from an initial human movement pattern.

Audible content: music and sound media

With the expansion of IT provision across the world more companies are posting free software known as 'freeware'. Using simple freeware software, such as Audacity (www.audacity.sourceforge.net), you can easily create your own podcasts that pupils could listen to as a recap of the main teaching points on their own generic MP3 players. This could be useful for some pupils as a description of the skills and techniques required as a prompt to engage in observation and analysis skills. These could then be verbalized onto a podcast to engage their particular learning style. Let us consider how our shot-put lesson could incorporate such elements. Practical PE is not renowned for setting homework or offering pupils a chance to engage with content prior to its delivery, so why not change that? As previously discussed, the schools' VLE could be used to post web links to specific sites that show images of the whole action. Also placed on the VLE could be links to a podcast that you have made. This could be as simple as verbalizing the main teaching points for the action or go into a little more detail explaining the action. By asking the pupils to visit such items beforehand, you could use this new-found knowledge as a stimulus for your starter activity in the shot-put lesson. Some pupils, with particular leaning needs, may even be allowed or encouraged to bring in their MP3 Players with the content on. With further explanation, the podcast could act as a 'self-paced' or pupil-led lesson programme; again, offering the pupil a personalized learning experience.

Although not directly concerned with our sample lesson, this is an ideal point to consider how audible content can stimulate learning across all PE-related areas. Music can create moods and, in particular to our area of study, can create affective engagement linking content to specific feelings hence developing learning bonds. Try and develop opportunities in your classroom for slow music to help in stressful situations (e.g. exams) and more up-tempo music for activity. If your classroom has a computer, remember most will have speakers and a disk drive so CDs could be used or if you have an internet connection and search engines are available, why not try to access sites, such as www.yahoo.com/music, which allow you to listen to new and old music and create a playlist.

TOP TIP: Be aware that most internet music sites require a username and password, so make sure it is not linked to your private email (e.g. your yahoo account) And also be aware of publicity laws that cover areas of public broadcast of material, which are now becoming more stringently enforced.

Mobile technology: PDAs/tablets/cameras/phones/GPS/media players

The boom in mobile technology is undoubtedly going to be of benefit to practical applications such as those found in PE. Technological developments allow electronic items to be made smaller, more powerful and self-sufficient. With regard to power, it allows the usability of each item to increase. Furthermore, the decrease in cost of such items makes them more attractive to an environment that is not always stable with regard to possible hard usage. Robust, cheap and effective items are a winner in the PE environment whether it is being used inside or outside. Alongside these key attributes, technology now allows you as practitioners to offer a wider range of learning experiences through modes that are often similar to those that pupils interact with on a daily basis.

In addition, mobile technologies allow pupils to gain greater control over where and when they learn and communicate, and blur the division between in- and out-of-school learning. Being less expensive than desktop computers or laptops, they allow more children access to the benefits that ICT can provide across areas of cognitive, personal and social development, reducing the impact of the digital divide.

(Becta 2005a)

For many years PE has embraced basic forms of handheld ICT such as stopwatches and heart rate monitors to measure and monitor performances. Outside of these items, it was usually the case of the PE department using a portable tape recorder for fitness tests and aerobic style lessons and the odd video camera or two. However, now it is possible to see PE departments brimming with handheld items. In the assessment section of this chapter, PDAs were highlighted as a way of taking basic computer packages out to the classroom or field. PDA's or pocket PCs are assisting PE teachers into becoming fully integrated into the handheld digital world and can be further developed with the integration of wireless networks around schools. Suggestions were made of recording our pupils' performance scores on a simple spreadsheet while in our shot-put lesson; however, these PDAs could be used in a media player mode allowing video clips stored on the memory to offer a visual representation of the performance in question. This could also be achieved through the use of a generic media player such as a video iPod or MP4 player. Tablet PCs can offer the same mobility as a PDA but offer more computing power and larger screen surface; however, they also cost more initially. More recently, the advent of 'solid state' computers, such as the ASUS Eee Personal Computer, create fully mobile computing with minimal cost outlay and a robustness never seen in personal computing.

Reflect

Go to www.asus-uk.com/eeepc/about/ and view solid state PCs. How will these benefit your pupils within PE? Think about how the robust nature of a PC without moving parts such as conventional disk drives could help.

Probably the most useful development is in the area of digital cameras in both still and video capabilities. Longer-life battery power, simple usability and greater robustness are key developments for these items to make them more attractive to the PE practitioner. Earlier, the use of computerized video analysis software was discussed and consideration given to the need for such items in everyday PE teaching. With digital cameras now available with reasonable sized screens and simple record and review functions, it is possible to provide pupils with observation and analysis, peer and self-evaluation opportunities on a regular basis though this medium. Our sample throwing lesson incorporates these items throughout the lesson as a way of self-checking performance and targeting future attempts. Not only does the use of such handheld videos embrace critical reflection, it also enhances social interaction leading to wider learning opportunities within the lesson. Koh and Khairuddin (2004) suggest ways in which video is used within PE. These are:

- as a visual demonstration to initiate the learning of a new skill;

- as a supplement to verbal feedback;

- to improve the learners' observational powers and to impart the skills necessary for good qualitative assessment of movement.

Furthermore, and on a more practical level, it is worthy of note that you do not have to have an all-singing, all-dancing camera to offer the above. Basic memory card-driven cameras are now available from as little as £30 that offer the record and playback facilities that provide the basis of Koh and Khairuddin strategies. It is worth noting here that the issue of compatibility with regard to the camera you use and how you intend to use the footage becomes important. In its simplest terms, once the performance has been recorded the image could be reviewed on the camera screen or by plugging it directly into a visual source (TV, projector, etc.). However, if you intend to use video analysis software packages with the recorded footage, you must check the format in which the camera records as many of the new 'hard drive' (where there is no tape) cameras will not work.

TOP TIP: Be aware of your schools policy with regard to taking and holding pupil information/images on file, tape or disk and be sensitive with its use. Some schools have image disclaimers, which the parents sign, giving permission for their child to be videoed and photographed whilst in education.

Other items that are becoming more prevalent in schools are games consoles and their additional features such as dance mats and sports equipment items. Developments in national curriculum content offer a fantastic opportunity for the forward-thinking practitioners to offer a variety of experiences through the ICT equipment available. Many of these games consoles offer the ability to engage with each other wirelessly and via the internet offering further dimensions to pupil interaction (such as dance mats and other systems mentioned earlier in this chapter).

With the huge rise in GPS being available, it is not uncommon to find small units in schools. You may find them in geography or science departments; however let us consider a use for them in our sample athletic throwing lesson. Many of the small 'outdoor pursuit' - style GPS trackers offer distance and time applications that are denoted from selecting two coordinates. Although less applicable to your shot-put lesson but yet more applicable to a javelin or ball throw, you could use the GPS system to give immediate readings of the distance thrown. More expensive units have the capability to log and store such information allowing for multiple distances to be gathered and offering a much more time-efficient solution to taking individual measurements with a tape.

TOP TIP: Look at other subject departments resources as they often have some good gadgets and toys that you can integrate within your lessons without having to buy them specifically.

Summary

The following are some of the key points raised within this chapter that you should try and 'do' on your school-based training:

- Look at ICT with an open mind, being open to the opportunities it can give you and your pupils.
- Consider the benefits to both you and your pupils when planning to integrate ICT. It is important to realize that ICT alone will not create a positive learning climate within your lesson.
- Find out what the school 'e-strategy' is and see if you can use this to gain resources through 'piggy-backing' this vision.
- See what the school currently has with regard to resources and see if you can beg, borrow or steal them rather than buying equipment initially to see if they impact positively on pupil learning.
- Look at sharing the workload and creating truly embedded examples of ICT usage through collaborative projects with other subject groups/teachers.
- Always have a back-up plan or plan B just in case something goes wrong.
- Share your good practice if it works.

A trainee teacher's lesson observation notes

Your use of ICT reinforced your pupils' learning and offered a self-paced climate that was appropriate to this group. The pupils continually revisited the 'looped' video clip of the high jump technique and their reciprocal teaching cards enabled them to better apply the techniques to each other.

Sample interview questions and developing a personal philosophy for teaching

---

Interview questions

- How would you contribute to the department's development of ICT?
- Can you tell us an occasion when your pupils successfully used ICT in one of your lessons?
- What do you think about the view that ICT in PE only reduces activity levels?

Is this you? Do you agree?

Q: Could you describe what you think makes a good PE teacher?
A: Enthusiasm. I think it helps if they are fit and good at the sports themselves as this gains respect.
Jenny Copnall, Mountain Bike Cross County Racer
www.sportingchampions.org.uk

Further reading

Becta (2003) *Celebrating ICT in Practice 2004.* Coventry: Bringing Educational Creativity to All.

Becta (2005a) *Body and Mind: A Report on the Use of ICT in Physical Education* (PE). Coventry: Bringing Educational Creativity to All.

Becta (2005b) *Personalised Learning with ICT.* Coventry: Bringing Educational Creativity to All (http://www.becta.org.uk/corporate/publications/documents/personalised_learning.pdf).

Condie, R. and Munro, B. (2006) *The impact of ICT in Schools: A Landscape Review.* Coventry: Bringing Educational Creativity to All.

Cox, M., Webb, M., Abbott, C., Blakeley, B., Beauchamp, T. and Rhodes, V. (2003), *ICT and Pedagogy. ICT in Schools Research and Evaluation Series, No. 18*: London: Bringing Educational Creativity to All/Department for Education and Skills.

DfES (2004) *High Quality PE and Sport for Young People.* Nottinghamshire: Department for Education and Skills.

Green, N. (2002) Using ICT within PE: its impact on a working department, *British Journal of Teaching Physical Education*, 33 (2): 25.

Higham, J. and Yeomans, D. (2005) *Collaborative Approaches to 14–19 Provision: An Evaluation of the Second Year of the 14–19 Pathfinder Initiative.* London: University of Leeds/Department for Education and Skills (www.dfes.gov.uk/research/data/uploadfiles/RR642.pdf).

Kennewell, S. (2004) *Meeting the Standards in Using ICT for Secondary Teaching: A Guide to the ITT NC.* London: RoutledgeFalmer.

Kibble, S. (2005) Beyond the gimmick: embedding ICT in everyday practice in PE. Paper presented at *One Day Conference*, 27th January, at University of Exeter (www.education.ex.ac.uk/research/pe_ict_event/presentations.htm).

Koh, M. and Khairuddin, A. (2004) Integrating video and computer technology in teaching: an example in gymnastics initial teacher-training programmes in Singapore, *British Journal of Teaching Physical Education*, 35(3): 43–66.

MacGilchrist, B., Myers, K. and Reed, J. (1997) *The Intelligent School.* London: Paul Chapman.

McBer, H. (2000) *Research into Teacher Effectiveness: A Model of Teacher Effectiveness.* Report to the Department for Education and Employment – June 2000. London: Department for Education and Skills.

Morgan, J. and Kinchen, G. (2003) At the heart of it all. *PE and Sport Today.* Spring: 68–9, New Opportunities Fund 1999. London.

Pachler, N. (1999) Theories of learning and ICT, in Leask and N. Pachler (eds) *Learning to Teach Using ICT in the Secondary School.* London: Routledge.

Poole, P. (1998) *Talking about ICT in Subject Teaching.* Canterbury: Christchurch University College.

OfSTED (2002) Ofsted report, in A. Thomas, and G. Stratton (2006). What are we really doing with ICT in physical education: a national audit of equipment, use, teacher attitudes, support, and training? *British Journal of Education Technology,* 37(4): 617–32.

OfSTED (2004) OfSTED Subject Reports 2002/03. *Physical Education in Secondary Schools* (accessed from HMI 18 July 2008).

QCA (2007), *Physical Education Programme of Study: Key Stage 3.* London: Qualifications and Curriculum Authority.

Stratton, G. and Finch, A. (2001) Information and communication technology in physical education: an ITTE-school partnership perspective, *British Journal of Teaching Physical Education,* Spring: 24–6.

TDA (date unknown) *ICT QTS Skills Test* (accessed 20 July 2008: http://www.tda.gov.uk/skillstests/ict.aspx).

Tearle, P. and Golder, G. (2008) The use of ICT in the teaching and learning of physical education in compulsory education: how do we prepare the workforce of the future? *European Journal of Teacher Education,* 31(1): 55–72.

Underwood, J. (2004) Research into information and communication technologies: where now? *Journal for Technology, Pedagogy and Education,* 13(2): 137–45.

Name:

Subject:

PE: Performing at maximum levels in relation to, distance, strength and accuracy in throwing event. (shot-put)

Trainee target(s):		Standards
Know how to use skills in literacy, numeracy and ICT to support their teaching and wider professional activities.		Q17
Design opportunities for learners to develop their literacy, numeracy and ICT skills.		Q23

Date & Time	Class & Attainment range	Lesson Sequence
	Year 7 3–5	1–8

Points from previous learning that need reinforcement e.g. misconceptions.

Curriculum references: (KS3/KS4/Post 16)

Key concepts: 1.1a, c; 1.2a, b, c; 1.3b; 1.4b
Key processes: 2.1a, c; 2.2b, c; 2.4a, b, c, d; 2.5b
Range and content: 3b, d
Curriculum opportunities: 4b, f, g

Pupil preparation for next lesson (homework)

Log on and go to the PE page on the school intranet. Find the lesson timetable code and watch the video performance of the shot put. Complete the tasks and bring them to this lesson.
(Use www.sportunterricht.de/animation/kugel.html for animated outline.)

The big picture

Shot-put is one of the throwing events in the field athletic activities. It requires both different and similar techniques to that of other throwing events in the field athletic category.

Learning objectives

By the end of the lesson pupils will:

- have demonstrated, practised and executed the linear (glide) shot-put technique using ICT to develop this technique where appropriate.

Pre-lesson tasks to involve pupils in the learned content through ICT medium.

Planning considers outcomes for whole unit to to place lesson in context.

Use of NC ref to map ICT planning and integration.

Trainee identifies key ICT standards in which they plan to include.

Inclusion of ICT allows for a variety of formative and summative assessment.

Outcomes expand upon actual skills derived through the use of ICT – that of observation and the ability to impact positively on performance for both themselves and others.

Learning outcomes

All pupils will:
- work both individually and as part of a team to analyse and improve performance;
- be able to identify the main elements of successful shot-put performance;
- identify strengths and weaknesses in their own performance with some assistance;

Most pupils will:
- work both individually and as part of a team to analyse and improve performance applying their knowledge of the activity
- be able to identify the main elements of successful shot-put performance and demonstrate them effectively;
- identify strengths and weaknesses in their own and others' performance with some assistance.

Some pupils will:
- work both individually and as part of a team to analyse and improve performance applying their critical and specific knowledge of the activity;
- be able to identify all the elements of successful shot-put performance and demonstrate them effectively;
- identify strengths and weaknesses in their own and others' performance making suggestions for future performance.

Addressing the needs of individuals – strategies you will use to ensure inclusion:

1. Setting suitable learning challenges – differentiate learning outcomes for the lesson, opportunity to take on different roles in activity – coach/evaluators, modifying the activity.
2. Responding to pupils' diverse learning needs – Set specific targets for individual in the roles they take, provide learning resources to support communication of objectives e.g. use mini camera replay of stored reference clip and MP3 audio.

How I will assess the learning objective/s (HIWALO):

- Questioning strategies to bring out knowledge and understanding of technique and performance.
- Activity 1 – set activity and observe pupils working to identify different methods used in final section – relate to DVD
- Activity 2 – set activity and observe and question pupils working to identify successful methods used to achieve final outcome.
- Activity 3 – allow pupils to adopt role of teacher using video to analyse and suggest ways in which to improve reflecting on performance.

Throughout lesson – observe detail/depth of involvement with ongoing observation and analysis using resources available to them.
Through catalogued examples of range of pupils attempts to give indication of level performances.

Cross-curricular elements offer opportunity not only for ICT to be integrated into lesson but expand upon work that may have been covered elsewhere in the curriculum and also offer further opportunities for pupil to apply the skills.

Cross-curricular links (with specific curriculum references)

PLTS	Functional skills and key skills	Other links
Effective participators: pupils have the opportunity to listen to others and to share and discuss their work. They provide constructive feedback and realize how their contributions can play a part in the success of others through observation and analysis skills.	Pupils will use ICT to find, select and bring together relevant information while reviewing shot technique. Pupils will apply ICT safely to enhance their learning and the quality of their work.	
Reflective learners: when analysing a performance, they identify and evaluate strengths and weaknesses finding ways of refining the quality of a performance. These are ongoing processes that underpin learning, improvement and success in physical activity.	Pupils will be able to validate and interpret results based on distance effectively and efficiently. Pupils will analyse how ideas and information are presented, evaluating their usefulness, e.g. in solving a problem	

Resources (including ICT)

- Measuring equipment, *e.g. tape-measures* and handheld GPS.
- Shot puts, enough for 1 per 3.
- Alternative/suitable balls – weighted/unweighted
- Cones/hoops
- Personal progress and performance log, *e.g. spreadsheets on PDA or equivalent*
- Video materials, *e.g. CD-ROM, slow-motion footage,*
- Mini video cameras – hard disk type (also double as a video player - see above)
- Audio teaching point recording – iPod/Mp3 player etc.
- Teacher PDA – register and method of assessment/recording performance

> Key items of equipment needed but could be substituted by cheaper or more expensive models. PDA could be laptop, mini cameras are as cheap as £30, video clips could be loaded onto video iPod. Expensive handheld GPS can store more than one distance making distance collection quicker.

> Creates inclusive access to all styles of learner or ability.

> Simple use of DEAD TIME in changing room by adding variety in learning opportunities. Ready-made by TV companies.

> Initial lesson content delivered through ICT. Engages and motivates.

TIME AND INTERACTION	ACTIVITY	ORGANISATION & EQUIPMENT	TEACHING POINTS	DIFFERENTIATION
	Resister and outline LO	Meet group in changing room – play looped DVD recording of 'Olympic events' the basic of shot-put from BBC coverage. Write LO on whiteboard.	As you're changing listen and watch (where possible). Find out 3 facts about shot put.	Ask specific pupils to find out specific number of key points from DVD.
	Movement to field	Take box of camera, 2 × MP3 players, portable GPS and collect resources from lock up/store on field.	Set specific individuals/groups tasks.	Give pupils with specific need MP3 players.
	Activity 1. Warm-up activities (specific) – sit/kneel/stand (non-shot use – replace with ball)	**Explain and demo simultaneously:** In 3's – 2 sit with 1 × ball behind red cone and 1 behind other facing inwards. On whistle chest pass ball to partner, get up and run to opposite side and sit down ready to receive (shuttle relay). Do until return to original place. Complete. ⊗ ● ⊗ ⊗ ● ⊗ ⊗ ● ⊗ **Explain and demo simultaneously:** as above but kneeling from behind yellow. Complete. **Explain and demo simultaneously:** as previously but use technique seen on DVD at green cone. Complete. Complete all stations (× 2 on each).	Watch and listen while this group show you what you are doing. Once you have got back to your original place hold the ball in the air. Think about the position you saw the athletes use on the video – can you copy and be accurate? Complete all three as quickly as you can. **QUESTION:** before complete again – what key points could you remember to make standing throw successful?	Different balls – weighted or non-weighted. Different distances between cones. Rephrase or prompt question for some.

Activity		
Activity 2. The standing frontal shot (use shot appropriate to age)	All three pupils standing behind green cone. Demo/explain: front on to use leg power and arm 'strike': • Stand feet TOGETHER. All have three attempts. (b) As previous but 'step' forward onto left leg and rise onto balls of feet. All have three attempts. **COMPETITION – HIGHEST AND SHORTEST** ⊗ ⊗ ⊗	Watch and listen. Be aware of command – THROW – COLLECT. When collected carry shot back and place onto floor before next gets ready. (right handed thrower) – face forward with feet shoulder width. Hold shot correctly in right hand – clean palm dirty neck. 'Wind up' by: • leaning back slightly; • bending knees. 'Unwind' and throw – keep elbow HIGH. As above but: • as unwind step with non-throwing leg. Using cones as in Activity 1, aim to land in between nearest yellow and red but go as high as possible.	Allow pupils to use non-weighted shot if needed. Give MP3 recording of instructions if not throwing as recap. More able also: • coil like a 'spring' twisting hip and shoulder to look behind you; • 'explode' in the opposite direction to face forwards.
Activity 3. Slip-sliders! – the glide	All three pupils stand behind green cone as before. Relay race: adopt starting shot position, **'Glide'** out to travelling backwards to opposite green cone – run return and tag next pupil. All complete (× 1). Students to observe and record peers – review and comment on: • height of body; • ability to keep same position throughout; • ability not to cross feet.	Watch and listen: demo. Adopt start position. Stay low. 'Chin knee toe' Bring legs together – then apart and repeat Press record on mini cams, pass camera to last person as teammate runs back. Review, comment and offer future advice.	Partner lightly hold non-throwing arm – add slight resistance to stay low. Use reference clip (loaded on camera) to compare if needed.
Activity 4 Complete the shot	All three pupils behind green cone. Combine glide and unwind activities. Maximum performance – use mini cameras to observe and analyse – peer – and self-review. Measure (tape or GPS) on best of three throws – use marker cone to show best attempt (from other cones that are present).	 (a) • clean palm dirty neck; • arm relatively horizontal to ground; • shot pushed against neck, underneath chin;	Level of feedback by peers and teacher dependent on ability. Recall using reference clip on mini camera screen if needed – reinforce main points.

Mini-cameras offer visual aids that assist social involvement and self reflection. Future strategies also considered through analaysing content.

	<ul><li>stand with back facing direction of throw at the back of the circle.</li></ul>(b) preparation for the glide<ul><li>chin knee toe – power position.</li></ul>(c) glide<ul><li>short body movement to give the shot momentum;</li><li>hop-like movement keeping the center of mass low and over the right leg;</li><li>ideally both feet arrive at power position at the same time.</li></ul>(d)<ul><li>body low and over right leg;</li><li>left leg extended with toe planted to form base of support;</li><li>base of support as wide as possible without hindering the throwing action.</li></ul>(e) putting action<ul><li>left arm swings over the top, opening the doorway for the throwing action;</li><li>lifting action is initiated by using the slower, stronger muscles of the leg, with forces then transferred to the trunk and arms to unwind;</li><li>shot released at a 40 degree angle over a straight left.</li></ul>	While reviewing use MP3 teaching points audio to assist. GPS units to assist in measurements.
Plenary and collection of data	Collect all items in. Recall to your team an area you focused on from observation during final event – select a target for yourself for future development (to be done individually while measurements are added to spreadsheet on PDA by teacher). **QUESTIONs**<ul><li>**What were key points of successful performance from DVD?**</li><li>**What was one area of performance someone else helped you with from your own video?**</li><li>**What target to develop do you have for the future?**</li></ul>	Rephrase or prompt question for some. Demo while recapping for visuals or allow replay using mini cameras.

ICT allows for quick storage of key data and offers tasks that engage and refocus students allowing recall of past experiences.

8 Teaching theoretical physical education

Harvey Grout and Gareth Long

A teacher's story

During my graduate teacher programme (GTP), I taught Year 10 PE revision to 25 boys for their upcoming GCSE examinations.

My mentor asked me to focus on components of fitness and methods of training. My knowledge of these particular areas was fairly good. However, I had only taught them in a practical setting and not in the classroom before.

I deliberated for what felt like hours on the best method to deliver the session. I had to consider differentiation, key points, making the lesson fun, catering for different learning styles and ensuring my subject knowledge was up to scratch.

The group had mixed academic ability so I ensured the pupils had as much interaction as possible. The start of the lesson was a quiz on the components of fitness. The class were split in half and we had a 'friendly' competition (boys love that!).

I then progressed to revising the methods of training and used practical examples to support their understanding. For example, for interval training the pupils sprinted on the spot for 10 seconds and then had 10 seconds' rest. This was repeated over and over again and the pupils were questioned on the energy systems being used and how they could tell, that is, when out of breath = anaerobic, when getting breath back (repaying O2 debt) = aerobic.

We finished with a series of questions linked to sporting videos I had downloaded from the internet. The pupils had to identify the different components of fitness and the methods of training the athletes were using to train them. I also designed worksheets as an extension exercise for the pupils to answer.

The plenary covered the lessons' learning objectives and a short but effective homework task. The homework was differentiated for the short-course pupils by multiple choice answers and easy-to-understand diagrams.

The class stayed on task throughout the lesson and were actively engaged in revising the key components required for their exam. Most importantly, they understood what they were being taught!

Richard, NQT teacher, age 24

Reflect

How do you feel about the prospect of teaching 'academic' PE in a classroom?

The learning outcomes of the chapter are:

☑ To develop effective teaching strategies for teaching theoretical PE
☑ To understand that pupils require a range of different teaching styles to ensure they improve their knowledge and understanding
☑ To explore a range of practical teaching ideas that engages the pupils and relates academic theory to real sporting examples

The professional standards for qualified teacher status (QTS) addressed in this chapter

Q10: Have a knowledge and understanding of a range of teaching, learning and behaviour management strategies and know how to use and adapt them, including how to personalize learning and provide opportunities for all learners to achieve their potential.

Q14: Have a secure knowledge and understanding of their subjects/ curriculum areas and related pedagogy to enable them to teach effectively across the age and ability for which they are trained.

Q22: Plan for progression across the age and ability range for which they are trained, designing effective learning sequences within lessons and across series of lessons and demonstrating secure subject/ curriculum knowledge

Q24: Plan homework or other out-of-class work to sustain learners' progress and to extend and consolidate their learning.

Q25: Teach lessons and sequences of lessons across the age and ability range for which they are trained in which they:

(a) use a range of teaching strategies and resources, including e-learning, taking practical account of diversity and promoting equality and inclusion;

(a) build on prior knowledge, develop concepts and processes, enable learners to apply new knowledge, understanding and skills and meet learning objectives;

(c)	adapt their language to suit the learners they teach, introducing new ideas and concepts clearly, and using explanations, questions, discussions and plenaries effectively;
(d)	demonstrate the ability to manage the learning of individuals, groups and whole classes, modifying their knowledge to suit the stage of the lesson.
Q26 (b):	Assess the learning needs of those they teach in order to set challenging learning objectives.

Introduction

Richard's initial apprehension towards teaching 'classroom' PE is a common trait among trainee PE teachers. The teacher's story addresses many of the fears trainee teachers have towards this environment. Reflections from trainee teachers we have mentored include statements such as:

"I felt comfortable in an 'outdoor' environment but the prospect of having pupils sat in front of me in a classroom was very nerve racking".

"I was initially very apprehensive about the prospect of teaching theoretical PE because of my subject knowledge".

"Initially I was very excited at the prospect of such a new challenge but I was very daunted to think there would be 25 sets of eyes focusing on just me at the front of the class for an hour's lesson".

"My main concern was with time management and if I would have enough information for the duration of the lesson and how can I engage the pupils to listen and learn?"

Reflect

Observe your mentor teaching in a classroom; which teaching strategies are similar or different to those they adopt in a practical environment?

GCSE and BTEC PE

This chapter seeks to make the relevance of the previous chapters apparent while recognizing the idiosyncrasies of teaching theoretical PE. Imaginative classroom activities are provided to show you how you can transfer all your teaching skills from the sports hall to the classroom.

> **Lesson Observation Notes** (Tony, PGCE Pupil): 'You are clearly torn at the moment between ensuring that your pupils write 'down' the information they require for their exam and being a "creative" teacher. Don't worry, you will be able to do both!'

The 'conflict' witnessed in the above extract from a lesson observation highlights a common problem for teachers of theoretical PE. Even in qualifications that are coursework based, the time pressures of covering specification details may lead teachers to worry more about the end result than the journey used to get there. 'The 'dangers' of the pressure of 'covering the specification' may lead teachers to a 'didactic transmission of content' (Harris et al., 1995: 253).

The following philosophy will argue that theoretical PE lessons need to help pupils maximize their grades in the subject. In turn, it will also show that effective learners should also be developed and supported through creative teaching of the specification.

Reflect

The following extract is taken from a GCSE 2009 specification:

> An understanding of the basic components of fitness to include the following: strength, endurance, flexibility, agility, balance, speed, power, co-ordination, reaction time and body composition and how they relate to selection into different activities.
>
> (AQA, 2007: 16)

Write down your initial ideas on how you would teach this to your own GCSE group.

Bringing the specifications 'to life': a philosophy of teaching theoretical PE

We learn:

10 per cent of what we read

20 per cent of what we hear

30 per cent of what we see

50 per cent of what we hear and see

70 per cent of what we say

90 per cent of what we read, hear, see, say and do.

(Edgar Dale, 1946)

We will assume that you are training to be a PE teacher because you love PE and sport. Similarly, the majority of pupils in your class will have chosen to study the subject further because they too love PE and sport. They will most probably play sport, watch sport, talk about sport and maybe read about sport. This is a great advantage, pupils in your class who love the subject! Admittedly, some may still not have realized that studying PE is much more than just 'playing' and actually involves 'studying'! However, the theoretical aspects of PE and sport are diverse and fascinating to both you and your pupils and therefore it is important that your lessons fuel (rather than quell) their desire to learn more about it.

The end result (the pupil's grade) should not be the only consideration that drives the teacher's planning and lesson objectives. Preparing pupils to become more effective learners is a responsibility of all teachers and therefore classroom PE needs to ensure that this also informs the planning of the lesson. After all, developing more effective learners in your group will better equip them to gain grades as well!

This chapter proposes that despite pupils' motivation for PE and sport, it is important that the teacher does not solely rely on the content of the subject to maintain and develop this motivation, but also provides stimulating and meaningful teaching and learning strategies to achieve this. Furthermore, the chapter advocates that 1<PE theoretical lessons should:

- be active – 'practical', fun and creative;
- apply to real life;
- be varied – teach and learn the content through a variety of methods/state; changes/resources;
- develop effective learners.

Keeping it active – teaching theory through 'practical'

Pupils require more than simply 'making notes from the textbook'. PE teachers must therefore create and use lots of imaginative ideas to engage pupils' learning.

Reflect

What methods/strategies used by your own teachers and lecturers were most effective for you to learn?

Presenting theoretical work in practical ways can be particularly important in terms of keeping pupils interested and engaged in learning (Macfadyen and Bailey, 2002).

Pupils can often understand theoretical concepts better if they are taught using practical examples. 'Practical' in this context can mean many things. Some schools and colleges have adopted a curriculum approach whereby theoretical concepts are taught entirely through the practical PE lesson. We argue that even in a classroom environment, PE teachers can 'play to their strengths' and pursue a 'practical' approach.

In its simplest terms we advocate 'practical' to mean:

> 'Activity' in the classroom. Play games, role-play, use case studies, and ensure the pupils are active/moving – in the classroom environment.

Examples

Arousal/Hormonal control of heart – create a competitive environment within the class and notify the class that you will be conducting a test to assess who is the fittest and the quickest – males or females.

Everyone must measure their heart rate. Publicize the results. Pick 2 (1 male/1 female) – inform the two competitors that they will be racing to a certain point and back. Weave an elaborate psyching-up scenario before the race where the girls are cheering on the female competitors and the boys in the class are cheering on the boys (keep this going for about 90–120 seconds) with the audience involved as much as possible. Just before you say 'go' or complete the countdown to the race – stop! Now measure the competitor's heart rates – it will have rocketed (hormonal control of the heart).

Feedback/proprioception – you will need big gloves, a bin, a tennis ball, eye mask or scarf. Pupils must try and shoot baskets into the bin wearing different sensory impairments. You can also offer differing feedback using knowledge of performance and knowledge of results and follow that way.

Type of muscle contraction/exercise – you will need a blood pressure meter. (Note: take a reading prior to and after each exercise.)
1 dumbbell curl (isotonic);
2 arm wrestle (isometric) and;
3 use a scarf and loop around hand – apply downward pressure when lifting arm up and upward pressure when pushing arm down (isokinetic).

Types of guidance – you will need a golf ball, golf putter and a golf hole (mug on its side). Ask three pupils to be golf coaches and send them out of the room to read the coaching sheet you have given them on putting (they will be coaching a beginner). Tell the rest of the class that they will be looking at how the coaches deliver the putting session and in particular whether they use verbal, visual or manual guidance. The coaches enter the room one after the other and coach a fellow pupil how to putt. The other pupils are recording the methods used.

> **Reflect**
>
> Were your ideas for teaching components of fitness 'active'?
>
> For example, could the pupils complete some 'tests' that demonstrate the components? How about putting up 'signs' for the components of fitness around the classroom – ask pupils to stand under the one that they think they are the best at. Go around and ask one pupil from each component of fitness to explain why they stood there and provide a sporting example.

Garnett (2005) recognizes that the middle part of a lesson may be the most appropriate time to use movement and to reignite learning at a time when pupils may potentially 'switch off'. The examples provided here are obviously only suggestions and you will undoubtedly come up with your own. The point is not to suggest that this is only or indeed the 'best' way to teach classroom PE, but instead that it will motivate pupils and begin to cater for a wider range of learning styles.

Applying the specification content to the 'real world'

The world of sport is often used excellently by other curriculum subjects to motivate their pupils. For example, in English pupils may write a newspaper report on a Wimbledon Final or provide the commentary for the Ryder Cup. In maths, graphs may be produced to represent the heart rates of Olympic 100m and 1500m gold medallists, while in science, the flight of a long jumper may be examined. In essence, modern and contemporary sport can 'bring to life' a subject for many pupils.

Classroom PE is no exception to this and the application of the theory to the experiences of elite sports' performers, coaches and teams will not only motivate pupils but will also develop their knowledge and understanding of the subject. A recent examiner's report advocated that examination answers were enhanced when pupils were able to provide contemporary sporting examples to demonstrate their knowledge:

> This type of up-to-date information and relevance is exactly what the candidates require in order to help their knowledge and understanding of the issues in modern day sport.

(AQA, 2006: 27)

By using 'real-life' examples, pupils will be able relate concepts and theories to what they already know.

> **Examples**
>
> **Sponsorship** – as a way of introducing types of sports sponsorship and exploring the benefits/limitations to sport, ask the pupils to name as many

sponsors of Premier League football teams as possible. After completing the list, ask them if any of the sponsors are 'dubious' (e.g. alcohol or gambling companies).

Training principles – show them a training programme/session of an elite athlete and ask the pupils to highlight where they believe it demonstrates one of the principles of training.

Anxiety and arousal – show a video clip of a penalty shoot-out (hopefully, not a particularly famous one). Ask the pupils to predict if the player will 'score or miss' based on their body language and the 'pressure' of the penalty. Ask the pupils to write down the cognitive thoughts and somatic responses the players who missed their penalty might have experienced.

By relating theoretical content to real sporting examples, it becomes more relevant to the pupils and they begin to understand the key principles of the topic. Real-life' examples do not always always need to be those of the elite sports performer. The pupils will also have their own sporting experiences that can help them make the crucial links between their personal understanding and the theory content. For example, ask them to write down the warm-up their own team perform before a game and evaluate it again once the theory of effective warm-ups has been taught. When the pupils start coming into your lesson saying they played football during their leisure time and were intrinsically motivated to succeed and felt their level of arousal was at point B on the Inverted U Diagram but the opponents' etiquette was poor because they failed to kick the ball out of play when their teammate was injured – then you know your pupils are engaged in learning!

Reflect

- Did your ideas for teaching the components of fitness relate to the 'real world'?
- Perhaps play a montage of sporting video clips and ask the pupils to write down what aspects of fitness they see contributing to performance.
- Ask the pupils to prepare an argument on 'who is the fittest sportsperson in the world and why?'
- Introduce the pupils to the concept of the classic TV programme *Superstars* and ask them to suggest a series of 'challenges' that will fairly test the fitness components of (insert your own names of top sports performers).

Variety is the spice of life! Use a range of teaching and learning activities

All the information your pupils may require for their course may well be found in the pages of a textbook. However, is the role of a teacher simply to guide the pupils to the correct pages and select the choice and sequence of tasks? If you have sat in a two-hour lecture when the only teaching method employed by the lecturer was them reading to you from PowerPoint slides, then you probably know this method is not conducive to effective learning.

A trainee teacher's lesson observation notes

You initially handled the 'question and answer' part of the lesson very well to extend the pupils' understanding; however, you may have overused this method as the pupils began to become restless and off task. This may have been a good time to refocus their attention with a different activity.

Pupils' attention will naturally wander and potentially become off task if your lesson does not succeed in 'keeping them on a crest of a wave' (Allan, 2006: 3). Changing the teaching and learning activity (a state change) can be as simple as 'talk to a partner for one minute about ...' or 'write down 5 things that ...'. Here are some state changes that you may consider to help keep the attention of the class.

Examples of possible state changes

- Read a newspaper report/magazine article/text book passage from an autobiography
- Draw a picture
- Create a model
- Visualize something as if it was you
- Take a photo/record a movement
- Highlight/shade/underline
- Produce a mind map
- Role play – for example press conference/after-match interview
- Crosswords, anagrams, puzzles – doing and designing
- Problem-solving tasks
- Use graphs/charts
- Reorganize/rank statements
- Play games/quizzes
- Write a play script
- Watch a DVD/video – sound/no sound
- Listen to/produce a podcast/audio commentary
- PowerPoint
- Question and answer
- Hold a debate
- Discuss
- Produce an advert
- Present to the rest of your group
- Research on the internet
- Tell a story

- Use humour
- Listen to music
- Mark your partner's work
- Teach to a friend
- Move and work at another table
- Make notes while listening
- Step forward to answer
- Reword a paragraph in your own words
- Use a case study
- Answer an exam question
- Do an experiment

The purpose here is certainly not for you to 'throw' all the above in a lesson plan but instead to recognize that there are many ways to achieve an objective and that by employing a variety of different teaching and learning activities (and changing them at the right time), you may be more succesful in keeping pupils on that 'crest of a wave'.

Reflect

Did your ideas for teaching the components of fitness use a variety of different methods? Could you use any of the ones on the list? Are there any others that you have seen used to good effect? How does the list relate to the work you have covered on learning styles?

Exercise the mind: developing effective learners in theoretical PE lessons

The Department for Education and Skills (DfES) produced a document called 'Developing Effective Learners' in 2004 and stated that pupils who are effective learners have the skills to learn on their own. By the age of 14 effective learners are:

- well organized, they plan their work independently so that it is completed on time;
- show confidence in the range of strategies they have to solve problems but are quick to realize when they need help and choose the most efficient means of getting an answer;
- when gathering information, understand the advantages and constraints of a range of resources and media including electronic and can use these independently and discerningly;
- take appropriate notes in a form that is suitable and can adapt information with a clear sense of audience;

- work well in a team, recognising the advantages of a collaborative approach; they take a lead role confidently when they see the need;
- look for reasons for learning, recognising when it is purposeful and when it is not; they are capable of linking ideas together so that the 'bigger picture' becomes clear;
- can set their own targets and evaluate their progress towards them.

(DfES 2004c: 4)

Reflect

In your plan to teach the components of fitness, consider how your lesson would also develop effective learners.

Planning

The importance of planning your lesson has been addressed in Chapter 1 but a few important aspects must be addressed. For theoretical PE, it is important to remember that you must teach the exam board's specification within a specified time period. As a result, the number of lessons allowed for each topic must be suitably planned for. Ask experienced members of staff how they break down the specification to ensure the pupils are taught all the topics in each module in time. You do not want to find that with only six weeks left before the pupils' exams, there is still over half of the specification to teach!

What do they need to know?

As already indicated, much of the lesson content will be dictated by the specification your pupils are following. It is important that you and your pupils know this document very well to plan the overall course timetable and for pupils to devise their own revision timetables.

The following is an extract from a GCSE exam board on the 'principles of training'; the candidates should be able to:

    i.   Define and explain the terms:
        overload
        progression
        specificity
   ii.   Describe what is meant by:
        meeting individual needs
        thresholds of training

    iii. Explain the FITT principle (frequency, intensity, time and type); Moderation and Reversibility

    iv. Understand and explain the use of these principles **and show how they may be applied** in planning a Personal Exercise Programme (PEP) to improve cardiovascular fitness, muscular strength, muscular endurance and flexibility.

(Edexcel, 2006: 22)

Reflect

- How much of the above content would you hope to teach in a one-hour theory lesson?
- Is the specification information given in enough detail to enable you to successfully plan for the content required?
- What lesson objective would you write based around the extract from the specification?

In addition to the particular specification, most qualifiactions will have a specific textbook that will provide you with more information (e.g. prefered terminology and definitions). It is also a good idea for you (and your pupils) to be become *au fait* with the qualification's past exam papers, examiners' reports, mark schemes and coursework guides.

For example, the following exam question is on the GCSE topic 'Principles of Training.'

A SAMPLE GCSE QUESTION

Ali plays badminton for the school team but is frightened of losing his place due to his lack of fitness. He has decided to plan a Personal Exercise Programme (PEP) to help him improve his fitness for badminton.

Overload and specificity are two important principles of training. Complete the table below to give an explanation of these two principles and specific examples of how Ali might apply them in his Personal Exercise Plan (PEP).

PRINCIPLE OF TRAINING	EXPLANATION OF PRINCIPLE	APPLICATION OF PRINCIPLE WITHIN ALI'S PEP
OVERLOAD		
SPECIFICITY		

(4 marks)

ANSWER

PRINCIPLE	EXPLANATION	APPLICATION
Overload	Increasing intensity of work/work harder	Start by working for 20 secs per station and increase to 25/quiv/figures showing an increase in workload from one session to the next
Specificity	Matching the training to the needs of the activity/ individual/ equiv.	Candidate gives examples of badminton related skills, e.g. shuttle runs, ghosting shots, court movement. Equiv.

N.B. Do not allow 'Specific'

(*Acknowledgement:* Exam question and answer taken from Exam Wizard: Edexcel available at www.edexcel.org.uk/quals/gcse/ri/examwizard).

The examination board's answer sheet provides you with the definitions and practical examples of overload and specificity. This specific terminology is what the pupils must understand and learn when being taught 'Principles of Training'. In turn, the importance of the application of these principles is highlighted. So, by becoming familiar with the appropriate 'support materials', you will gain a good idea of what content is required to teach. Remember that your lesson objectives may also include how the lesson will encourage the pupils to learn to become more effective learners.

Now that you have decided what to teach let us explore some of the factors involved with how to teach it.

Lesson starters: starting with a bang!

The start of your lesson can help create the learning environment you want to achieve. You can inform your pupils that you need to 'warm up the brain' because a good starting activity will engage the whole class in a purposeful and challenging manner.

Your lesson can start as soon as the pupils walk through the classroom door if an appropriate starting activity is in place. This prevents pupils drifting in, chatting to each other and creates a positive purpose to the lesson. A video playing, a picture or discussion topic on the board or a game on their desk as they enter the classroom will instantly get their brain thinking on the topic you are about to teach.

Setting a starter activity sets a good pace to the lesson ensuring the pupils are on task. The activity must provide pupils with a challenge and engage their motivation. Provide something too easy and they will become bored but provide something too challenging and they will become frustrated and stressed. As MacFadyen and Bailey (2002) state, any task set should be challenging but achievable.

When you are thinking of an appropriate starter activity for your lesson, it is imperative you consider the purpose of the activity and the lesson objective. The activity might be a good way to assess their learning from the previous lesson or it could be used to assess their knowledge of the topic you are about to teach. How are you going to organize the activity? Does it require the pupils to work individually, in pairs, groups or as a whole class? Can pupils that arrive late quickly join in without causing disruption to the lesson also?

Phillips (2001) describes the use of a wide variety of stimulus materials teachers can use for their starter and plenary activities, such as visual sources, text and stories and music. Whatever stimulus material you choose for your activity, it is important you plan key questions and that the pupils have instructions to follow.

Let us take an example of the muscular system and three examples that could be used as effective lesson starters:

1   *Situation*: The teacher is confident in the maturity of the class and wants to recap definitions learned from last lesson.

As the pupils enter the class, they are given a 'Post-it note', which they stick to their forehead without looking at it. When the teacher gives the signal, the challenge is for those with a name of a muscle to find their 'partner' (the pupil with the appropriate definition). So, for example, 'bicep' has to find the pupil with 'the muscle that causes flexion at the elbow' written on their head! When a pair have found their partner, they can help others until the group have succeeded. The teacher may set a time limit for all partners to be united.

2   *Situation*: The teacher wants a more 'controlled' start to the lesson but still wants to recap definitions from last week.

On each table an envelope is placed. Each envelope contains a 'starter' card that has a definition on it, for example, 'The muscle group which are the antagonistic muscles for the hamstrings'. The group have to find the card with the correct answer on it, 'Quadriceps', and place it above the starter card. The quadriceps card will have a definition written on the other side, for example, 'The muscle which causes extension at the elbow' and the pupils now have to find the correct card. This continues until the table have a 'chain' of cards where each definition correctly matches the muscle name.
To download a set of these cards visit www.sport-IQ.com.

3   *Situation*: The teacher wants to introduce some of the key concepts in an interesting way in a group and assess the class's existing knowledge.

Each table has a poster of a sports star. In a similar style to 'pin the tail on the donkey', the group have to attach the muscle 'Post-it notes' to the correct part of the body (you could use one of the group as the sports star). After two minutes, each group can send one 'spy' to go and look at where the other groups have put theirs. They then have one minute to rearrange anything. A PowerPoint slide then provides a diagram that shows the answers.

Reflect

What starter activities could you use to create a 'memorable' start to your components of fitness lesson?

One idea would be to show a pre-prepared video of members of the PE department each demonstrating a component of fitness (badly!), for example, one of the 'bigger' male members of staff trying to convince the group that he is in fact flexible (going through a stretching routine dressed as a ballerina!).

Teaching and learning considerations for theoretical PE

The outlined philosophy at the beginning of this chapter will have hopefully provided you with some ideas on teaching and learning activities that may be suitable for your lesson. This section of the chapter now introduces some other considerations that can bring variety and interest to your lesson and create a positive learning environment.

Reflect

Look at the two pupil case studies provided. How would you adapt your components of fitness lesson to successfully engage both Paul and Felicity?

Pupil 1: Paul chose this course because he loves playing sport (football) and if he was honest, he thought he would be spending an extra two hours a week out on the field. He struggles in most of his 'classroom' lessons and is often sent out for being disruptive. Paul has an extensive knowledge of football and this is pretty much all he talks about! Recently, Paul handed in his coursework and it showed very little understanding or effort.

Pupil Two: Felicity is the brightest pupil in your class; sometimes, you even think she may know more than you! She is also an able practical performer and excels in the school's Sports Day. You are confident that she will gain the top grade possible and you think she would be an excellent pupil at the next level of study. However, Felicity is very shy and prefers to work on her own and does not get involved in class discussions/group tasks.

Did you adapt your lesson to focus on their strengths or to help them improve their 'problems'?

The sound of music

You will probably already use music in your practical lessons; possibly as a motivational tool while pupils are completing circuit training or to create excitement in a basketball shooting competition. Music can also be a very powerful tool in your classroom teaching. It can be used not only to create and reinforce a suitable learning atmosphere (e.g. lively, thoughtful), but also as a management tool. For example, as already discussed, the start of the lesson is crucial. Entering the classroom to music can put the pupils in a 'good frame of mind'. Additionally, once the pupils are sat down if the music is turned up then quickly turned off, more often than not pupils recognize this as a signal that the lesson is about to begin and stop talking; you have not even had to say anything! (Try it and see!).

Music can also be used as a 'timing' method for activities – "you have until the end of this song to complete the next task". Moreover, the correct choice of music can also encourage discussion (pupils are less worried that you and others in the class will hear what they are saying in their group) and music will help their concentration by blocking out distracting noises (e.g. passing cars, playground noise).

If you really want to experiment, then some of the music can 'match' the lesson content (see the lesson plan at the end of this chapter for a 'fun' example). The point here is that the music should enhance learning as opposed to distracting from it and as with any teaching and learning strategy, the choice and timing of its use is important.

Me, myself and I

It is clear that our philosophy encourages a range of teaching and learning activities to enhance learning and maintain pupil motivation. It is very rare in practical PE lessons that a pupil will work on their own for the full duration of that lesson. We propose that partner and group work can be a valuable learning experience in theory lessons as well. To highlight how this can be achieved, let us take the example of pupils undertaking a 'practice exam'.

Traditional activity: pupils are given a diagram of a skeleton and have to label the correct bones. The first letter of each bone has been provided and the pupils work individually on the worksheet. After a set time period the teacher asks the pupils for the correct answers and the pupils mark their own work and make any corrections.

Alternative approaches:

1   Adopt the same approach as above but give pupils time to discuss their answers (and fill in gaps) with their partner/table before the teacher provides the correct answers.
2   Before completing the sheet, the pupils pair up and play 'Name those bones'. Partner A begins by stating "I can name five (or whatever they think) bones", partner B has to raise, for example, "I can name six bones" or call them by stating "name them". The game continues until one of the pair 'calls' and then the player has to successfully name that number of bones (a textbook can settle any dispute!). After the game the players find another opponent.
3   Pupils complete the sheet and then join a group of four. After a set time of discussing their different answers, the teacher will call out the 'answers'.

The teacher will deliberately get some wrong and the group can 'challenge' the teacher. A correct challenge will earn the group points and an incorrect challenge will lose the group points.

4   'Speed dating': the challenge is for the group to get everyone to have the correct answers by the end of a set period of time. Everyone completes the sheet individually as in the traditional activity, and then they pair up and have 30 seconds to check/discuss/amend each other's sheet. When 30 seconds are up, they have to find another partner and repeat. Can the group achieve the challenge in the allocated time?

It is important to clarify that individual study is an important skill for pupils to learn and the argument here is certainly not that all class work must be completed in groups (after all, exams and coursework will need to be completed individually). However, by creating a supportive learning environment in which the pupils are involved in their own learning, as well as the learning of others, a less teacher-dependent atmosphere may prevail.

Reflect

Consider the seating arrangements for your classroom lesson. Should it always stay the same or should it match the activities you are using?

Resources, resources, resources

There are now an abundance of resources available that are designed to make help teaching theoretical PE more innovative and motivating for the pupils. The days of purely making notes from pages 24–46 of a textbook are hopefully long gone.

While the use of textbooks have a place in your teaching and provide a very useful source of information and subject knowledge, they should not be the sole teaching tool you rely on. The use of a variety of resources within your lesson is good pedagogical practice. Resources should be viewed as supportive instruments to pupil learning and should be varied in order to maintain pupil engagement. It is important to remember learning will only be effective in the long term if pupils understand what is being taught first of all, so the resource you choose for each particular topic should only be used if it meets this objective.

Digital cameras, movement analysis programmes, DVDs, interactive white-boards, the internet, CD-ROMs, heart rate monitors, newspapers, magazines, board games and interactive quizzes are all tangible resources that provide teachers with strategies to develop pupils' knowledge and understanding.

Reflect

If you are teaching 'sponsorship', list the resources you have access to that will aid your teaching and the pupils understanding of the topic.

Reflect

What resources did you decide would be useful for teaching the topic of sponsorship? Why did you choose these resources? How can you ensure 'learning' takes place?

Lesson plenaries: finishing on a high!

The plenary follows many of the same objectives as the starter activity. It draws together the learning of the pupils and provides you with a good assessment of how much they have learned from the lesson. Spontaneous plenaries that are squeezed in just as the bell is about to go are not effective at all. Link the activity to the lesson objectives and teaching points. Perhaps the pupils have been sat down for the entire lesson and absorbed a lot of information, so an active, enjoyable activity for the last 10 minutes will refresh them. It also provides you with a wonderful opportunity to provide feedback to the pupils and reward their achievements at the end of the lesson.

Connect 4

You do not need to buy a load of Connect 4 board games but if you find this activity beneficial, it does provide a better stimulus to the pupils as opposed to drawing their own board on a piece of paper.

Work in pairs on the lesson's topic for the class, for example, the skeletal system.

Pupils take it in turns to name a bone of the human body and point to it on their body. If they are correct, the pupil chooses where to place their colour in the board. First person to 'Connect 4' is the winner.

Differentiation

- Vary the questions to multiple choice, true or false.
- Class ladder competition so equal ability play each other.

Similiar style games include Blockbusters and Noughts and Crosses.

Who wants to be an A * Candidate?

Devise a set of questions and answers for the pupils on task cards. Work in pairs, groups or as a whole class.

One pupil asks the questions and the other pupil answers the questions. They must answer eight questions correctly to achieve an A*.

The pupils answering the question have three lifelines:

1   50/50, where they are offered two possible correct answers.
2   Ask a friend, where they choose one person from the class to help them answer the question.
3   Ask the class, where they offer the class two possible answers and ask for a show of hands for each answer.

A question of sport

Devise a sports quiz for the pupils to answer a range of questions that link with your lesson topic.

Use pictures/photos for the 'picture board' round, for example, a picture of the human heart and pupils label parts such as the vena cava, right atrium, left ventricle, pulmonary vein and aorta.

Questions such as '1984 Los Angeles hosted the Olympics, what happened next'? Offer pupils the opportunity to apply, analyse and evaluate areas of the specification.

Walkabout

Turned face down on the floor are a series of A4 sheets with one key word written on. The pupils walk around the class, meet another pupil and both pick up a sheet. They then attempt to explain to the other pupil what the word is and how it relates to the lesson just gone. The sheets are then returned face down and the pupil walks to meet another pupil.

Homework and feedback

Setting homework is something you will factor into your planning. Will the homework relate to the pupils' next lesson? Or assess their learning from the lesson you have just taught? Do your pupils have access to the internet at home?

Setting homework that relates to the next lesson will give pupils a chance to research the area they will be studying. Initial class discussions could give them a chance to highlight their knowledge and provide examples from the world of sport in this particular area.

However, homework that relates to the lesson you have just taught will give you a good opportunity to assess their level of understanding.

> **Reflect**
>
> What different tasks or types of homework can you set a class?

Providing feedback to the pupils on their thoughts, beliefs, attitude and homework is a vital tool for teachers to develop effective learners. By spending time and effort on constructive feedback, it portrays to pupils that their answer, opinion and work is valued.

Providing a pupil with a mark of 14 out of 20 or simply writing Grade C on their work will do little to help them improve their work. Providing pupils with questions can act as a stimulus for further thought. Why do you think this achieved a Grade C? What aspects of your work were written well? How could you improve this piece of work?

Developing revision techniques

Examinations seem to be 'just around the corner' all the time now with pupils able to sit exams throughout the academic year. This can be a stressful time for teachers and pupils because the implications for both parties are significant.

Revision techniques are a very useful tool to teach pupils. Part of the philosophy of this chapter is that developing revision and examination techniques should not just be left to the end of the course but instead taught and emphasized throughout. This can be done not only to recap and embed crucial information but also to educate your pupils to the strategies that work best for them. Like most ideas we have written about the best method of revision is diversity.

What they do

Think what actions may help you understand and remember (e.g. hold your bicep muscle, raise and lower your hand to feel when the bicep contracts and relaxes. Hold your ribs as you breathe in and out to remember what happens as you inspire and expire). Talking and presenting topics to pupils' parents and classmates is another useful revision tool. Creating revision groups gives pupils an opportunity to ask questions to their peers they might otherwise feel intimated to ask their teacher. It also provides a vehicle for them to communicate what they know and boost their confidence. The specification can be divided into topics and pupils can 'teach' each other. Encourage your pupils to discuss and argue. They can produce 'documentaries' or 'TV news items' on areas of the specification. Play active revision 'games' such as 'balls of fire'. In this example, teams are shown a multiple choice question on the whiteboard and the first person from each team runs out and places their team's ball (different colour) in the correctly labelled (A, B or C) bucket. Points are awarded for the correct answer and for being the first team to get the right answer.

What they read

Pupils can read textbooks and make notes; this is fine but how should they present their notes? Can they 'chunk' information and make lists rather than write in continuous prose? Acronyms can help us remember information quickly (e.g. SPORT as the principles of training is often used – Specificity, Progression, Overload, Reversibility, Tedium/Type). These can also become extended acronyms such as Some Naughty Athletes Perform Better Drugged to help recall types of drugs (Stimulants, Narcotics, Anabolic Agents, Peptide Hormones, Beta Blockers and Diuretics).

What they hear

Obviously, pupils listen to everything you say! But, in addition, they can listen to podcasts. Even better, they can produce their own revision podcasts and listen to them when out jogging. Auditory material can be repeated over and over again. If we listen to a song we like so many times, we begin to learn the words. The same principle can work for revision tapes and podcasts. In addition, stories can be a useful way of pupils remembering detail. Most of us can retell what happened in our favourite film and certain aspects of the specifications (e.g. Olympic controversies) can be woven into a good story!

What they see

Notes do not always have to be written. Encourage pupils to draw diagrams, pictures, memory maps and posters. The brain's ability to store visual images is almost limitless, so they make a sensible option for presenting class material and revision notes. Figure 8.1 is an example from Sport IQ 16–19 Magazine of how a visual poster can help support pupils' learning, understanding and memory.

Figure 8.1

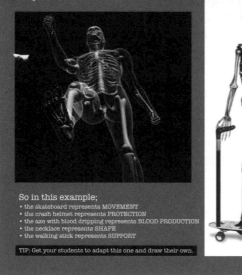

REVISION

Brain Power:
Developing Memory
to Aid Revision.

Revision Technique: Using pictures!

Recognise the face but can't remember the name?
The brain's ability to store visual images is almost limitless
so they make a sensible option for presenting class material
and revision notes. The visual representation will help
students learn without always reading.

Example: The Functions of the Skeleton

So in this example;
• the skateboard represents MOVEMENT
• the crash helmet represents PROTECTION
• the axe with blood dripping represents BLOOD PRODUCTION
• the necklace represents SHAPE
• the walking stick represents SUPPORT

TIP: Get your students to adapt this one and draw their own.

The skateboard represents MOVEMENT
The crash helmet represents PROTECTION
The axe with blood dripping represents BLOOD PROTECTION
The necklace represents SHAPE
The walking stick represents SUPPORT

Every pupil will have their preferred method of revising but by offering them
new ideas it can help develop 'effective learners' in your class as discussed at the

beginning of the chapter. Pupils can become responsible for their own learning and as a result develop a higher level of knowledge and understanding.

Examination techniques

Some examinations play an important contribution to a pupil's final grade in PE, so it seems important that the necessary skills should be taught early. This does not mean simply reproducing exam conditions in your classroom – after all you wouldn't begin training for the marathon by running 26 miles on your first training session! What follows are some ideas to emphasize examination techniques and even keep practising examination technique fun!

Begin slowly

Present pupils with an exam question, and ask them to write down the key words they think will need to be included (this will encourage pupils to begin to think about 'planning' answers). Play a short music track to 'time' this process (get them to think about what music helped them concentrate or distracted them).

Next, ask the pupils to check their books, look in textbooks, or chat with their partner to add any other information and again play some music (this will highlight any existing gaps in knowledge that need to be learned and remembered).

The third stage is for the pupils to write their answer (again to music). By doing this, the pupil will gain an appreciation of the time required to be spent on writing an answer to the question.

The final stage is for the pupil to 'tick' where they think they have gained the marks. By doing this, the pupil will have to think as the examiner and begin to appreciate what the examiner needs to see to be able to give a mark. The teacher can then show the mark scheme and the pupils can evaluate their knowledge of the question, their own revision notes and their examination technique.

Getting in the mind of the opponent

A good way of enabling pupils to appreciate the importantance of 'key words' in an exam question is to show them the answer from the mark scheme and then ask them to write the question. As well as seeing if they understand the content shown, it will also bring out the type of response required by pupils for words such as 'state' compared to 'discuss'. Another useful class activity is to set the class the challenge of 'examiner tennis'. Show the class a question and although it may be worth 5 marks, the class have to come up with all answers covered on the mark scheme, if they do they are 15–0 up!

Overload the examination training

The following activity will encourage pupils to begin thinking about the technique of undergoing examinations beyond 'just knowing the answers' and should initiate their thoughts regarding the planning time required per question, the level of response required and 'self-marking' as they answer the question. The pupils are shown an exam question and can play one of their 'faster' or 'higher' cards to gain more points. If they play their faster card, they have less time then the rest of the class to answer the question. If they choose to play their higher card, the question is marked for a higher score (e.g. a question originally worth 5 marks will now be worth 6 so a more detailed response is required).

The academic year

The register provides you with a record sheet for this ongoing task. 'The Champions League' is a fun, ongoing assessment tool that helps create a quick, purposeful start to each lesson and pupils find enjoyable.

Pupils earn points for different tasks and these points are transferred to their league position on the Champions League table. This table could also become a visual table in the classroom as an incentive for them to improve or sustain their league position.

Points can be awarded for homework handed in on time or late, the quality of their homework, successful answers in the starter and plenary activities, as well as for remembering what the key words from the last lesson were, what the main outcomes and objective of the last lesson was and to make pupils forecast what they are for future lessons.

Reflect

Can you incorporate a sport education model into your theory lessons?

Summary

We began this chapter by highlighting that it is not uncommon to feel nervous about the prospect of teaching classroom PE. However, while many trainee PE teachers start the course apprehensive about the prospect of teaching theoretical PE, many go on to find it is the most rewarding aspect of their teaching. Here is a quote from one of our PGCE students nearing the end of their qualification. Hopefully, the ideas throughout this chapter and their comments will actually make you excited to teach classroom PE rather than being apprehensive:

> 'Having taught classroom PE I can honestly say I thoroughly enjoy engaging the pupils and having the opportunity to find different ways for the pupils to learn. From starting off worried, I have become more confident and therefore more creative in my teaching. My lessons have progressed from command style, PowerPoint lessons to more interactive lessons where the pupils have the opportunities to contribute to their own learning'.

Sample interview questions and developing a personal philosophy for teaching

Interview questions

- What would you say to a parent who felt that GCSE PE was not worth their daughter studying?
- Where do your strengths in teaching theoretical aspects of PE lie?
- What are your thoughts regarding GCSE PE as a preparation for advanced level study?

Is this you? Do you agree?

Could you describe what you think makes a good PE teacher?

I'm a PE teacher and I think what makes a good one is someone who inspires their pupils by what they do, how they conduct themselves and what they say. My aim as a teacher is to find some activity for everyone and to re-engage those who lack enthusiasm and confidence, not just focusing on the high-achieving 'sporty' pupils.

Rachel Brown, Women's Football
www.sportingchampions.org.uk

Further reading

DfES (2004) *Pedagogy and Practice: Teaching and Learning in Secondary Schools. Unit 17: Developing Effective Learners*. Nottingham: Department for Education and Skills: Crown.

Macfadyen, T. and Bailey, R. (2002) *Teaching Physical Education 11–18*. London: Continuum.

Name:		Mr PE	
Subject:		GCSE PE	

Target(s) from:			Standards	Pupil preparation for next lesson (homework)
Have a knowledge and understanding of a range of teaching, learning and behaviour management strategies and know how to use and adapt them, including how to personalize learning and provide opportunities for all learners to achieve their potential.			Q10	Research blood doping.
Know how to use skills in literacy, numeracy and ICT to support their teaching and wider professional activities.			Q17	Research the procedures for drug testing.
Evaluate the impact of their teaching on the progress of all learners, and modify their planning and classroom practice where necessary.			Q29	

Date & time	Class	Lesson sequence	Curriculum references: (KS3/KS4/KS5)	
09.00 – 11.00	Year 11	1st lesson on the topic	KS4 GCSE PE	

How does this lesson address gaps in pupils' learning from the previous lesson?

Pupils are studying 'health and fitness' and the effect this has on athletes' performances. This specific lesson is on the topic 'drugs in sport'.

Planning considers prior learning of pupils to set suitable challenge and progressions.

Learning objectives

(This is what the pupils are going to learn by the end of the lesson – what the pupils should know, understand and do. It should be presented to pupils as 'We are learning to: WALT')

By the end of this lesson pupils will know detailed information about performance-enhancing drugs, they will be able to understand how to recognize symptoms in relation to the different types of performance drug and they will experience different learning styles and roles in each activity.

The big picture

Pupils are working towards achieving the highest possible grade in their GCSE exam.

Learning outcome *(This is what the results of the teaching will look like – the success criteria. It should be presented to pupils as 'What I'm looking for: WILF')*

All pupils will:

- work as part of a team or pairs in different activities;
- be able to identify three types of performance-enhancing drugs;
- be able to identify three side-effects/symptoms of performance-enhancing drugs.

Most pupils will:

- work as a team or in pairs in different activities using verbal communication to help the team improve their knowledge and understanding;
- be able to identify four types of performance-enhancing drug;
- be able to identify four side-effects/symptoms of performance-enhancing drugs;
- to act in two different roles during the group task.

Some pupils will:

- work as a team using effective communication skills and identifying what the strengths of the team was;
- be able to identify all of the performance-enhancing drugs groups;
- act in two different roles, one of which being group leader, listening to ideas and making effective decisions.

How I will assess the learning objective/s *(HIWALO)*:

- Questioning strategies to bring out their knowledge and understanding of the topic.

- Challenge 1 – set activity and observe pupils working to identify different roles they take on.

- Challenge 2 – assign particular roles to individuals in groups and observe how they carry out the roles.

- Challenge 3 – allow pupils to give roles to different people in the group based on reflection of previous challenges.

- Between each activity ask the pupils to evaluate the success and shortcomings of how well they have achieved the lesson objectives.

Addressing the needs of individuals: strategies you will use to ensure inclusion.

Questions will be levelled to a suit level for each pupil.

Cross-curricular links (with specific curriculum references)

PLTS	Functional skills and key skills	Other links
Independent enquirers	Spend time planning and developing their work.	
Reflective learners	Make choices and decisions, think creatively and act independently.	
Team workers		

Resources (including ICT)	Tic tacs in a medicine bottle www.en.wikipedia.org/wiki/BALCO_Scandal www.100percentme.co.uk Substance Abuse Crossword Puzzle

ACTIVITY	ORGANIZATION & EQUIPMENT [PLEASE USE DIAGRAMS TO ILLUSTRATE]	TEACHING POINTS	DIFFERENTIATION
Add music			
Starter Activity Often 'drugs' is a difficult area to stimulate debate as the majority of pupils see the issue of drugs in sport as cheating and the debate is often one-sided	Before the lesson place some white tic tacs in a medicine bottle. No lesson objectives or lesson content written on the board. Explain to the class that the examination board and a leading university have developed some 'memory sweets' that have been proven to improve exam results by 15%. Offer the 'memory sweets' to the class and see how many pupils are happy to take one to improve their memory.	• Improve exam results by 15% • They enhance brain capacity to store information Ask the pupils why some did take a 'memory sweet' and some did not take a 'memory sweet'? Why do you think some athletes are tempted to take performance-enhancing drugs?	

This is an interesting and novel way to begin to enable the pupils to understand why athletes may take drugs.

Lesson objective

Place the lesson objectives on the board

By the end of this lesson you will have a good understanding of the following:

- What are the different types of drugs athletes take?
- What effect do drugs have on the athlete's body and performance?
- What punishments are given to athletes caught taking drugs?

Lesson content matches information taken from the exam board specification.

Class discussion

Ask the pupils questions to assess their existing knowledge surrounding drugs in sport

Applies the specification to the 'real world'.

A sample that may appear on the whiteboard after the 'discussion'. This highlights the big picture of the lesson.

DRUGS IN SPORT

- Athletics (Dwain Chambers)
- EALCO Scandal
- Cycling (Tour de France)
- Blood doping
- Anabolic steroids
- Rio Ferdinand missed drugs test (9-month ban)

Name a famous sports star who has been banned for doping offences.

What drug was found in their system?

What was the punishment handed out?

Questions to the pupils are levelled.

Find newspaper articles/website articles of athletes being caught using drugs in sport. Distribute to some pupils to stimulate answers.

Ranking game

Individual task

Place these eight 'reasons' athletes have given for taking performance-enhancing drugs on the board.

- To be the best
- Because other athletes are doing it
- Fame
- Money
- Coach recommends it
- To improve body image
- To get over injury
- To lose weight/get fit

Rank 1–8 these 8 factors.

These can be used as potential answers for an exam question.

Extend – rank the eight reasons directly to a specific famous drugs case (e.g. Ben Johnson)

Pupils have to emphasize with another person's point of view.

Pupils are reminded of links to exam (or coursework).

Music can be played at this point to help create a suitable learning environment for 'discussion'.

Extension exercise – In groups of four compare your individual answers and agree on a group list.

Discuss and agree the ranking of the eight reasons and explain to the rest of the class your justification for these rankings.

Revision/memory techniques are introduced.

Performance-enhancing drugs

Place the following sentence on the board:

Some Naughty Athletes Perform Drugged

Ask the pupils if they can name the 5 performance drugs that are banned by the IOC.

Pupils write the five types of drug category under the heading 'types of drug'.

- Stimulants
- Narcotic Analgesics
- Anabolic Agents
- Peptide Hormones
- Diuretics

Group research task			
Group research task	five groups and each group are assigned to research one of the performing-enhancing drugs. Either in the IT suite so pupils can research their own research or gather a file of information on each drugs group before the lesson. Answer the four questions for the performance-enhancing drug you are researching. www.bbc.co.uk/schools/gcsebitesize/pe/fitness/ www.100percentme.co.uk www.wada-ama.org/en/ www.s-cool.co.uk	Questions on a sheet to complete. 1. What physiological effect does the drug have on the athlete's body to enable them to improve their performance? 2. What symptoms/side-effects could taking this drug have on an athlete? 3. What types of sport performer may use this drug? 4. Find a case study of an athlete banned for using this drug. **Stimulants** • Increase heart rate • Stimulate the nervous system • Improve reaction time Examples of stimulants • Caffeine • Amphetamines Possible side-effects • Increase in hostility • High blood pressure • Irregular heart beat • Addiction **Narcotic analgesics** • Kill pain allowing the athlete to train and perform when injured • Illegal	Provide some groups with more information than others. Decide the number of websites you will provide to each group to assist them. Provide question sheets with multiple choice answers.
Class 'news report' task Pupils will now have all notes relating to the five categories of drug.	Present your information as if an athlete has been caught taking a performance-enhancing drug in a 'breaking news' broadcast for TV. The pupils whose group is not 'presenting' are reporters needing to make notes on the four questions.		

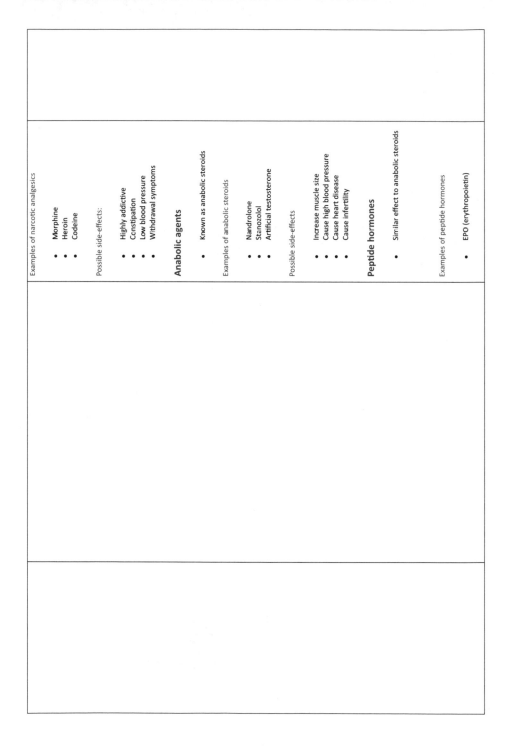

Examples of narcotic analgesics

- **Morphine**
- **Heroin**
- **Codeine**

Possible side-effects:

- **Highly addictive**
- **Constipation**
- **Low blood pressure**
- **Withdrawal symptoms**

Anabolic agents

- **Known as anabolic steroids**

Examples of anabolic steroids

- **Nandrolone**
- **Stanozolol**
- **Artificial testosterone**

Possible side-effects

- **Increase muscle size**
- **Cause high blood pressure**
- **Cause heart disease**
- **Cause infertility**

Peptide hormones

- **Similar effect to anabolic steroids**

Examples of peptide hormones

- **EPO (erythropoietin)**

Possible side-effects of peptide hormones

- Cause strokes
- Abnormal growth

Diuretics

- Make you urinate and enable quick weight loss (boxers and horse jockeys must be under a certain weight before competing)

Examples of diuretics

- Fruscmide probenicid

Possible side-effects

- Cause cramp
- Dehydration
- Nausea

Allow some pupils to use their text books for reference.

FINAL ACTIVITY

1. IT Suite – www.100percentme.co.uk

- 100% ME programme
- Education for schools
- Play the 100% ME challenge

Homework	Prepare questions for next week's Question Time		Teacher provide a few sample questions.
	• A panel of six pupils at the front of the class and the remainder of the class ask the panel questions e.g.:		
	a. What punishment would you hand out to a winner of the 100m Olympic sprint final found guilty of using a banned substance?	Pupils must answer the question from the audience.	
	b. If you were looking to get involved as a sponsor in sport would you sponsor the Tour De France?	Consider each question carefully and provide a response based on facts.	
	c. What punishment would you hand out to an athlete who missed an out-of-competition drugs test?		
	d. Should we have two Olympics? One for those who take drugs?		
EXTRAS	TV programmes		
	The Great Olympic Drugs Scandal – Channel 5 *Drug Runners* – Panorama *The Drugs Olympics* – Panorama *The Beijing Olympics* – Inside Sport BBC1		

9 Conclusion

By the time you read this, we will assume that you are very close to or will have completed your qualified teacher status (QTS). First, congratulations! As you will no doubt be aware, to get this far has involved a tremendous amount of work but also we hope you have found that it has also been a very rewarding experience.

Of course, we all never stop learning and trying to improve our teaching. It is important you continue to develop your teaching philosophy and pedagogy into and beyond your new qualified teacher (NQT) year.

A brief outline of the process of your NQT year is addressed but also ideas of how your role as a PE teacher can expand and grow beyond the lesson.

Before you start your teaching position, you will no doubt visit the school to familiarize yourself with your new department. What is the purpose of this visit? What do you want to know by the end of the day? For most of you the priority will be *'what and who am I teaching?'* Other considerations should be to:

- collect the school staff handbook to familiarize yourself with the school's policies and procedures;
- introduce yourself to your induction tutor, and provide them with a copy of the outcomes from Transition Point 1 of your career entry and development profile (CEDP);
- perhaps have an initial discussion with your department about areas that you are interested in improving; for example, you might have limited experience refereeing rugby games and so it would be sensible to ask the department if they can book you on a rugby referee's course if this will be an expectation of you once you commence your new position, or you may feel you need more support working with Key Stage 5 pupils.

Your NQT year

The first year of teaching is an exciting and demanding time for most teachers and so your school and local education authority (LEA) will offer you a comprehensive induction programme. This induction programme offers you a range of opportunities to further develop your teaching skills and subject knowledge.

There are two main aspects to the induction period (three terms): an individual programme of professional development and monitoring; and an assessment against national induction standards. You must complete this induction period successfully to continue teaching in a maintained school or non-maintained special school in England.

Your induction programme

Your induction programme offers you the support and advice you might need during your NQT year. Your main point of contact will be your 'induction tutor'. Their responsibility is to provide an induction programme that meets your needs and offers you appropriate monitoring, support and assessment.

Individualized programme

Near the end of your QTS year, you will need to complete a CEDP. You and your induction tutor will formulate a programme based on this CEDP. The aims of the programme are for you to:

- develop the strengths and development priorities identified in your CEDP file;
- achieve the induction standards;
- understand the demands of the teaching post in which you are about to start your career.

You and your induction tutor will use your CEDP profile to map out your development priorities and set objectives for you to achieve throughout your NQT induction.

It is important not to underestimate how much you can offer your new school. While you might be fairly 'inexperienced' as far as years of teaching goes, the fact remains that you have fresh ideas and an understanding of the new developments occurring nationally in schools. As the new National Curriculum for PE rolls into schools, some of the teachers in your department may not know as much as you on this development and so do not be afraid to offer ideas in department meetings. You can develop your teaching pedagogy from observing other teachers, either within your department, another department within the school or even from teachers from another school. Your induction programme offers you scope to do this.

Reflect

What teacher/department would you like to observe? What can you learn from observing this lesson that will help your teaching?

The school and/or the PE department you are going to should also be keen to use your talents and knowledge to improve their practice. They might be interested in setting up a BTEC course, for example, and ask you for your assistance. However, it is important to stress to your school that you must not be disadvantaged by agreeing to take on additional roles, or by shouldering additional responsibilities without the adequate support in place.

Continuing professional development (CPD)

CPD courses are available and aimed at improving your attributes, skills, knowledge and understanding.

There are many different methods of CPD. Your school will provide a lot of your CPD training. Remember those four or five random days off you had as a school pupil? Well, your teachers were more than likely in school doing some CPD training! Methods of CPD within your school will include observing your lessons and offering you constructive feedback, mentoring you during your NQT year, offering you the opportunity to share good practice and shadow a teacher within your department. The school will also run whole-school CPD where every teacher is expected to attend. These can be run internally or externally in an area that will benefit every department.

External providers also offer CPD courses outside of school. Your school will have a designated budget for staff to attend these courses. Try and book onto these courses if at all possible. Whatever area of the curriculum you feel you need further assistance with, then there is an external course available. It might be that the school offer trampolining in PE and so you need to go on an instructors' course or you are teaching A Level PE and need ideas on ways to teach the specification in an innovative and engaging way that aids your pupils' knowledge and understanding.

Another area to be aware of is postgraduate professional development (PPD). While the thought of more study and assignments might not sound appealing just yet, as you approach the end of your QTS degree, it is worth remembering that some of your assignments might include credits towards a master's degree. Effective learning and development can come from studying pupils in action and some teachers do see this as a good method for improving their attributes, skills, knowledge and understanding. A master's degree might also prove beneficial if you have aspirations to climb to the top of the teaching ladder and join the senior management team in later years.

National induction standards

Teachers are always required to follow professional standards. You will be required to meet the 'Q' professional standards as a NQT. These standards will assess you on your:

- relationships with children and young people;
- understanding of your professional duties and statutory requirements;
- ability to communicate and work with others effectively;
- progress of your personal professional development;
- teaching and learning;
- assessment and monitoring;
- knowledge and understanding of the curriculum;
- literacy, numeracy and ICT skills;
- ability to provide an inclusive lesson for all pupils;
- awareness of the requirements of the health and well-being of your pupils;

- planning, teaching and assessing skills;
- ability to provide a safe learning environment;
- your ability to work in a team.

Your induction tutor will regularly be monitoring your progress towards these standards. After you have completed three terms and have achieved these standards, you have passed your NQT year!

In 10 years' time?

It is not the place for this book to decide that question, but now more than ever there are plenty of career opportunities available as your teaching career progresses, so it is worth beginning to consider where you want to be in 10 years' time.

As you become more experienced, there will be opportunities within your department or at another school for promotion or more responsibility. This could include being in charge of a particular area of the curriculum, for example, BTEC PE, Key Stage 3 PE.

One day you might have aspirations to become a Head of Year or a Head of Department. Another career path is working within the Government's Physical Education Sport Strategy and Young People (PESSYP) policy. Your school will likely be part of a School Sport Partnership (SSP) and within this partnership will be a Partnership Development Manager (PDM) and a School Sport Coordinator (SSCo) and these may be careers that interest you. You may also look ahead and have ambitions to become an Advanced Skills Teacher or Excellent Teacher.

Although you are probably rightly focused on making the right impression, improving as a teacher and surviving your first year of teaching, it will not hurt to take time to consider your future development within the profession.

Further reading

www.tda.gov.uk/teachers/induction

Summary

This book has been about the PE lesson. Its aim was to help you as a trainee PE teacher to plan, teach and evaluate effective PE lessons and develop an understanding of your teaching philosophy and pedagogy. Ultimately this book was about helping you to become the teacher you want to be.

We hope somewhere within the book we have been effective in your continued professional development and we wish you all a very long and rewarding career in teaching.

References

AALA (2004) *Adventure Activities Licensing Regulations*. Cardiff: AALA

AfPE (2008) *Making the High Quality Connection: How Do the Physical Education and School Sport Quality Outcomes Relate to Ofsted Criteria and Evey Child Matters?* (Accessed 18 May 2008 from Teachernet: www.teachernet.gov.uk/_doc/10679/ HQ%2poster.pdf.

Allan, R. (2006) *Impact Teaching*. Unpublished manuscript.

AQA (2006) *General Certificate of Education, Sport and Physical Education 5581/6581 Report on the 2006 examination. June Series*. Manchester: Assessment and Qualifications Alliance.

AQA (2007) *Physical Education 3581 Specification A 2009*. Manchester: Assessment and Qualifications Alliance.

Armour, K.M. and Yelling, M. (2003) The truth and the trouble with CPD, *PE and Sport Today*, 13: 40–3.

Assessment Reform Group (2002) *Assessment for Learning: 10 Principles – Research-based Principles to Guide Classroom Practice*. London: QCA.

Association for Physical Education (2008) *Safe Practice in Physical Education and School Sport*. Leeds: Coachwise Business Solutions.

BAALPE (1995) *Safe Practice in Physical Education*. Dudley: British Association of Advisers and Lecturers in Physical Education.

BAALPE (2004) *Safe Practice in Physical Education*. Dudley: British Association of Advisers and Lecturers in Physical Education.

Bailcy, R. (2001) *Teaching Physical Education: A Handbook for Primary and Secondary Teachers*. London: Kogan Page.

Bailey, R. and Morley, D. (2008) *Physical Education Quality Standards for Talent Development* assessed 26 July, 2008 from Youth Sport Trust: http:// www.youthsporttrust.org/downloads/cms/Xchange/ TALENT_DEVELOPMENTFINAL.pdf.

Beaumont, G. (2006) Health and safety: safety education, *Physical Education Matters*, 2: 56.

Beaumont, E.G., Kirkby N.G. and Whitlam P. (2008) in Association for Physical Education (2008) *Safe Practice in Physical Education and School Sport*. Leeds: Coachwise Business Solutions.

Becta (2003) *Celebrating ICT in Practice*. Coventry: Bringing Educational Creativity to All.

Becta (2005a) *Body and Mind: A Report on the Use of ICT in Physical Education (PE)*. Coventry: Bringing Educational Creativity to All.

Harris, S., Wellade, G. and Rudduck, J. (1995) 'It's not that I haven't learnt much. It's just that I don't really understand what I'm doing': meta cognition and secondary-school students, *Research Papers in Education*, 10(2): 253–71.

Higham, J. and Yeomans, D. (2005) *Collaborative Approaches to 14–19 Provision: An Evaluation of the Second Year of the 14–19 Pathfinder Initiative*. University of Leeds/DfES, London: Department for Education and Skills (www.dfes.gov.uk/research/data/uploadfiles/RR642.pdf).

Holt, J.E., Ward, P. and Wallhead, T.L. (2006) The transfer of learning from play practices to game play in young adult soccer players, *Physical Education and Sport Pedagogy*, 11(2): 101–18.

HMSO (1974) *Health and Safety at Work etc Act. SI1974/1439*. London: Her Majesty's Stationery Office.

HMSO (1984) *The Occupiers Liability Act*. London: Her Majesty's Stationery Office.

HMSO (1999) *Management of Health and Safety at Work Regulations (MHSWR). SI1999/3242*. London: Her Majesty's Stationery Office.

HSE (1999) *5 steps to Risk Assessment*. Sheffield: Health and Safety Executive.

Jones, A. and Moreland, J. (2005) The importance of pedagogical content knowledge in assessment for learning practices: a case-study of a whole-school approach, *The Curriculum Journal*, 16(2): 193–206.

Kennewell, S. (2004) *Meeting the Standards in Using ICT for Secondary Teaching: A Guide to the ITT NC*. London: RoutledgeFalmer.

Kibble, S. (2005) Beyond the gimmick: embedding ICT in everyday practice in PE. Paper presented at a *One Day Conference*, 27 January, University of Exeter. (www.education.ex.ac.uk/research/pe_ict_event/presentations.htm).

Koh, M. and Khairuddin, A. (2004) Integrating video and computer technology in teaching: an example in gymnastics initial teacher-training programmes in Singapore, *British Journal of Teaching Physical Education*, 35(3): 43–6.

Kolb, D.A. (1984) *Experiential Learning: Experience as the Source of Learning and Development*. Englewood Cliffs, NJ: Prentice-Hall.

Lambert, D. (1995) Assessing and recording pupils' work, in S. Capel, M. Leask, M. and T. Turner (eds) *Learning to Teach in the Secondary School: A Companion to School Experience*, pp 262–314. London: Routledge.

Luke, I.T. (1998) An examination of pupils' metacognitive ability in physical education. Unpublished doctoral thesis, Loughborough University.

Luke, I.T. and Hardy, C.A. (1999) Appreciating the complexity of learning in physical education: the utilization of a metacognitive ability conceptual framework, *Sport, Education & Society*, 4(2): 175–91.

McBer, H. (2000) *Research into Teacher Effectiveness: A Model of Teacher Effectiveness: Report by Hay McBer to the Department for Education and Employment – June 2000*. London: DfEE.

McCormick, J. and Leask M. (2005) Teaching styles, in S. Capel, M. Leask and T. Turner, (eds) *Learning to Teach in the Secondary School*, pp. 276–91. London: Routledge.

Macfadyen, T. and Bailey, R. (2002) *Teaching Physical Education 11–18*. London: Continuum.

MacGilchrist, B., Myers, K. and Reed, J. (1997) *The Intelligent School*. London: Paul Chapman.

McNamara, S. (1999) *Differentiation: An Approach to Teaching and Learning*. Cambridge: Pearson.

Morgan, J. and Kinchen, G. (2003) At the heart of it all. *PE and Sport Today*, Spring : 68–9.

Mosston, M. and Ashworth, S. (2002) *Teaching Physical Education,* (5th edn). San Francisco, CA: Benjamin Cummings.

National Curriculum (2008) *Physical Education: Video Case Study 2: Planning Cross-curricular Opportunites with Physical Education*. London: Crown.

Nisbet, J. and Shucksmith, J. (1986) *Learning Strategies*. London: Routledge & Kegan Paul.

O'Brien, T. and Guiney, D. (2001) *Differentiation in Teaching and Learning Principles and Practice*. London: Continuum.

OfSTED (2006) Ofsted report, in A. Thomas and G. Stratton. What are we really doing with ICT in physical education: a national audit of equipment, use, teacher attitudes, support, and training. *British Journal of Education Technology*, 37(4): 617–32.

OfSTED (2003) *Good Assessment Practice in Physical Education*: HMI 1481. London: Crown.

OfSTED (2004) *Ofsted Subject Reports 2002/03: Physical Education in Secondary Schools*. London: Crown.

OfSTED (2005) *Ofsted Subject Reports 2003/04: Physical Education in Secondary Schools* . London: Crown.

OfSTED (2006) *School Sport Partnerships: A Survey of Good Practice.* HMI 2518. London: Crown.

Pachler, N. (2005) *Theories of Learning and ICT*, in Leask and N. Pachler (eds), *Learning to Teach Using ICT in the Secondary School*. London: Routledge,

Phillips, R. (2001) Making history curious: using initial stimulus material (ISM) to promote enquiry, thinking and literacy, *Teaching History*, 105: 19–24.

Pickup, I., Price, L., Shaughnessy, J., Spence, J. and Trace, M. (2008) *Learning to Teach Primary PE*. Exeter: Learning Matters.

Piotrowski, S. and Capel, S. (eds) (2000) *Issues in Physical Education*. London: Routledge Falmer.

Poole, P. (1998) *Talking about ICT in Subject Teaching*. Canterbury: Christchurch University College.

Powell, S. and Tod, J. (2004). *A Systematic Review of How Theories Explain Learning Behaviour in School Contexts* (accessed 21 July 2008 from behaviour4learning: www.behaviour4learning.ac.uk).

QCA (2005) *Physical Education: 2004/05 Annual Report on Curriculum and Assessment.* London: Qualifications and Curriculum Authority.

QCA (2007a) *Physical Education Programme of Study.* Assessed 2 July 2008, from Qualifications and Curriculum Authority: (www.curriculum.qca.org).

QCA (2007b) *Physical Education: Programme of Study for Key Stage 3 and Attainment Target.* London: Qualifications and Curriculum Authority.

QCA (2007c) *Physical Education Programme of Study: Key Stage 3.* London: Qualifications and Curriculum Authority.

QCA (2008a) *National Curriculum* (accessed 18 May 2008 from www.curriculum. qca.org.uk).

QCA (2008b) *Physical Education Programme of Study* (accessed 2 August 2008 from Qualifications and Curriculum Authority: www.curriculum.qca.org).

QCA (2008c) *Every Child Matters: At the Heart of the Curriculum.* London: Qualifications and Curriculum Authority.

Raymond, C. (1999) *Safety Across the Curriculum.* London: Falmer Press.

Rowntree, D. (1977) *Assessing Students: How Shall We Know Them?* London: Harper & Row.

Salvara, M., Jess, M. Abbot, A. and Bognar, J. (2006) A preliminary study to investigate the influence of different teaching styles on pupils' goal orientations in physical education, *European Physical Education Review*, 12(1): 51–74.

Siedentop, D. (ed.) (1994) *Sport Education: Quality PE Through Positive Sport Experiences.* Champaign, IL: Human Kinetics.

Severs (2006) Accidents in physical education: An analysis of injuries reported to the Health and Safety Executive (HSE), **Physical Education Matters**, 1(1) : 19–21.

Skills Active and DCSF (2007) *Guidance Document: Roles, Skills, Knowledge and competencies for Safeguarding and Protecting Children in The Sports Sector.* London: Department of Children, Schools and Families.

Stratton, G. and Finch, A. (2001) Information and communication technology in physical education: an ITTE-school partnership perspective, *British Journal of Teaching Physical Education*, Spring: 24–6.

TDA (date unknown) *ICT QTS Skills Test* (accessed 20 July 2008: www.tda.gov.uk/ skillstests/ict.aspx).

TDA (2007) *Professional Standards for Teachers in England* (QTS). London: Teacher Development Agency.

Tearle, P. and Golder, G. (2008) The use of ICT in the teaching and learning of physical education in compulsory education: how do we prepare the workforce of the future? *European Journal of Teacher Education*, 31(1): 55–72.

TGAT (2007) *National Curriculum Task Group on Assessment and Testing: A Report.* London: Department of Education and Science/Welsh Office.

Torrance, H. and Pryor, J. (2001) Developing formative assessment in the classroom: using action research to explore and modify theory. *British Educational Research Journal*, 27(5): 615–31.

Underwood, J. (2004) Research into information and communication technologies: where now? *The Journal for Technology, Pedagogy and Education*, 13(2): 137–45.

Whitlam, P. (2006) Health and safety: avoiding risk + avoiding challenge = avoiding high quality: understanding the management of risk in physical education and school Sport, *Physical Education Matters*, 1(3): 48.

Whitlam, P. (2007) Health and safety, *Physical Education Matters*, 2(2): 32.

Whitlam, P. (2008) Health and safety: best practice guidance on the effective use of individual and agency coaches in physical education and school sport, *Physical Education Matters*, 2(4): 47

Williams, M.A. and Hodges, N.J. (2005) Practice, instruction and skill acquisition in soccer: challenging tradition, Journal of Sports Sciences, 23(6): 637–50.

Wood, P. (2008) Classroom management, in S. Dymoke, and J. Harrison (eds), *Reflective Teaching and Learning: A Guide to Professional Issues for Beginning Secondary Teachers*, pp. 109–54. London: Sage Publications.

Woods, P. (ed.) (1980) *Pupil Strategies: Explorations in the Sociology of the School*. London: Croom Helm.

Wright, D. (2005) *There's No Need to Shout: The Secondary Teacher's Guide to Successful Behaviour Management*. Cheltenham: Nelson Thornes.

INDEX